Origins
of the
Synoptic Gospels
Some Basic Questions

Origins

of the

Synoptic Gospels

Some Basic Questions

Ned B. Stonehouse
Foreword by William L. Lane

BAKER BOOK HOUSE
Grand Rapids, Michigan

PHOTOLITHOPRINTED BY CUSHING - MALLOY, INC.
ANN ARBOR, MICHIGAN, UNITED STATES OF AMERICA
1979

FOREWORD

It is refreshing to reread the chapters of this book. They convey a vivid impression of the intellectual maturity and profound Christian commitment of the man whom many of us regarded as the dean of evangelical New Testament studies. As the successor to J. Gresham Machen in the chair of New Testament at Westminster Theological Seminary in Philadelphia, Ned B. Stonehouse had selected the Gospels and the distinctive witness of each to Jesus Christ as the area of his concentration. Contemporary discussion of the Gospels and of Gospel tradition had brought forward what he considered the most basic question of all, namely, What are we to think of Jesus Christ? He recognized that critical decisions regarding the authority, reliability, and adequacy of the testimony of the Gospels inevitably conditioned a response to that ultimate question. He therefore determined to enter the arena of debate as a responsible spokesman for what the Gospels actually said concerning the person and message of Jesus. The publication of *The Witness of Matthew and Mark to Christ* (1944) was followed by a sequel, *The Witness of Luke to Christ* (1951). A projected volume on the Fourth Gospel never appeared, and in his research, writing, and teaching Stonehouse seems to have narrowed his concentration to the Synoptic Gospels.

The quality of Stonehouse's work did much to strengthen confidence in the integrity and reliability of the evangelists as witnesses to the history of Jesus. He was prepared, for example, to acknowledge the gulf that separates Mark's historical method from the historiographical standards in force in our own century, but insisted that this gulf was the result of Mark's theological interest rather than evidence of an indifference toward historical facts. Stonehouse's insistence that a decision regarding an evangelist's intention must rest upon data supplied by the Gospel narrative itself permitted a significant exegetical advance in defining the character of each of the Synoptic Gospels. In assessing the nature of his primary sources, Stonehouse had drawn attention to the importance of the framework of the Gospels, a feature which was almost totally neglected in contemporary studies, and had allowed the total witness of each evangelist to define the character of his witness to Christ. His commitment to the primacy of exegesis made it possible to exhibit the precise features of that testimony. By focusing upon the distinctive message of each of the Synoptic Gospels, he made a permanent contribution to evangelical scholarship.

Ned Stonehouse's stature as an interpreter of the Synoptic Gospels was recognized in the invitation extended to him by the faculty of Fuller Theological Seminary in Pasadena, California, to deliver the tenth series of the Payton Lectures during March 1962. The invitation was accompanied by the challenging proposal that he address himself to the vexing theme of the Synoptic Problem. After considerable hesitation Stonehouse agreed to seize the opportunity to mature his reflections on several themes that bear on Synoptic origins. Of particular importance to him was the question of the historicity of the Synoptic tradition in the light of the contemporary discussion of source and form criticism. In preparing his lectures for publication he acknowledged that "in the nature of the case, many aspects of the Synoptic Problem do not allow of confident solutions. My impression in brief is that the data available are not sufficient to justify firm and final conclusions with regard to many matters concerning which we are understandably curious." Nevertheless, he was convinced that some progress might be made if it was recognized that the Synoptic Problem could not be treated as "an isolated and rather narrow question, but rather that it involves one necessarily in a wide range of New Testament studies"; "ultimately one is confronted here with nothing less than decisions regarding the relationship between the Gospels and Jesus Christ. For one cannot seriously evaluate the history of the Christian Church in which the Gospels came into being apart from conclusions as to the place of Jesus Christ within this history."

That way of seeing things "in the large" was typical of Ned Stonehouse. Consequently, the lectures he produced and then expanded for publication possess a distinctive character in which careful exegetical consideration of what was actually said in the tradition and the self-witness of the Gospels is sharpened by lively interaction with the proposals of such major representatives of current scholarship as G. D. Kilpatrick and G. Bornkamm on Matthew, C. H. Dodd on the *kerygma,* H. Riesenfeld on the character of early tradition, and a host of others. In addressing himself to such basic questions as the authorship of the Synoptic Gospels, their relationship to one another, the transmission of the tradition into the hands of the evangelists, and the source of their ultimate origin, Stonehouse succeeds in drawing his readers into a conversation with major spokesmen on crucial issues which affect the stance of faith. On the question of the ultimate origin of the Synoptic Gospels, Stonehouse's own position is un-equivocal in his assertion of unqualified continuity between the historical Jesus and the gospel tradition. The Jesus to which the evangelists bear witness in their respective Gospels is the Jesus of history. The synoptic witness finds its explanation and validation in a divine Messiah who imparted his God-given authority to the apostles. The priority of Mark, and the dependence of Matthew upon Mark, simply attests the integrity and reliability of the apostolic tradition.

No summary could do justice to the manner in which Stonehouse assesses the evidence. His respect for the tradition is evident in his sober and cautious handling of the text, and is balanced by the incisive character of the pointed and searching criticism that he directs toward his professional colleagues who were prepared to go beyond the weight of the evidence or who had failed to respect its witness.

Origins of the Synoptic Gospels was to be the last volume from Stonehouse's pen. In November of 1962 he died unexpectedly, and the book was published posthumously. The reviews were favorable. The "basic questions" which Stonehouse had addressed were the decisive ones. They continue to be discussed with utmost seriousness in academic circles today. Stonehouse's mature reflections are as contemporary and trenchant in 1979 as they were when first published sixteen years ago.

Men of the stature of Ned B. Stonehouse appear rarely in any given generation. They exert an enormous influence for Christ and the Church through their teaching, preaching, and writing. Then suddenly they are gone. Of their teaching there remain only cherished notebooks and the anecdotes of the "old guard" who were privileged to know them as mentors. Of their preaching there remain individuals and congregations who were strengthened and nurtured in faith, who find occasion in their memories to thank God for the fidelity of his servants. But of their writing there remains a legacy which can perpetuate the power of a mind in disciplined submission to the Word of God. It is an occasion for celebration that Ned B. Stonehouse's *Origins of the Synoptic Gospels* has now been reprinted and is again available to students who are prepared to find themselves engaged by the self-witness of the Synoptic Gospels in a compelling and responsible way.

WILLIAM L. LANE
Western Kentucky University

To
MARGARET

THE PAYTON LECTURES

T HE present volume is an expansion of the tenth series of Payton Lectures delivered by Professor Ned B. Stonehouse March 27-30, 1962, at Fuller Theological Seminary, Pasadena, California.

The Payton Lectureship was instituted in memory of Dr. and Mrs. John E. Payton, the parents of Mrs. Charles E. Fuller, wife of the founder of Fuller Theological Seminary. The bequest provides for an annual series of lectures by a competent scholar. The lectures must fall within these areas: the uniqueness or confirmation of the historic Christian faith, the confutation of non-Christian or sub-Christian views, or the formulation of Biblical doctrines.

PREFACE

T HE invitation to give a course of Payton Lectures, graciously
extended to me by the Faculty of Fuller Theological Seminary
several years ago, was accompanied by the challenging suggestion that I should treat the theme of the Synoptic Problem.
Because of my agreement as to the continuing importance and
relevance of this topic for students of the Scriptures, and the
interest I had developed in it over a period of many years of
teaching in the area of Gospel origins, it could not easily be
set aside. Nevertheless, my reaction at once was one of considerable hesitation as to whether I should attempt to lecture
on that theme, and it may be useful even now to give some
account of the reasons for this reluctance. For the reader may
thus be able to understand why, having chosen not to make
use of the liberty granted to select another topic, I approach
this general subject as I do.

One perhaps rather obvious reason for a somewhat negative
attitude was that any really adequate treatment of the Synoptic
Problem would necessarily involve one in the presentation of
many minute and technical details, and I rather despaired of
being able to sustain the attention of my audience even for an
hour, not to say four or five hours, of public discourse. A
more basic deterrent, however, was the conviction that if I were
to announce this subject I might properly be expected to offer
a solution of the problem or at least to try to settle many of
the thorny questions that have arisen in connection with the
problem as a whole. I happen however to hold that, in the
nature of the case, many aspects of the Synoptic Problem do
not allow of confident solutions. My impression in brief is
that the data available are not sufficient to justify firm and
final conclusions with regard to many matters concerning which
we are understandably curious. The intrinsic difficulties are
so considerable that, as I see it, much more reserve and caution
are demanded of students of this field of research than are
commonly manifest. And at least one other weighty factor,
bound up with my own analysis of the problem, commends due
restraint. It is my belief that the Synoptic Problem cannot,
as many discussions seem to suggest, be treated as an isolated

and rather narrow question, but rather that it involves one necessarily in a wide range of New Testament studies including general and special introduction and historical and theological interpretation. Ultimately one is confronted here with nothing less than decisions regarding the relationship between the Gospels and Jesus Christ. For one cannot seriously evaluate the history of the Christian Church in which the Gospels came into being apart from conclusions as to the place of Jesus Christ within this history.

The reasons just stated are presumably sufficient to indicate why I should have hesitated to treat the Synoptic Problem, particularly in the course of a few public lectures. These same reasons may nevertheless suggest why I should have been challenged to say something on this great theme. If because of the inherent difficulties of the problem, as well as the limitations imposed upon a special lecturer, indubitable results all along the line might not be expected, some progress might still be possible by way of a more modest estimate of the undertaking.

A few comments on the development of the lectures and the book may be in order. Adopting a highly selective approach, I chose to lecture on four topics, treating in turn certain aspects of the questions of authorship, order and interdependence, apostolic tradition, and ultimate origin. In expanding and revising the original manuscript for publication two chapters were devoted to each topic with the exception that three seemed necessary for the second question. Although, as a result of this selection of subjects, and further narrowing of treatment of various themes, many facets of the Synoptic Problem remain undiscussed and the resultant work may appear somewhat arbitrarily eclectic, other factors hopefully may serve to disclose a pervasive unity and coherence. One is the persistent concern to integrate the treatment of the various topics with the profound issue of the witness of Jesus Christ and one's response to him. Another hardly less basic issue joined here is that in which, drawing a clear line of demarcation between Scripture and tradition, I seek to apply this distinction consistently in the final evaluation of various questions.

One of the opportunities which I wish to seize here is that of expressing my hearty thanks to the Faculty of Fuller Theological Seminary for the extraordinarily generous hospitality and brotherly kindness shown me during my stay in Pasadena

as well as for the honor conferred in the invitation. My thanks
are hereby also expressed to many others who in one way or
another have contributed to the completion of this work: the
students of Westminster who have stimulated my thought and
teaching; the audience of Fuller students and guests for their
kind attention and response; the publishers who have granted
permission to quote from their books; my secretary, Miss Doro-
thy Newkirk, who has gone well beyond the call of duty in
rendering skillful services at every stage of the enterprise; and
Messrs. Wm. B. Eerdmans, Sr. and Jr., for their cordial interest
in undertaking the publication of the volume.

N. B. S.

Note

Upon the death of the author, the Reverend Professor Paul
Woolley, professor of Church History at Westminster Theological
Seminary, proofread the text and made slight revisions in the
manuscript, and Mr. Bernard J. Stonehouse, the author's son,
compiled the index of subjects. We wish to thank both of them
for their careful work.

THE PUBLISHERS

CONTENTS

Preface   vii

Abbreviations   viii

I   TRADITION AND AUTHORSHIP   1
    Irenaeus   4
    Tertullian   7
    Papias   10
    The Superscriptions   15

II   THE SELF-WITNESS OF MATTHEW   19
    Some Basic Objections   22
    Kilpatrick's Reconstruction   25
    The Appeal to Matthew 22:6   35
    Conclusion Regarding Matthean Authorship   43

III   THE QUESTION OF ORDER AND
      INDEPENDENCE   48
    Opinions Concerning Priority   49
    The Testimony of Tradition   54
    Is Mark the First Gospel?   56
    The View of Chapman   73

IV   THE FACTOR OF LANGUAGE   78
    General Appraisal   78
    The Original Language of Matthew   82
    The Papian Declaration   90

V   THE RICH YOUNG RULER   93
    Introductory Considerations   94
    The Young Man: Inquiry and Response   97
    Followers of Jesus: Questions and Disclosures   101
    Some General Observations   108

VI   THE APOSTOLIC TRANSMISSION OF THE
       GOSPEL   113
       Apostolic Transmission   115
       Cadbury's View of the Lucan Prologue   118
       Other New Testament Evidence   128

VII THE APOSTOLIC TRADITION: THE MESSAGE   132
       Dodd and the *Kerygma*   135
       Riesenfeld's Hypothesis   138
       Critical Evaluation   142

VIII THE MODERN DEBATE CONCERNING
       ULTIMATE ORIGIN   146
       Adolf Harnack   149
       Strauss and Baur   154
       Wilhelm Wrede   158
       Albert Schweitzer   160
       Rudolf Bultmann   168

IX   THE SELF-REVELATION OF JESUS CHRIST   176
       Analysis of Messiahship   178
       The Deity of the Messiah   185
       Conclusion   190

     Indices   193

ABBREVIATIONS

ANF	*Ante-Nicene Fathers*
ASV	*American Standard Version*
CCL	*Corpus Christianorum, Series Latina*
CBQ	*Catholic Biblical Quarterly*
ExT	*The Expository Times*
HE	*The Ecclesiastical History of Eusebius*
HNTC	*Harper's New Testament Commentaries*
IB	*The Interpreter's Bible*
ICC	*The International Critical Commentary*
JBL	*The Journal of Biblical Literature*
JTS	*The Journal of Theological Studies*
KNT	*Kommentaar op het Nieuwe Testament* (Grosheide and Greijdanus)
KNTTM	*Kommentar zum Neuen Testament aus Talmud und Midrasch* (Strack and Billerbeck)
KV	*Korte Verklaring der Heilige Schrift*
NICNT	*The New International Commentary on the New Testament*
NPF	*Nicene and Post-Nicene Fathers*
NTD	*Das Neue Testament Deutsch*
NTS	*New Testament Studies*
PBA	*Paul Before the Areopagus and Other New Testament Studies* (Stonehouse)
PL	*Patrologiae cursus completus, Ser. Latina:* Migne
SNT	*Die Schriften des Neuen Testaments*
TC	*Tyndale New Testament Commentaries*
TS	*Theological Studies*
TU	*Texte und Untersuchungen*
TWNT	*Theologisches Wörterbuch zum Neuen Testament*
WC	*Westminster Commentaries*
WLC	*The Witness of Luke to Christ* (Stonehouse)
WMMC	*The Witness of Matthew and Mark to Christ* (Stonehouse)
WTJ	*The Westminster Theological Journal*
ZKNT	*Kommentar zum Neuen Testament* (Zahn)
ZNW	*Zeitschrift für die neutestamentliche Wissenschaft*

CHAPTER ONE

TRADITION AND AUTHORSHIP

IF any one feature of the inquiry concerning Synoptic origins may be singled out as particularly crucial for the explication of Gospel relationships, it is surely that of authorship. And if any one decision regarding authorship is more far-reaching than others in its bearing upon one's total estimate of the historical situation to which our attention is being directed here, it is certainly that of the authorship of Matthew. These evaluations have in any case influenced the approach taken in these studies. Two chapters are being largely devoted to this one matter: in the first, authorship, though not wholly to the exclusion of other aspects of origins, is reflected upon in the light of tradition; in the second, the self-witness of Matthew to its own origin comes under review and critical judgment.

In using the terms "tradition" and "self-witness," it may be well to point out, I am deliberately abandoning the older terminology employed in my undergraduate course of studies, namely, "external and internal evidence." Since I have exactly the same contents in view in my distinctions as my teachers had in theirs, the difference being pointed up hardly involves a serious dispute with them. There is nevertheless, I believe, a distinct advantage in rejecting the older terminology in favor of that which is used here because in this fashion greater justice can be done to the profound difference between external and internal evidence, especially as this difference is related to the contents of Scripture. It is difficult indeed to exaggerate the value of the knowledge gained from tradition; without it we should be in a position of incomparably deeper ignorance than we now are. Nevertheless, the testimony of tradition cannot rise above the level of tradition whereas the self-witness of the Gospels and other writings of the Scriptures, in the very nature of the case, is of a qualitatively different kind. In coming to ultimate

1

judgments concerning a document nothing can be alleged against that which it discloses itself as being by its very contents. And the qualitative nature of this difference is underscored when, as in the case of the Gospels, we are dealing with the witness of Scripture itself.

In concentrating upon the subject of authorship other questions such as when and where the several Gospels were written, and to whom and for what purpose, recede somewhat into the background, although they are not entirely neglected. It is legitimate, however, to center one's thought upon authorship as the factor of most basic import. This question enjoys preeminence especially if the authors were apostles of Jesus Christ or associates of apostles, for then their place in history may be assessed with a high degree of precision. And by the same token the repudiation of such a view as to the relationship of the authors to Jesus Christ would compel one to adopt an essentially different estimate of Gospel origins.

So, for example, one's final evaluation of the Gospel according to Mark, and especially of its peculiar niche in the history of the Synoptic Gospels, will be deeply affected by one's attitude toward the tradition that its author was intimately associated with the apostle Peter and that the contents of this Gospel depend significantly upon the message he proclaimed. If this tradition is accorded a large measure of historical credibility, all other data connected with Synoptic origins will have to be integrated with it. On the other hand, if the tradition is largely or wholly discounted, one might feel constrained to allow seriously for such a theory as that of F. C. Grant that this Gospel was essentially a social product, combining various factors within the expanding life of Christianity as it was transplanted from Jewish soil to the pagan environment of Rome. According to the "fantasy" which Grant allows himself, its author, rather than being the John Mark of Scripture, was perhaps a young clerk in a Roman mercantile establishment who was commissioned to put together in his free time the Gospel tradition as it circulated in the church of that city in the late sixties.[1]

Similarly, if one accepts the tradition that the author of Matthew was one of the twelve apostles, there will be far-reach-

---

1. F. C. Grant, *The Earliest Gospel* (Nashville: Cokesbury, 1943), pp. 34ff., 53ff. Cf. my review of this book in *WTJ*, VI (May, 1944), 199-206.

ing implications for one's judgment as to the place of this Gospel in the unfolding of the Synoptic witness to Jesus Christ. On this view Matthew would constitute one of the earliest of the authentic testimonies. On the other hand, if at most the apostle Matthew was the author of a source used by an unknown evangelist, or the name of Matthew was perhaps attached to the Gospel merely as a pseudonym, the association with the history of Jesus Christ might well be quite tenuous or even non-existent. Then one would have to allow for a much broader range of possibilities concerning its date, *raison d'être* and essential character.

A brief explanation of the concentration on the authorship of Matthew rather than that of Mark or Luke may be in order.[2] In the first place, in spite of notable exceptions, the traditions of the authorship of Mark by John Mark and of Luke by the companion of Paul are generally accepted even by Liberals. With regard to Matthew, however, there is a strong critical consensus that it is not apostolic. And in the second place, the disjunction: (1) apostolic *or* not apostolic, as this applies to Matthew, confronts one with a far more crucial and basic issue as regards Christian origins than the disjunction: (2) apostolic associates-companions *or* other early Christian disciples, as this would apply to Mark and Luke. To be sure, the issue whether the witness of the Gospels is essentially apostolic is faced also in the evaluation of Mark and Luke, but it is most sharply joined as one grapples with the fact that Matthew, if tradition is to be accepted, constitutes a witness to Jesus Christ on the part of one who belonged to the small circle of those who were intimately associated with Jesus during his public ministry on earth. Matthew is the only one of the Synoptic Gospels for which this claim is made, and thus the rejection of apostolic origin would tend to affect more or less radically one's judgment concerning its peculiar place within the development of primitive Christianity.

In presenting and reflecting upon the testimony of tradition in this chapter I have chosen to be selective rather than broadly comprehensive. To restrict myself as I do here to Irenaeus and Tertullian, to Papias and the superscriptions of the Gospels, admittedly has certain disadvantages. Selectiveness was

2. The authorship of Luke is discussed in *WLC* (London: Tyndale; Grand Rapids: Eerdmans, 1951), Chapter I.

however dictated by the consideration that presentation to a public audience was in view. Moreover, it is likely to be acknowledged that the materials chosen for discussion are second to none in importance, and that through reflection upon them one may gain a rather adequate insight into the situation as a whole.

Irenaeus

That Irenaeus, at first presbyter and later bishop of Lyons in Gaul, and author of the invaluable refutation of Gnosticism, *Against Heresies* (written 181-189), is deserving of priority in our discussion will hardly be challenged. His stature as a churchman and theologian was distinguished. Moreover, his early life in Asia Minor and his personal contacts there with Polycarp and the Elders of Asia demonstrate that he was not a spokesman merely for an isolated and remote part of the Church. In sum, he was in the position of being better informed with regard to earlier tradition than many of his contemporaries.

In a passage that has been preserved in a Greek text by Eusebius, Irenaeus says:

> Matthew published a writing of the Gospel among the Hebrews in their own language while Peter and Paul were preaching in Rome and establishing the Church. And after their departure Mark, the disciple and interpreter of Peter, delivered over to us in writing the things which were preached by Peter. And Luke also, the follower of Paul, recorded in a book the gospel preached by him. Afterward John, the disciple of the Lord, who had also leaned upon his bosom, himself also published the gospel, while he was residing in Ephesus of Asia.[3]

This tradition of the fourfold gospel, associated with the names of Matthew, Mark, Luke and John, as we shall be observing somewhat more particularly, is fully representative of the viewpoint of the Church in this period. It is illuminating to take further account of the context in which this quotation appears, and to note several points that expand our understanding of the testimony of Irenaeus.

(1) There is a noteworthy emphasis upon the apostolic preaching as constituting the specific background for the publication of the Gospels, a declaration which establishes at least

---

3. *Adv. Haer.* III 1:1 (ed. Stieren I, pp. 422f.; *cf. HE* V 8:2). The English translation in *ANF* has been partially utilized.

a point of contact with the modern discussion concerning the *kerygma*. Irenaeus, we should note, declares, moreover, that the apostles handed down the written publication of their proclamation in the Scriptures.

(2) In keeping with this evaluation of the apostles, and by way of refuting the Gnostic depreciation of them, Irenaeus rejects the charge that the apostles represented an inferior stage in the history of revelation. "It is not lawful to say," he declares, "that they preached before they had perfect knowledge, as some even venture to say, boasting themselves as improvers of the apostles." In this context he also insists that the apostles did not carry out their teaching mission until after they had been invested with the power of the Holy Spirit from on high.

(3) Evidently because of this enduement of the Spirit and their possession of perfect knowledge the result of their proclamation is but a single gospel. Though many were involved in this proclamation, and they preached to the ends of the earth, "all equally and individually have the gospel of God." As Irenaeus says somewhat later on in a context where he is stressing the fourfold aspect of the gospel, they are "bound together by one Spirit."[4]

(4) As to its contents, the gospel is concerned with the one God, Creator of heaven and earth, and with one Christ, the Son of God. And anyone who does not accept the gospel is spurning not only the apostles but Christ the Lord and the Father also and stands self-condemned as resisting and opposing his own salvation.

(5) When in this same chapter Irenaeus marshals arguments from the four Gospels against the Gnostics, he identifies the four somewhat more particularly. Of special importance is the fact that Matthew is specifically designated as "the apostle." Mark is said to be "the interpreter and follower of Peter" and Luke "the follower and disciple of the apostles."[5]

(6) It is in the latter part of this same chapter that Irenaeus develops at great length his argument that the gospel as received in the church has, and necessarily must possess, a fourfold form. By way of observations and exegesis that may perhaps leave us more amused than persuaded, Irenaeus declares:

> It is not possible that the Gospels be either more or fewer than they are. For since there are four regions of the world in

4. *Ibid.*, III 11:8.
5. *Cf. ibid.*, III 9-11.

which we live, and four principal winds, and the Church is scattered over the whole earth, and the pillar and ground of the Church is the gospel and the Spirit of Life, it is fitting that she should have four pillars, breathing forth immortality on every side, and giving life to men. From this it is evident that the Word, the Artificer of all, who sitteth upon the cherubim and who contains all things and was manifested to men, has given us the gospel under four forms, but bound together by one Spirit.[6]

Appealing now to Psalm 80:1 ("Thou that sittest between the cherubim, shine forth") and finding agreement, in turn, between these descriptions of the Living Beings in Revelation 4 and John, Luke, Matthew and Mark, Irenaeus concludes:

And therefore the Gospels are in accord with these things, among which Christ Jesus is seated. . . . Such then as was the course followed by the Son of God, so also was the form of the living creatures; and such as was the form of the living creatures, so also was the character of the gospel. For the living creatures are quadriform and the gospel is quadriform, as is also the course followed by the Lord.[7]

Although, as I have suggested, one may not be inclined to take this line of argument in full seriousness, it should not be overlooked that there was impressive force in an appeal to a gospel which enjoyed the attestation of no fewer than four men, and these either apostles or associates of apostles, over against the appeal of various heretics to single Gospels. In this context he refers to the use which the Ebionites made of Matthew, Marcion of a mutilation of Luke, and Valentinus of John.[8] And later he returns to this same subject and condemns those "who destroy the form of the gospel" by representing "the aspects of the gospel as being either more in number than as aforesaid, or, on the other hand, fewer." Here we encounter particular references to Marcion, the Montanists and Valentinus. His castigation of the Valentinians for designating their own publication "The Gospel of Truth" is especially memorable; "for if what they have published is the Gospel of truth, and yet is totally unlike those which have been handed down to us from the apostles, any who please may learn, as is shown from the Scriptures themselves, that that which has been handed down from the apostles can no longer be reckoned the Gospel of

6. *Ibid.*, III 11:8.
7. *Ibid.*
8. *Cf. ibid.*, III 11:7.

truth." Irenaeus himself is of course not in doubt on this issue. As he at once adds, the apostolic Gospels "alone are true and reliable."[9]

Tertullian

That Irenaeus' viewpoint concerning the fourfold Gospel canon was not simply his own but representative of the Church of his time receives noteworthy confirmation from the testimony of Tertullian. The weight of this testimony from North Africa is borne in upon us with greater force if we take account of the fact that even Tertullian's conversion to Montanism did not produce any essential change in his view of the New Testament Canon.[10]

In his work *Against Marcion*, which incidentally belongs to the latter period, for example, he sets forth his views in the following terms:

> We affirm first of all that the evangelical *instrumentum* had apostles as authors, to whom this duty of publishing the gospel was assigned by the Lord himself. If there were also apostolic men (*apostolicos*), nevertheless they did not stand alone but with apostles and after apostles, since the preaching of disciples could be suspected of a zeal for glory if there did not accompany it the authority of the masters. Of the apostles therefore John and Matthew instil faith into us; of the apostolic men Luke and Mark renew it, proceeding upon the same principles, so far as relates to the one God the Creator and his Christ, born of a virgin, fulfilling the law and the prophets.[11]

The rather extraordinary way in which Tertullian at once proceeds, by way of a critique of Marcion, to underscore the distinction between apostles and apostolic men is illuminating. In passing, he points out that, over against Marcion, the apostolic writings, though differing in the order of the narratives,

---

9. *Cf. ibid.*, III 11:9. In concluding that the apostolic Gospels are *sola illa vera et firma* Irenaeus is evidently contrasting those which are *sola . . . vera* with the Valentinian (alleged) *veritatis evangelium* (ed. Stieren I, p. 474). On the recently discovered Gospel of Truth, see especially *The Gospel of Truth: A Valentinian Meditation on the Gospel*, translation from the Coptic and commentary by Kendrick Grobel (New York: Abingdon, 1960) and the article by W. C. van Unnik in *The Jung Codex* (London: Mowbray, 1955), translated and edited by F. L. Cross.

10. See my *The Apocalypse in the Ancient Church* (Goes, 1929), pp. 86ff.

11. *Adv. Marc.* IV 2 (*CCL* I, pp. 547f.). English translation in *ANF* in part.

agree in the essential matter of faith. Briefly he also criticizes
Marcion's Gospel for its anonymity: ". . . a work ought not to
be recognized which holds not its head erect, which exhibits no
consistency, which gives no promise of credibility from the
fullness of its title and the just profession of its author." And
then Tertullian proceeds at some length to ring the changes
on the observation that Marcion had singled out for his mutilat-
ing process a gospel which was "not of an apostle, but only an
apostolic man, not a master (*magister*) but a disciple and so
inferior to a master." And not content with this form of his
polemic, Tertullian goes on, apparently with the thought of
counteracting anyone who might appeal to Luke's association
with the apostle Paul, to insist that

> had Marcion even published his Gospel in the name of Paul
> himself, the single authority of the document, destitute of all
> support from preceding authorities, would not be a sufficient
> basis for our faith. There would still be wanted that gospel
> which Paul found in existence, to which he yielded his belief,
> and with which he so earnestly wished his own to agree, that
> he actually on that account went up to Jerusalem to know
> and to consult the apostles, lest he should run or had been
> running in vain. . . . Inasmuch, therefore, as the enlightener
> of Luke himself desired the authority of his predecessors for
> both his own faith and preaching, how much more may not I
> require for Luke's Gospel that which was necessary for the
> Gospel of his master.[12]

Although one may not agree with Tertullian's exegesis of
Galatians offered in support of the proposition that Paul to an
extent derived the authority of his message from the earlier
apostles, one may discern a sound historical insight as to the
course of Christian history so far as it relates to the earliest
preaching of the Christian message. And to concentrate more
particularly on the point at issue here, one wonders how
Tertullian could have drawn the line between apostles and
apostolic men more sharply.

A little later as he argues for the antiquity of the form of
Luke's Gospel known to the Church, and the secondary character of Marcion's form, he develops his distinction between
the Gospels of the apostles and those of apostolic men to the
point where he is prepared to assert that the former must have
been earlier than the latter. Maintaining that Marcion has

12. *Ibid.*, IV 1.

acted arbitrarily and irresponsibly in ignoring John, Matthew, and Mark he declares that

> Marcion ought to be called to a strict account concerning these also, for having omitted them, and insisted in preference on Luke; as if they, too, had not had free course in the churches, as well as Luke's Gospel, from the beginning. Nay, it is even more credible that they existed from the very beginning; for, being the work of apostles, they were prior, and coeval in origin with the churches themselves. How comes it to pass, if the apostles published nothing, that their disciples were more forward in such a work; for they could not have been disciples, without any instruction from their masters?[13]

In most basic respects, therefore, the witness of Tertullian is in agreement with that of Irenaeus. There is the same clear-cut testimony to the fourfold character of the gospel, and the same four books are obviously in view. There is moreover a similar emphasis upon the apostolicity of the gospel as over against the essential novelty of Marcion's publication of an anonymous radical redaction of Luke. But there is in Tertullian a far stronger stress upon the pre-eminence of John and Matthew than appears in Irenaeus. For both fathers, indeed, Mark and Luke are to be associated with the names of the apostles Peter and Paul. In both Irenaeus and Tertullian this feature is introduced in the interest of explaining their authority. In Tertullian, however, there is besides, manifestly as a consequence of the development of his polemic against Marcion, what amounts at times to a distinct depreciation of these Gospels. If the traditions concerning the origins of Mark and Luke had been more fluid, would not their history of usage and regard in the church have been essentially different from what they actually were? To suggest that they might have been rejected outrightly, with the result that we would have had a twofold rather than a fourfold Gospel, is perhaps too radical. But there are other possibilities. Might not, for example, these Gospels have been relegated to some sort of deutero-canonicity? Their subordination to the others on the part of Tertullian might suggest this, but as a matter of fact he does not distinguish between the four Gospels in terms of variant degrees of authority. And is it not possible that the tendency to associate them with the names of Peter and Paul might have been carried through more radically with the result

13. *Ibid.*, IV 5.

that they might have come to be known in the church as the Gospel according to Peter and the Gospel according to Paul? The fact that none of these things happened constitutes the most weighty evidence in support of the conclusion that the names of Mark and Luke, as well as those of Matthew and John, were joined to these Gospels from the earliest times, and that this tradition was so fixed and universal that it could not be set aside even by acute pressures arising from polemical and apologetic interests.[14]

Papias

When one turns backward from the latter part of the second century to the evidence bearing on the subject of Gospel origins in the first half of the century, one is bound to be impressed with its paucity and to some extent even with its obscurity. There are proofs enough to be sure of the existence of the several Gospels within this period. For example, Ignatius writing about A.D. 115 quite unmistakably reveals that he possessed Matthew. And, to utilize another kind of evidence, the Rylands Papyrus shows that the Gospel according to John had reached Egypt within this period. Interested as we are, however, in data which bear upon questions of authorship, and

---

14. Among other more or less contemporaneous witnesses to the four-fold Gospel are Clement of Alexandria (*cf. HE* VI 14:5) and the Muratori Canon. Of special interest also is the witness of the Anti-Marcionite Prologues to the Gospels, which may be conveniently consulted in Huck's *Synopsis of the First Three Gospels*. Since 1928, as the result of the investigations of De Bruyne and Harnack, the Prologues have widely been recognized as having been written between the years A.D. 160 and 180, and thus as forming a highly significant witness for the period between Papias and Irenaeus. A survey article which supports this position was published by W. F. Howard in *ExT* 47 (Sept., 1936), pp. 534ff. The validity of this dating of the Prologues is, however, still being challenged — recently, for example, in an article by Engelbert Gutwenger in *TS* (Sept., 1946), pp. 393-409, and in A. H. McNeile, *An Introduction to the Study of the N.T.*, 2d rev. ed. (Oxford: Clarendon, 1953), p. 26.

The Matthean Prologue has been lost, and there are certain difficulties in the interpretation of the Marcan and Johannine Prologues, but the Lucan Prologue speaks of Matthew and Mark as Gospels which were written before Luke, the one in Judea and the other in Italy. In attesting the Lucan authorship of both the Gospel and Acts it identifies Luke as a follower of Paul and among other things contains the interesting tradition that he was of Antioch in Syria. Moreover, John the Apostle, one of the Twelve, is designated as author both of the Apocalypse and the Gospel.

hopefully on other questions of origin, we cannot but be distressed that either these questions were not generally in the forefront of interest or that documents dealing directly or incidentally with them have not been preserved. Were it not for this general famine one would be at a loss to explain the extraordinary interest in the few small fragments of Papias, as preserved by Eusebius, that has been displayed in the modern discussion.

Papias indeed, in spite of the criticism of Eusebius, is a figure who is eminently worthy of our close attention. Described as he was by Irenaeus as a hearer of John (by whom Irenaeus certainly meant the apostle), a companion of Polycarp and an ancient man, and having written his *Exposition of Dominical Oracles* by A.D. 125 or not long thereafter, we would be bound to assign to him a place of intense historical interest if only his book had been substantially preserved. Considering that we have but the two brief excerpts concerning Matthew and Mark and nothing relating to Luke and John, would we not be willing to sacrifice at least a few Dead Sea scrolls if only we could recover the whole of Papias' book? The lack of reference to Luke and John, to be sure, as Bishop Lightfoot demonstrated with his usual distinguished perception, by no means implies that Papias had no acquaintance with Luke and John; the silence at this point is the silence of Eusebius. On the basis of a careful study of the contents of the *Ecclesiastical History* as well as of sources which were known to be available to the author, Lightfoot concludes that "his main object was to give such information as might assist in forming correct views concerning the Canon of Scripture"; that accordingly "he was indifferent to any quotations or references which went towards establishing the canonicity of those books which had never been disputed in the Church"; and that as regards these undisputed canonical works, including the four Gospels, the Acts and the thirteen Epistles of Paul, "he contents himself with preserving any anecdotes which he may have found illustrating the circumstances under which they were written, *e.g.* the notices of St. Matthew and St. Mark in Papias and of the Four Gospels in Irenaeus."[15]

Though we must exercise due caution because of the brevity

15. J. B. Lightfoot, *Essays on the Work entitled Supernatural Religion* (London: Macmillan, 1889), p. 46; *cf.* also pp. 178, 186.

and the isolated character of the references to Matthew and Mark, their early date constrains us to give them our very best attention. The longer and clearer passage concerning Mark may be treated to advantage first because it contains terms and evaluations which are crucial for the understanding of the declaration concerning Matthew. It reads as follows:

> And the Elder used to say this, "Mark having become Peter's interpreter wrote accurately whatever he remembered, not, indeed, in order, of the things said or done by the Lord"[16] for he neither heard the Lord nor did he follow him but afterward, as I said, followed Peter, who adapted his teaching to the needs of his hearers, but not with the intention of making a composition of the Dominical Oracles so that Mark did not err in thus writing some things as he remembered them. For of one thing he took forethought, not to omit any of the things which he heard nor to state any of them falsely.[17]

Several pertinent evaluations and conclusions may be noted:

(1) Regardless of decisions one might reach as to the identity of "the Elder" whom Papias quotes and the precise extent of the quotation, it is noteworthy that at least to a substantial extent Papias' testimony concerning Mark is not presented as his own opinion but as that of an earlier authority. We have to do here, therefore, with a tradition that apparently goes back at least as far as the beginnings of the second century.

(2) The tradition that the author of the Marcan Gospel was intimately associated with the ministry of the apostle Peter, and that its origin is connected in some basic way with the preaching or teaching of Peter, is now observed to have been present in the church well over half a century before the time of Irenaeus. Although the figure of the apostle Peter looms large in the background of Mark's Gospel, and its contents are viewed as derived wholly or substantially from Peter, there is a somewhat greater recognition of the initiative and independence of Mark as an evangelist than appears in some of the later testimonies. It is specifically denied that Peter was responsible for a composition of dominical oracles. And since Papias immediately thereafter dwells upon Mark's activity as author, there appears to be the plain implication that what Peter did not do Mark accomplished, namely, the preparation

---

16. It remains uncertain exactly how far the quotation from the Elder is meant to extend.

17. *HE* III 39:15 (ed. Schwartz, 1914, p. 122).

of a composition of dominical oracles. This significant conclusion with regard to Mark then would be equal in force to the declaration concerning Matthew that he composed the oracles. This understanding of the term "oracles" as descriptive of the contents of Mark and Matthew, and of the terms "arrangement" and "arranged" as referring to the actual compositions, has not, to be sure, found general acceptance. Partly because the term "oracles" has been widely understood as referring to "sayings," and partly also because of an apparent tendency in Gospel criticism to preserve Papias' support for the Q hypothesis on the assumption that the apostle Matthew could not have been the author of the Gospel, sight has generally been lost of the implications of Papias' statement regarding Mark. Of most immediate weight here is the fact that Papias implies that Mark's arrangement or composition consisted of the things said or done by the Lord. In brief, Papias himself is an important witness for the view that "oracles" may by no means be confined to "sayings."[18]

Altogether congruous with this estimate of Papias' characterizations of Mark and Matthew is the form of the title of this work as that may be interpreted in the light of the Preface which has been preserved, in whole or part, by Eusebius. The final sentence of the Preface, "For I did not suppose that the things to be gotten from books would profit me so much as what came from a living and abiding voice," is often interpreted as a sweeping depreciation of such writings as make up our New Testament. But such interpreters fail to notice precisely the context of this observation in the Preface. Papias stresses indeed his concern with the traditions of the Elders but he states quite precisely that his procedure is to "join them to the interpretations."[19] His primary interest is therefore in the interpretations; only secondarily is it in oral tradition. The "interpretations" are then naturally in view in the word "Exposition" in the title. Briefly stated, Papias' exposition of dominical oracles may be most appropriately understood as interpreting the things either said or done by the Lord, in short, with the contents of the Gospels themselves.

That Papias may not fairly be understood as depreciating

18. On the meaning of λόγια, see especially G. Kittel, *TWNT* IV, 140f. *Cf.* also B. B. Warfield, *Revelation and Inspiration* (New York: Oxford, 1927), pp. 333ff.

19. συγκατατάξαι ταῖς ἑρμηνείαις (*HE* III 39:3; *cf.* 1-4: ed. Schwartz, p. 119).

written works in general is strongly confirmed by the high praise he accords Mark's Gospel. For in the foreground of his description of Mark's activity he includes the declaration that he wrote "accurately" and he concludes with an attestation of its trustworthy character. One is thus reminded in some ways of the competence claimed by Luke in his Gospel prologue to supply a completely trustworthy account of what had happened so as to provide certainty to his readers. On the background of this high praise of Mark, the assertion that his composition was "not indeed in order" may hardly be pressed to support the thesis that there is a measure of downgrading of Mark in favor of another Gospel. To establish such a thesis one has to read quite dogmatically a great deal into Papias' simple phrase. On the other hand, the explanation of Zahn commends itself because it is substantially drawn from Papias' own language: the lack of order is that of one who was not himself an eyewitness but was dependent upon Peter who was concerned only to adapt his teaching to the needs of his hearers.[20]

We now turn to Papias' statement concerning Matthew itself. Initial appearances to the contrary notwithstanding, a rather broad background has already been provided. When Eusebius quotes Papias as saying,

> Matthew made an arrangement of the oracles in the Hebrew language, and each translated them as he was able,[21]

it is perfectly clear that he understood Papias to be referring to the Gospel according to Matthew. And while many modern scholars have sought support in Papias' statement for a connection of the apostle Matthew with a source of the Gospel rather than with the Gospel itself,[22] it is noteworthy that many others including Jülicher, Bacon, Ropes, Kittel, and Kilpatrick, as well as Lightfoot and Zahn,[23] have firmly insisted that the

---

20. T. Zahn, *Einleitung in das N. T.*, (Leipzig, Deichert, 1907), II, 212; *Introduction to the N.T.* (Edinburgh: Clark, 1909), II, 439. A somewhat different explanation, which also maintains a high view of Mark, is that of F. C. Burkitt, *The Earliest Sources for the Life of Jesus* (London: Constable, 1922), pp. 82f.

21. *HE* III 39:16 (ed. Schwartz, p. 122).

22. *Cf. e.g.* B. H. Streeter, *The Four Gospels* (London: Macmillan, 1930), pp. 500f.

23. A. Jülicher, *Einleitung in das N.T.*, 7te Aufl. (Tübingen: Mohr, 1931), p. 280; B. W. Bacon, *Studies in Matthew* (New York: Holt, 1930), pp. 13, 443f.; J. H. Ropes, *The Synoptic Gospels* (Cambridge: Harvard University Press, 1934), pp. 107f.; G. Kittel, *TWNT*, IV, 144; G. D.

statement clearly must have been intended to refer to the Gospel.

The conclusion of Ropes that Papias "was unquestionably interested in reporting a tradition bearing on the origin of our Greek Gospel of Matthew"[24] might be discounted by some because of this scholar's outright rejection of the Q hypothesis. Of special interest at this point, therefore, is the position of Kilpatrick, a defender of Q, who writing as recently as 1946 trenchantly argues against the theory that by "the oracles" Papias meant the document Q:

> On this hypothesis Q was originally written in Aramaic, and later a number of Greek translations of it were made, one of them being used in both our Matthew and Luke. But, if there were several translations of Q, how is it that Matthew and Luke independently use the same one, while of the others there is no sign? Again, it is not surprising that an anonymous document incorporated in both Matthew and Luke should later disappear, but it is surprising that a document, accepted as the work of the Apostle and in sufficiently widespread circulation in the latter part of the first century to be used by these two evangelists, should have disappeared without a trace.[25]

The Superscriptions

Passing by for the time being (until Chapter IV) an evaluation of the declaration of Papias concerning the language of Matthew, we observe that apart from the superscriptions of the manuscripts of the Gospels themselves there are no additional witnesses to the authorship of the Gospels within the first half of the second century. It must be admitted, moreover, that the superscriptions cannot be dated with absolute precision. Decisions reached in this area are necessarily bound up with broader conclusions especially concerning the text and canon of the New Testament. Nevertheless, there is substan-

---

Kilpatrick, *The Origins of the Gospel According to St. Matthew* (Oxford: Clarendon, 1946), p. 3; J. B. Lightfoot, *op. cit.*, pp. 171f.; T. Zahn, *Geschichte des ntl. Kanons* (Erlangen: Deichert, 1888), I, 860f.; *Einleitung* II, 260f. (E.T., II, 509ff.). See also the recent comments of F. V. Filson, *The Gospel according to St. Matthew*, HNTC (New York: Harper, 1960), p. 17.

24. Ropes, *op. cit.*, p. 107.

25. Kilpatrick, *op. cit.*, p. 4. Kilpatrick's comments on the view that τὰ λόγια might be understood as a kind of testimony book are also weighty. *Cf.* pp. 4f.

tial agreement that the superscriptions, in the forms According to Matthew, According to Mark, According to Luke, and According to John, originated no later than A.D. 140 and in all probability were handed down with the Gospel texts as early as A.D. 125. The four names, moreover, were evidently understood as referring to authorship.

J. H. Ropes favors a date c. A.D. 125. Appealing to the uniformity of the titles and taking account of the history of the fourfold Gospel, he declares:

> Probably as early in the second century as the year 125, someone, in some place, or some group of persons, assembled for the use and convenience of the churches the only four Greek books describing the life and teachings of Jesus Christ which were then believed to be of great antiquity and worthy of a place in such a collection. To them were assigned as such a collection required, uniform titles, the Gospel according to Matthew, to Mark, and the others . . . .[26]

Ropes' general conclusion, accordingly, is that the Synoptics are not pseudonymous, that they are so old that it was possible to claim that actual apostles and their associates had written them, and that about A.D. 125 all the Gospels were already relatively ancient books associated with an earlier generation.

Alfred Plummer stated the matter somewhat more cautiously but nevertheless hardly with less emphasis as regards the force of the intent of the superscriptions:

> In no case is the title to a book of the New Testament part of the original document. It was in all cases added by a copyist, and perhaps not by the first copyist. Moreover, in all cases it varies considerably in form, the simplest forms being the earliest. Thus "according to" neither affirms nor denies authorship; it implies *conformity to a type,* and need not mean more than "drawn up according to the teaching of." But it is certain that the Christians of the first four centuries who gave these titles to the Gospels meant more than this: they believed, and meant to express, that each Gospel was written by the person whose name it bears. They used this mode of expression, rather than the genitive case used of the Epistles, to intimate that *the same subject had been treated of by others;* and they often emphasized the oneness of the subject by speaking of "the Gospel" rather than "the Gospels."[27]

26. Ropes, *op. cit.,* pp. 103f. Quoted by permission.
27. Alfred Plummer, *An Exegetical Commentary on the Gospel According to St. Matthew* (London: Scott, 1910), p. vii.

Kilpatrick is in agreement with regard to the date of the superscriptions, at least so far as this relates to Matthew, but in other respects his position is unique. He states specifically that the superscription, understood as having reference to the apostle Matthew, "came into being not later than A.D. 125."[28] Thus on his view also the earliest extant testimony ascribed this Gospel to the apostle Matthew. At first blush Kilpatrick's position with regard to the superscription of Matthew might seem the more weighty because of his own personal rejection of apostolic authorship. But it must not be overlooked that what he actually holds is that the real evangelist — not the apostle Matthew — in the interest of clothing a non-apostolic work with the authority of an apostolic name deliberately joined the name Matthew to the document as a pseudonym and that this action was approved by the church with which he was associated. On Kilpatrick's understanding, accordingly, the superscription "according to Matthew" does not presuppose a belief in apostolic authorship on the part of the church most intimately associated with the origin of this Gospel, nor does it allow for the possibility of a somewhat earlier tradition of association of Matthew's name with the Gospel as its actual author. This view of Kilpatrick will be critically examined at the end of the next chapter.

The evidence of the superscriptions, accordingly, unless some such view as that of Kilpatrick were to be accepted, constitutes exceedingly early second century testimony to the authorship of the four Gospels. It shows that the traditions reported by Irenaeus, Tertullian, and other patristic witnesses were maintained by or were current in the Church no later than c. A.D. 125. The view that the superscriptions came to be associated with the several Gospels about that time because the four were brought together and henceforward largely circulated as a fourfold Gospel is plausible in the light of all that we know concerning the history of the text and canon.

Nevertheless, it of course does not follow that the traditional names of the evangelists were, as it were, drawn from a hat on that occasion. On the contrary, since half of these names are not of apostles, there is confirmation of the view that in the Church for a considerable time prior to A.D. 125, and perhaps

28. Kilpatrick, *op. cit.,* p. 138; *cf.* p. 5.

as early as the time of their individual publication, these very persons were associated with the Gospels as their authors.

Granted that the testimony of Papias is in some respects intrinsically difficult and that one may not anticipate a consensus as to its precise meaning in detail, my own considered judgment is that it also serves to demonstrate that well before the middle of the second century the later, more precisely formulated traditional views concerning Gospel origins had been accepted in the Church. And it is noteworthy that Papias also regards his evaluations as expressing, at least to an extent, earlier tradition.

The testimony of tradition regarding authorship appears to be marked by clarity and consistency. As I have been emphasizing, however, such testimony cannot in the nature of the case be accorded a place of absolute authority. It is necessary, therefore, to proceed in the next chapter to the Gospel according to Matthew itself, asking what its contents may have to tell us concerning its origin.

CHAPTER TWO

THE SELF-WITNESS OF MATTHEW

TRADITION may be quite specific regarding the authorship of the Gospels, but the fact must be squarely faced that they themselves are anonymous writings. None of them follows, for example, the practice of the apocryphal Gospel of Peter in including such a statement as the following: "But I, Simon Peter, and Andrew my brother, took our nets and went into the sea. . . ."

With respect to their anonymity one should observe, even though it must be in passing, that there is a noteworthy difference between Matthew and Mark on the one hand, and Luke and John on the other. For in the latter two Gospels there are arresting elements of reflection upon origins including features of self-disclosure on the part of the authors.[1] But there is nothing of this character in either Matthew or Mark.

Confining the discussion now to Matthew, one may take note particularly that this Gospel makes no claim whatsoever that would directly account for the tradition that it was written by the apostle of that name. Nor does this evangelist anywhere take pains to suggest that he was an eyewitness of various events which he records. And, for that matter, there are no features of an explicit or incidental kind that suggest that a later, presumably non-apostolic, writer was seeking to clothe his work with apostolic authority.

There are indeed certain peculiarities in the references to the apostle Matthew in this Gospel. In the Synoptic accounts of the call of the apostle who was once a publican, it is of interest that, whereas Mark and Luke identify him as Levi, our Gospel

---

1. For Luke the prologues of the Gospel and Acts are chiefly in view but the "we"-passages are also significant (cf. WLC, pp. 10ff.; 24ff. and below pp. 113ff.) ; for John, cf. especially Jn. 21:24f. together with Chapter 21 of WLC and such passages as Jn. 13:23ff.; 19:26f., 35; 20:2ff.

19

uses the name Matthew. These narratives agree so fully in detail that Matthew and Levi must be thought of as names for the same person (Mt. 9:9-13; cf. Mk. 2:14ff.; Lk. 5:27ff.). That Mark and Luke presuppose this identification is confirmed by the observation that in their catalogues of the apostles they include Matthew but not Levi (Mk. 3:18; Lk. 6:15; Acts 1:13; cf. Mt. 10:3). Zahn has made the interesting suggestion in explanation of the foregoing that the name Matthew, as the one used in Christian circles, was preferred by one who, formerly known as Levi, had been a hated publican.[2] On the other hand — and I now draw attention to another peculiarity of reference to Matthew in this Gospel — only in the catalogue of Matthew 10:3 is he designated as "the publican." Still another detail which distinguishes the account of the call of Matthew as found in our Gospel from that of Mark and Luke is that only the latter report that, following the call itself, Jesus sat at meat in the house of Matthew; they have the reading "his house" whereas Matthew has merely "the house."

On our part, we do not believe that these data, however interesting, provide any sound basis for the conclusion that this evangelist intends his readers thereby to ascertain his identity. To allow for such a conclusion one would almost have to assume that the evangelist is playing at games, perhaps at "hide-and-seek" or "hidden treasure." Although not in the nature of self-witness, however, these data are distinctly consonant with the tradition of Matthean authorship. This is especially true with regard to the witness of the Synoptics that the person whom the Church acknowledged as the author of the First Gospel had been a tax official. As such he was evidently not a Roman official but one who served Herod Antipas.[3] Laboring in his domain — "Galilee of the Gentiles" — he would probably have spoken Greek as well as Aramaic, and at least a partial background is provided for the understanding of his activity as a writer.[4]

In view of the fact that Edgar J. Goodspeed, as a feature of his rather sensational conversion to the acceptance of the apostolic authorship of Matthew, laid such extraordinary emphasis upon Matthew's qualifications as a tax collector, it seems

2. Zahn, op. cit., II, 259. In English translation, II, 507.
3. Ibid.
4. Cf. E. Schürer, Geschichte des jüdischen Volkes im Zeitalter Jesu Christi, 4te Aufl. (Leipzig: Hinrichs, 1901-1909), I, 57ff., 84ff.

appropriate to make a few observations concerning his book at this point.[5] To do justice to it one would have to make mention of several salutary features. There is, for example, a far wiser appraisal of the strength of the tradition of apostolic authorship than appears in most modern critical discussions. And it may be acknowledged that Goodspeed has helped to fill out our knowledge of the qualifications and activities of the ancient tax collector. This he does, not merely by way of a specific chapter devoted to the subject, but throughout the book as he rather repetitiously develops his thesis that Matthew of all persons was pre-eminently qualified to write the Gospel that has come down under his name. Nevertheless, his thesis does not at every point carry conviction, as for example when he seeks to support it by referring to the evangelist's interest in numbers in the genealogy. Nor is he persuasive in his development of the view that the tax collector, as one "who wrote everything down,"[6] was virtually a secretary of Jesus who had a primary interest in committing his teachings to writing. Some of the argument, especially as it is developed in detail, impresses one as being rather imaginative and even speculative.[7] While therefore Goodspeed must be credited, among other things, with an enlargement of one's understanding of the activities of ancient tax collectors, it must be borne in mind that this does not constitute a positive argument for apostolic authorship. None of this evidence falls in the category of self-witness to authorship. However important the details that have been passed in review are for the identification of the person to whom the ecclesiastical tradition attributed the authorship of our Gospel, he remains after all a relatively obscure figure.

5. E. J. Goodspeed, *Matthew, Apostle and Evangelist* (Philadelphia: Winston, 1959).
6. *Ibid.*, p. 99.
7. In evaluating Goodspeed's "conservative" conclusion one should not overlook the consideration that his predilection for Matthew may find a motive, as it evidently did in the case of F. C. Baur, in his special enthusiasm for the Sermon on the Mount and other discourses as supposedly supporting his essential Liberalism. Moreover, one should keep in view that from the standpoint of the characteristic modern criticism of Matthew, to which attention will be given below, Goodspeed's argument will remain unconvincing because he fails to take account of the historical and theological arguments generally offered as reasons for not accepting apostolic authorship.

Some Basic Objections

It is now necessary to address ourselves seriously to some of the objections which have been raised against accepting the tradition of apostolic authorship. The tradition, we have observed, is early and it is consistent. And it is difficult to account for the origin of the tradition, especially if one bears in mind the relative obscurity of the apostle Matthew, except on the assumption that from the very beginning of its reception on the part of the Church it was known to have come from him. Nevertheless, as I believe we must continue to emphasize, tradition may not be assigned a place of authority on a level with the witness of the Gospels themselves. And so if one's study of Matthew should bring to light elements that contradict the tradition, we ought to be prepared to jettison the tradition and to hold on firmly to what the Gospel discloses concerning itself.

The first objection to be considered briefly involves the question of the sequence of the Gospels, a subject that will come before us for more particular evaluation in the following chapters. Presupposing the priority of Mark to Matthew, a conclusion largely developed by way of comparison of the contents and form of these Gospels, it is maintained — to use the words of Ropes — that "it is inconceivable that one of the twelve . . . should have been so dependent as the author of the First Gospel shows himself to have been on an informant whose opportunities for knowledge of the event were incomparably inferior to his own."[8]

This objection is widely held to be valid. And under the conviction of its cogency conservatives sometimes have insisted that the only way to maintain the apostolicity of Matthew is to repudiate the hypothesis of Mark's priority. At this point of discussion I do not want to assume either the priority of Mark or that of Matthew. But I wish to point out briefly that, in my judgment, the argument in question is completely lacking in force, and that it is not only unnecessary but also unfortunate to link up indissolubly the question of the authorship and order of the Gospels as indicated above. In brief, I hold that those who present this argument unwittingly are in general involved in a modernization of the circumstances of publication in the ancient world and in particular of the publica-

8. Ropes, *op. cit.*, p. 38. Quoted by permission.

tion of the Gospels. There was of course no such thing as copyright. And plagiarism evidently did not enter the picture as a possible factor in the use of one document by the author of another as it does today. The Gospels in particular were not private literary productions. Their anonymity underscores this fact. There was a single gospel in the Christian Church, proclaimed by the apostles, and handed down to all. As the tradition concerning our four Gospels was wont to stress, there was but one gospel, howbeit in a fourfold form. On this perspective it would not be surprising at all if the apostle Matthew should have utilized Mark, assuming that it had come into his hands and he himself recognized it as a genuine publication of the Christian gospel. Such a use of Mark is even more explicable if Matthew previously knew, as tradition later affirmed, that in some significant way the preaching of Peter — which, as Acts discloses, had a pre-eminent place in the earliest Christian Church — contributed to the contents of Mark.

A rather different type of argument than the one which has just been under discussion has evidently, however, contributed far more decisively to the rejection of the apostolic authorship of Matthew. Stated in most general terms this is the argument that a careful study of this Gospel will disclose historical and theological perspectives which are irreconcilable with what an eyewitness and hearer of Jesus in the days of his flesh would presumably have reported. In somewhat more specific terms the argument has characteristically taken the form that there are distinctive tendencies in Matthew — whether legalistic, or ecclesiastical, or universalistic, or eschatological — which betray the fact that the evangelist has rather freely interpreted, that is altered, his sources or has fashioned largely new material as he addressed the Church of his day.[9]

It is rather obvious that this approach involves one not only in judgments concerning authorship but also in the entire gamut of Gospel studies. The question of the order and interdependence of the Gospels is bound to enter into the discussion.

---

9. Among influential modern representatives of this general point of view mention may be made of A. Jülicher, *op. cit.*, pp. 287ff., and J. Moffatt, *An Introduction to the Literature of the New Testament*, 3rd ed. (New York: Scribner's, 1925), pp. 244, 248f. See also A. H. McNeile, *op. cit.*, pp. 8ff. and F. V. Filson, *Origins of the Gospels* (New York: Abingdon, 1938), pp. 162f.; *The Gospel according to St. Matthew*, HNTC, pp. 20f., 41ff.

In this connection it is interesting that Kilpatrick re-formulates the argument which was considered above concerning the implications of Matthew's (supposed) use of sources. "It is incredible," he says, "that an apostle should, for the greater part of his material, depend on written sources and, where he revises them, betray the outlook of a later period."[10] These latter words really constitute the nub of the question at issue. And they point up the fact that the question of date is also in the foreground of attention.

But even these weighty matters of authorship and date and of sequence and interdependence do not stand alone. They are bound up with profound questions of interpretation of the person and ministry of Jesus Christ and of the whole course of the history of the Christian Church within which the Gospels came into being. Such questions as the following are in the center of discussion or are at least implicitly in view. What place did the apostles occupy within this history? Were they actually eyewitnesses? Were they mainly responsible for the proclamation of the Christian message, and did it receive a definite form and authority from them? Was their activity ultimately decisive for the fashioning of the Gospels and the rest of the New Testament? And what -- this question is the most basic of all — are we to think of Jesus Christ? Was he the divine Messiah? Did he intend to establish the Christian Church, and did he deal with his disciples in such a way as to intimate that he regarded them as already constituting the new messianic community? What was the nature of his teaching concerning the kingdom of God, and what of his teaching concerning the parousia? Was his expectation wholly and exclusively futurist, or did he envisage a manifestation of his presence and of the kingdom of God following upon his resurrection and prior to the consummation?

The answer to these important questions is surely to a large extent a matter of exegesis, and since the New Testament is open to all there may be highly fruitful exchanges of varied observations and a testing of conclusions reached in the light of the evidence. Nevertheless, as the history of the study of the New Testament, and of the Gospels in particular, has made abundantly clear, philosophical and theological presuppositions constantly are seen to be basically determinative of hermeneu-

10. Kilpatrick, op. cit., p. 3.

tics and so also decisive for ultimate conclusions. It is a merit of Bultmann's controversial essay on the demythologizing of the New Testament proclamation to have placed this point in sharp focus. I am far from wanting to suggest that one can come to grips with the subject of presuppositions apart from a vigorous grappling with the texts which contain the New Testament message. Nevertheless it is impossible to understand the varied conceptions of the New Testament which have come to prominence in modern times unless one inquires as to the philosophical backgrounds, whether they be rationalistic, Kantian, Hegelian, existentialist or some variation or combination of these classic modern philosophical points of view.

Moreover, it is helpful to observe that, in spite of the tensions and contradictions which often come to expression in the exposition of various modern points of view with reference to the Gospels, there are also features that indicate that these constructions or reconstructions of Christian history are characterized by a greater or lesser measure of inner consistency. Because of such coherence it is possible oftentimes to distinguish between that which is primary and that which is secondary, between the more central aspects and others which are more peripheral, and thus to avoid the necessity of a piecemeal evaluation. To be concrete, it is usually observable that a radically negative view concerning the purpose of Jesus with regard to the Church is bound up with a basic skepticism concerning the testimony of the Gospels to his messiahship. On the other hand, if the messianic claims are taken at face value there is likely to be little difficulty in accepting the view that for Jesus those who followed him and believed on him constituted already in the days of his public ministry a messianic community which was distinguishable from Israel as a whole. Though not precisely identifiable with the Christian Church this community was its forerunner; and its life, even while it looked forward to a fulfillment bound up with the exaltation of Christ, was understood as being in continuity with the Church that Christ promised to build.

Kilpatrick's Reconstruction

So far I have spoken in very general terms as I have endeavored to sum up the main thrust of modern criticism in this area. In the interest of greater particularity and contemporaneity, however, I wish now to draw attention especially to the recently published position of Kilpatrick.[11]

Discussing "The Gospel and Judaism" (Chapter VI of his book), Kilpatrick propounds his thesis that Matthew betrays the outlook of a later period in the fact that it reflects the Judaism of A.D. 70-135. It was within this period, Kilpatrick contends, that the breach between Judaism and Christianity developed; Matthew indeed is not thought of as marking the full climax of this process but rather the conditions that led to the breach. During these decades, he further avers, the controversy with the Jews was heightened and Christians were persecuted, the Pharisees became the dominant party in Judaism, and the liberal attitude towards the Gentiles asserted itself. Although it is maintained that this Gospel manifests a distinctly Christian character, it is insisted that as the Gospel "closest to Rabbinical Judaism," it reflects a time of "re-Judaization" in which "much Jewish moral and religious teaching was transmitted to later Christianity."[12]

That this reconstruction of the relations between Judaism and Christianity and of the place of the Gospel according to Matthew within it is by no means established from the evidence, and indeed at times begs the deeper question at issue, could perhaps be fully shown only by a study in depth and great detail. The following considerations may however suffice for our present purposes:

(1) The question of the so-called Jewishness of Matthew's Gospel must be assessed with the greatest possible care. On the one hand, it may freely be acknowledged that in no other Gospel does the continuity of Christianity with the Old Testament appear with such emphasis. The distinctive introduction of Old Testament quotations most conspicuously makes this point. Moreover, these and other features demonstrate that

11. *Ibid.* See note 23 in Chapter I above. As another current example of this basic point of view one may profitably take account also of recent writings of G. Bornkamm. See especially his article entitled, "Enderwartung und Kirche im Matthäusevangelium," in the volume *The Background of the New Testament and Its Eschatology* (eds. W. D. Davies and D. Daube, Cambridge: University Press, 1956) and his *Jesus von Nazareth* (Stuttgart: Kohlhammer, 1956). An English translation of the 3rd edition of the latter was published by Hodder & Stoughton (London, 1960) and Harper & Brothers (New York, 1961). See my review in *WTJ*, XXIII (May, 1961), 181ff.

12. *Ibid.*, pp. 101, 103, 122f.

the evangelist evidently had a Jewish or Jewish-Christian audience chiefly in view. And thus he takes pains to report at length Jesus' maintenance of the authority of the law and the prophets and at the same time their fulfillment in his life and teaching.[13] Kilpatrick substantially recognizes this point so far as the teaching of the Gospel is concerned, for he says:

> The doctrine of Christ is introduced, not as in Marcion's teaching like a razor which shears off every Jewish feature, but as the true end of Judaism on which all the wealth of Jewish life and teaching is focused. We have, in fact, not an elimination of Judaism, but a reorientation.[14]

But may this statement not be regarded as a rather fair summary of Jesus' own point of view rather than as one which emerged in the Christian Church in the latter part of the first century? Kilpatrick, in my judgment, offers only the most slender kind of support of his own thesis, evidence that fails to bring conviction.

As an example of his argument one may note his appeal to Mark 10:12 compared with Matthew 5:32 and 19:9:

> In Mark, the possibility of a woman divorcing her husband is taken into account, a possibility which existed in Roman but not in Jewish law. In the Matthean passages this provision is omitted, so that the saying conforms to Jewish practice.[15]

13. *Cf. WMMC* (Philadelphia: Presbyterian Guardian, 1944; 2d ed. Grand Rapids: Eerdmans, 1958), pp. 198, 253.
14. Kilpatrick, *op. cit.*, p. 122.
15. *Ibid.*, p. 102. A similar view of Mk. 10:12 has frequently found expression in the commentaries, *e.g.*, Meyer, Gould, Menzies, Grant *(IB)*, Johnson *(HNTC)*, and elsewhere. On the other side, however, see F. C. Burkitt, *The Gospel History and Its Transmission* (Edinburgh: Clark, 1906), pp. 100f.; W. C. Allen *ad* Mk. 10:12 (New York: Macmillan, 1915); John Murray, *Divorce* (Philadelphia 1953), p. 53, n. 15. Strack-Billerbeck *(KNTTM) ad loc.* note certain exceptions to the rule that a woman might not obtain a divorce.
V. Taylor, *The Gospel according to St. Mark* (London: Macmillan, 1953), here favors the D text: "If a woman go away from her husband." Burkitt seems to follow this text and W. C. Allen allows for it. Then Jesus would not be speaking specifically of divorce but of desertion and remarriage. Taylor thinks the Aleph text and the A variation may be explained as efforts to adapt an original saying of Jesus addressed to a Jewish situation to conditions which obtained at Rome. Burkitt, however, maintains that the textual variations do not touch the main point, *viz.*, that "the woman that deserts her husband to marry someone else is blamed as well as the man who divorces his wife" (p. 100). He observes further that while "it was no doubt monstrous to imagine that a Jewess should desert her husband to marry another man," there is the instance of

Apart from the general consideration that it is hazardous to enter a dogmatic judgment as to why Matthew in this case, as in so many others, is briefer than Mark, it is particularly unconvincing to imply that Matthew would have eliminated the teaching concerning the possibility of a woman divorcing her husband simply because he had a Jewish audience or a life-situation in a Jewish-Christian Church in view. In our Lord's teaching on divorce, in Matthew as well as Mark and Luke, there is a central concern to set aside current Jewish views and practices and to insist that the woman's status be elevated. And even if, for the sake of the argument, one were to acknowledge that Matthew might have omitted the teaching of Mark 10:12 because he was thinking in terms of specifically Jewish situations, it would of course not follow that this decision could have emerged only some time after the year A.D. 70.

Murray meets the deeper issue forthrightly in his statement: "Suffice it to say here that it would be wholly indefensible to suppose that our Lord confined himself, particularly in his more private instructions to his disciples as in this instance, to what would have strict and exclusive appurtenance to Jewish custom." He further concludes:

> This text does not of itself prove that the right of the man to divorce his wife for adultery, established by Matthew 5:32; 19:9, belongs also in like manner to the woman. But it does point in the direction of a distinct provision in the Christian economy to the effect that the woman is accorded an equal right with the man in the event of marital unfaithfulness on the part of her spouse. In the Old Testament there is no provision for divorce by the woman. There does not appear to be any such provision in Jewish custom at the time of our Lord. But in this saying (Mark 10:12) there is an indication that our Lord in the exercise of the authority that belonged to him not only provided that a man may divorce his wife for the cause of fornication but that the wife also may divorce her husband for the same offence.[16]

Herodias' desertion of Philip to marry Antipas and this was probably specifically in view. For Burkitt the question whether Herodias actually obtained a divorce is immaterial: "Our Lord's previous words shew that he did not regard an immoral act as being any less immoral for being carried out according to law" (pp. 100f.). Cf. also D. Daube, The N.T. and Rabbinic Judaism (London: Athlone, 1956), pp. 365ff.
16. Murray, op. cit., pp. 53f. On the status of woman in the teaching of Jesus, cf. e.g. also V. Taylor, op. cit., p. 421: "From x. 2-12 it is clear that Jesus regarded marriage as an indissoluble union and that He

(2) As one evidence "that Matthew is closely connected with the Rabbinic Judaism of the end of the first century," Kilpatrick states that the points of controversy "are made more precise and take us further into the Rabbinic tradition."[17] As illustrations he cites (a) the Matthean words, "for every cause," in Matthew 19:3 as an addition to the question of Mark 10:2 "which adapts the question to the form in which it was debated in Scribal circles" and (b) in the story concerning plucking corn on the Sabbath (Mt. 12) the addition "they hungered" in verse one, and of verse five, as making the issue more detailed and illustrating it "with an exception recognized in Rabbinic law."[18]

These data hardly add up to a weighty case for the thesis that Kilpatrick is seeking to establish. Confining myself to the latter point as being the more substantial, I am bound to ask whether Jesus himself might not, quite independently of the scribes, have appealed to the practice of the priests in the temple on the Sabbath. But even if contact with the scribal tradition were established, this would surely not require a date near the end of the first century. The beginnings of the literature of Rabbinical Judaism may with Kilpatrick be dated after A.D. 70. Moreover, Rabbinical Judaism undoubtedly came thereafter to a place of pre-eminence beyond that of the earlier, more complex situation. Nevertheless, there is a broader sense in which the term Rabbinical Judaism also applies to a central, if not to the main, current of Jewish religious life before A.D. 70. It is strange therefore that Kilpatrick places such a sharp disjunction between the "earlier Judaism" and "the Rabbinical Judaism" of the Talmud which he finds reflected in Matthew.

G. F. Moore is representative of authorities on Judaism who stress the continuity of Rabbinical teaching:

> The series of Tannaite sources begins to flow in any volume only with the reestablishment of the schools at Jamnia after the destruction of Jerusalem, that is, about the time when our trio of Gospels may be supposed to have attained the form in which we know them. But the task of Johanan ben Zakkai and his fellows was one of conservation, not of reformation. . . . The

---

placed husband and wife in a relationship of equality. In these respects His teaching went beyond Jewish and Pagan conceptions, giving to marriage a position of the highest dignity."
17. Kilpatrick, *op. cit.*, p. 106.
18. *Ibid.*

Gospels themselves are the best witness to the religious and moral teaching of the synagogue in the middle forty years of the first century, and the not infrequent references, with approval or dissent, to the current Halakah are evidence of the rules approved in the schools of the Law and taught to the people. It is this relation between the Gospels and the teaching of the rabbis, whether tacitly assumed or criticized and controverted, which makes them the important source they are for a knowledge of the Judaism of their time, and on the other hand makes the rabbinical sources the important instrument they are for the understanding of the Gospels.

Long before the Qumran discoveries, it was widely recognized that Moore, in connection with his occupation with so-called "normative Judaism," had somewhat oversimplified the historical developments. And his statement above may not do full justice to the factor of change within Rabbinic tradition. Nevertheless, his central point as to continuity and the relevance of important segments of this tradition for the study of the period before A.D. 70 is still valid.[19]

---

19. G. F. Moore, *Judaism* (Cambridge: Harvard University Press, 1927), I, 131f.; *cf.* also 251ff., 262. Quoted by permission. Moore also stresses the "Jewishness" of Matthew (*e.g.*, pp. 184f.), but this is not tantamount to Kilpatrick's thesis that Matthew definitely reflects the period of Jewish life beyond A.D. 70.
D. Doeve, *Jewish Hermeneutics in the Synoptic Gospels and Acts* (Assen: van Gorcum, 1954), pp. 42ff., holds that Moore's statement concerning "conservation, not of reformation" is faulty, and maintains that one must recognize that that which became normative *c.* A.D. 70 was still in process of growth and restricted to certain circles *c.* A.D. 30 (*cf.* pp. 45f.). Nevertheless, in the main he defends the propriety of the use of Rabbinic data for the study of the N.T. including the teaching of Jesus (*cf.* p. 42 and *passim*).
Cf. Kilpatrick, *op. cit.*, pp. 101ff. For additional evidence he appeals to E. von Dobschütz, "Matthäus als Rabbiner und Katechet," *ZNW*, XXVII (1928), 338ff.; Bacon, *op. cit.*, pp. 71ff., 131ff. Von Dobschütz falls far short, in my judgment, of establishing his thesis that this evangelist had been a rabbi and he is even less plausible in his conjecture that, as a rabbi, he had been a disciple of Rabbi Johanan ben Zakkai, who was active after the destruction of Jerusalem in Jabneh. Bacon also leans on von Dobschütz, and appeals *e.g.* to Matthew's supposed neo-legalism.
The supposedly more Jewish character of Mt. 19:9 as compared with Mk. 10:12 (see note 16 above) is held by Kilpatrick to be an illustration of the way in which a saying of Jesus, first modified by conditions in the Graeco-Roman world, later on in a strongly Jewish church could be adjusted anew to Jewish ways (pp. 102f.). At this point Kilpatrick's discussion merely shows that such a development is theoretically possible but

(3) Nor does Kilpatrick make out an impressive case for his central contention that Matthew, in contrast with Mark, reflects a late state in the history of the Jewish parties and groups when "the Pharisees were the one important Jewish sect contemporary with Matthew."[20] The record of controversy with the Pharisees is to be sure conspicuous in Matthew, but this creates no special problem if only the *Sitz im Leben* in which Jesus carried on his ministry and the audience which the evangelist Matthew is particularly addressing are kept in view. In the light of the actual evidence of the Gospels, Kilpatrick is really far too sweeping in his statement: "In Matthew, the Herods and the Herodians almost disappear from the story and only archaism keeps them there at all, and the same is true of the Sadducees of history."[21] Even this declaration, it will be noted, by way of its reference to "archaism," shows the tendentious character of his position at this point. It is interesting, moreover, that later on he admits that the name "Sadducees" occurs seven times in Matthew, "as often as in the whole of the rest of the New Testament together."[22] Moreover, he is on highly conjectural ground in appealing to Matthew 22:23, as compared with Mark 12:18, as expressing the view that, according to Matthew, "there were Sadducees who denied a resurrection, not that they did so as a party," and especially in his further conclusion that "this suggests that, in Matthew, Sadducee was a more inclusive term than it was in Mark and in history, that it embraces all non-Christian, non-Pharisaic Jews, corresponding to the Rabbinic use of Minim, with the Christian Jews excluded."[23]

(4) Of more substantial moment perhaps is the contention that, whereas "in Mark the differences between the Pharisees lie in certain controversial issues. . . . In Matthew the animus is directed more and more against the Pharisees themselves in

---

does not demonstrate that this was the actual course of events. Moreover, he assumes a rigid approach to Synoptic literary relationships which, in evaluating parallel passages, denies to Matthew access to other sources. Personal recollections are of course excluded on his conclusion that the evangelist was not the apostle Matthew. For other points made by Kilpatrick, see below.

20. *Op. cit.,* p. 121; *cf.* pp. 106, 120ff.
21. *Ibid.,* p. 106.
22. *Ibid.,* p. 120.
23. *Ibid.*

distinction from the controversial issues."[24]   The use of the
phrase "offspring of vipers", directed in part at least against
the Pharisees, in Matthew 3:7 and 12:34, and the declarations
of Matthew 15:12-14, with their strong condemnation of the
Pharisees as "blind guides," are among the evidences offered as
supporting this conclusion. But "the most explicit statement of
the community's attitude" is said to be in Matthew 23:2f. where
a distinction is drawn between the teaching and the works of
the scribes and Pharisees: "The scribes and Pharisees sit on
Moses' seat; all things therefore whatsoever they bid you, do
and observe; but do not ye after their works; for they say and
do not." Kilpatrick immediately concludes: "From this we
must not infer that the controversy had been lost sight of in
a mutual antipathy, but that they had hardened into a sectarian
hostility. The issue of Christ against the Law had become
also the opposition of the Church and the Synagogue."[25]

As to this argument it may be acknowledged that there are
data in Matthew which supplement the testimony of Mark
with regard to the attitude of Jesus towards the Pharisees. But
the issue presented here may not be resolved simply in terms
of a disjunction between issues and persons. In part, we are
faced again with the larger question of Jesus' affirmation of
the law: to the extent that the Jewish teachers affirmed the
law and, sitting on Moses' seat, faithfully expounded it, they
were to be obeyed. At the same time, Matthew 23:2f. can hardly
be pressed to mean that all of the content of Pharisaic teaching
was approved, for the Gospel is replete with testimony to the
contrary.[26] On the other hand, in speaking with new authority

24. *Ibid.,* p. 121.
25. *Ibid.*
26. The leaven of the Pharisees and Sadducees is definitely identified with
their teaching (Mt. 16:12). And their teaching is specifically distinguished
from that of Jesus with respect to table fellowship (9:11), the sabbath
(12:2), ceremonial cleansing (15:2) and marriage and divorce (19:3). The
righteousness with respect to which the Pharisees are deficient relates not
merely to lack of attainment but also to erroneous interpretation (5:20,
21ff.; *cf.* also 3:7f., 9). The Pharisees are directly accused of transgressing
and making void the Word of God because of their tradition (15:3, 6) and
their designation as "blind guides" (15:14) applies most pointedly to their
instruction. Finally, the denunciation of them as "offspring of vipers"
(3:7; 12:24) may be explained, in part at least, by their charge that Jesus
cast out demons by the prince of demons (9:34, 12:24ff.), which Jesus responds to by drawing the lines between himself and the Pharisees in the
strongest possible antithetical terms (12:25ff., 31f.).

and not as the scribes, Jesus confronted men with the living God
as only lawgiver and judge and exposed the formalism and
hypocrisy of those who yielded up to God anything short of
perfect devotion to him and love of their neighbors as themselves. His indignation at such hypocrisy was so profound and
his exposure of it so soul-searching and wrathful that his language at times may even appear to be severe and harsh. But
if only one recognizes the claims which Jesus makes as sovereign
Judge, it is not necessary to project into the distant future a
time when these words of condemnation would have relevance.

(5) Nor is Kilpatrick persuasive when, discussing the subject of the relation between Christians and Jews from the standpoint of the activity of the Jewish synagogue, he argues that
Matthew reflects a time of persecution late in the century.
There are to be sure evidences from Jewish and Christian
documents from approximately that time that Jewish measures
against Christians "included controversy and propaganda, exclusion from the synagogues, persecution, and even death."[27]
When, however, Kilpatrick turns to present some of the evidence of Matthew which supposedly demonstrates that the opposition of the Christian Church to Judaism had led to persecution from the side of the synagogue, he can hardly expect
to gain ready assent except from those who fully share his
presuppositions with regard to Matthew. To do justice to
Kilpatrick one ought to take account of his entire statement,
which reads as follows:

> The following passages suggest that propaganda and delation
> were practised, v. 11 beside Luke vi. 22, Matt. xv. 19, [false
> witness],[28] xxiv. 10, though we cannot be sure that the delators
> were Pharisees. After A.D. 135 the Jews themselves suffered
> considerably from delation. The Jewish Christians experienced,
> as had St. Paul, the discipline of the synagogue, xxiii. 34, with
> which we may compare x. 17 from Mark xiii. 9. They were
> chased from town to town, x. 23, xxiii. 34, and were put to
> death, xxii. 6, by stoning, xxi. 35, or by crucifixion, xxiii. 34.
> These references are to passages which are in their form peculiar
> to the Gospel and are frequently due to the rewriting of the
> sources, which suggests that the statements are true for the
> evangelist's own time.[29]

27. *Op. cit.*, p. 115.
28. In place of "false witness" in brackets Kilpatrick quotes the plural
Ψευδομαρτυρίαι.
29. *Ibid.*, pp. 121f.

One need not linger long over the former passages inasmuch as Kilpatrick himself admits that there is no evidence that the accusation in view was thought of as being Pharisaic in origin. Moreover — and this is a point which Kilpatrick simply ignores — these references to delation are not restricted in any respect from a temporal point of view. Is it not therefore most arbitrary and even irresponsible to insist, for example, that the Matthean beatitude, "Blessed are ye when men shall reproach you, and persecute you, and say all manner of evil against you falsely, for my sake," must be explained in terms of, and even as derived from, the life-situation of the Church towards the end of the first century? This criticism applies substantially to the latter group of passages as well. The prophecies of Matthew 10:17 and 23, uttered in connection with the sending out of the Twelve, and the prophetic words of Matthew 23:34 are without further discussion summarized by Kilpatrick *in the past tense* as descriptive of the historical situation on which he had been centering our attention. The prophecy of Matthew 23:34, "Wherefore, behold, I send unto you prophets, and wise men, and scribes; some of them shall ye kill and crucify; and some of them shall ye scourge in your synagogues, and persecute from city to city," does not support the thesis that at the time of the composition of Matthew Christians experienced the discipline of the synagogue, were chased from town to town and were put to death by crucifixion.

The appeal to Matthew 21:35 and 22:6 may well be considered separately because they are parts of parables rather than prophetic utterances. Only the Matthean form of the parable of the wicked husbandmen mentions stoning, but obviously a really satisfactory evaluation of such a detail cannot be undertaken hopefully apart from a broader study of the other peculiar features of the Synoptic accounts. Such a study will not be entered upon here. For our present purposes it is enough to note that the servants were beaten and killed and stoned prior to the mission of the Son. The reference therefore is to the prophets of the old dispensation. It is interesting that Jeremias, even though he holds that the Matthean form of the parable is the latest of the three and reflects substantial editorial modification of an allegorical character, interprets the stoning as having special reference to the fate of the prophets.[30]

30. J. Jeremias, *The Parables of Jesus* (London: SCM, 1954), translated from *Die Gleichnisse Jesu,* 3te Aufl. (Zürich: Zwingli, 1954), pp. 56f.

The Appeal to Matthew 22:6

The final reference which is thought to reflect the discipline
of the synagogue is Matthew 22:6 where the response of those
who were bidden to the royal marriage feast included the
feature that they killed the servants who had conveyed the
king's invitation. In contrast to the reference in the parable
of the wicked husbandmen which has been under consideration
this statement concerning murder seems, at first blush at least,
not to presuppose any specific historical situation. The terms
employed are quite general, and in particular there would
appear not to be anything that would precisely delineate the
historical situation that Kilpatrick has in view. Nevertheless,
it is clear that this writer presupposes a modern interpretation
of this parable which puts an entirely different face upon the
question. Some intimation of this has been given by Kilpatrick
himself where, in connection with his discussion of the date
of Matthew, he appeals to Matthew 22:7:

> A comparison of Matt. xxii. 1-10 with Luke xiv. 16-24 suggests
> that the story at Matt. xxii. 7 has been rewritten to make
> explicit reference to the destruction of Jerusalem. Before this
> alteration could be effected it was necessary for the fall of
> Jerusalem to lead to a change in the interpretation of the
> passage, and this modified interpretation had to become fixed
> before it could be written into the text as it is in our Gospel.
> This seems to require a date after A.D. 75.[31]

In order to understand Matthew 22:6, 7 we ought to consider the interpretation of the parable as a whole. And inasmuch as Bornkamm — who, as has been noted, substantially
shares Kilpatrick's view of Matthew — has recently made a
striking appeal to this parable and the companion parable in
Luke 14, we may profitably center attention upon his discussion. The fact that Bornkamm dwells upon these parables not
from the point of view of their possible bearing upon the dates
of the Gospels but rather in the interest of establishing the
correctness of his total estimate of the witness of the Gospels
(according to which we are meant to understand the past
history of Jesus as concerned not with who Jesus was but who
he is), does not detract from our interest in what he has to say.
On the contrary, this confirms the observation previously made
that decisions regarding questions of special introduction in-

31. *Op. cit.,* p. 6.

evitably entail broader historical and theological implications.
Bornkamm's comments are as follows:

> For the clarification of this contemporary nature of the word
> of Jesus, let us here refer to a single obvious example, to which
> we can find many parallels. When one compares the different
> versions of Jesus' parable of the Great Supper (Mt. xxii. 1ff.;
> Lk. xiv. 16ff.), one sees that Luke tells it differently from
> Matthew, and moreover provides the older text. A rich man
> invites his friends to the feast, but the guests refuse the invita-
> tion with plausible though fatuous excuses. The account in
> Luke remains in the quite natural setting of a parable. In
> Matthew the telling is strengthened by lurid features. The man
> of means has become a king. The meal has become the marriage
> feast for his son. The servants (no longer only one) are mal-
> treated and killed. We read further in Matthew that the
> infuriated king sends out his armies against the thankless and
> murderous guests and burns down their city. One sees at once
> that this is no longer a simple parable. Each special feature de-
> mands interpretation and understanding. The king is a standard
> picture of God. The king's son is the Messiah. The marriage
> is a picture of the joy of the Messianic age. In the fate of the
> servants we recognise the martyrdom of God's messengers. In
> the military campaign we recognize the Jewish war, and in the
> destruction of the city, the catastrophe of A.D. 70. The old
> people of God, having become rebellious, will be rejected and
> a new people will be called. But this new people is still a
> mixture of good and bad on the way to judgment and the
> final separation of the unworthy. (Only in Matthew does the
> parable end with the rejection of the man who came to the
> wedding without a wedding garment.) In Matthew's version
> we find clearly worked into the parable of Jesus his own story,
> a picture of Israel and the picture of the early Church. The
> word of Jesus long ago has become today's word.

Luke, at least at first, has better preserved the original
character of the simple parable, but he also reveals the tendency
of the word of Jesus to become contemporary. He makes the
servant of the nobleman go out not only twice but three times;
after the first refusal he is sent to the poor, lame and crippled
in the town, and after that once again to those in "the highways
and hedges" *outside* the town. There can be no doubt that
the evangelist intended to represent thereby the advance of the
mission from Israel to the heathen world.

One learns from the example of such a text how strongly the
tradition collected in the Gospels has been influenced by the
believing interpretation of the history and person of Jesus.
The understanding of the "once" of the history of Jesus in its

significance for the "today" of his lordship over the Church and for the divine consummation that lies ahead was able to lead to what in our terms would be considered a relativisation, often even to an elimination of the historical boundaries between the period before and after Easter.[32]

With regard to Bornkamm's comments on these parables and Kilpatrick's appeal to them, several observations may be made: (1) We do well perhaps to remind ourselves first of all that we are confronted here with presuppositions and interpretations of form criticism which are radically at variance with those of historic orthodoxy. The issue concerns not merely minor details which might be regarded as more or less peripheral. Nor is the question simply one of a lack of precise notarial exactitude in the transmission of the words of Jesus.[33] Here we have to do rather with records which are conceived of as substantially reflecting highly distinctive ecclesiastical situations of later decades rather than as trustworthy, though not necessarily verbatim, reports of the actual teaching of Jesus.

(2) In spite of the prevalence of opinions to the contrary I cannot but regard it as gratuitous to insist that these two parables are really only one. The parables of the royal marriage feast and of the great supper, though similar in various respects, are also pervasively different.[34] And certainly no evi-

---

32. *Jesus of Nazareth*, pp. 18f.

33. Bornkamm, it is true, also asserts that "the word of Jesus is preserved, and yet not with the piety of an archivist, nor is it passed on like the utterances of famous rabbis with expositions attached" (p. 17). This statement is as such unobjectionable. See discussion below, pp. ......ff. But the deeper issue relates to the historical setting in which the tradition of Jesus' teaching is to be envisioned, whether within the framework of Jesus' own life on earth or the *Sitz im Leben* of the Church, Palestinian or Hellenistic, of the decades following the conclusion of Jesus' earthly ministry.

34. There is, to be sure, an element of agreement in the insistence of the host that the feast shall be well-attended in spite of the negative response of those who are invited. For the rest, however, the differences throughout are so many and substantial that anyone who takes pains to compare the two parables with any care will be impressed with the divergences. These disagreements are as a matter of fact largely or wholly observed and admitted by modern scholars who maintain that originally they were but a single parable, but these differences are appealed to in support of their hypothesis that the original parable has been radically modified within the course of its transmission in the Church, and that in its divergent forms it reflects variant ecclesiastical situations and points of view. Thus C. H. Dodd, *The Parables of the Kingdom* (London: Nisbet,

dence exists which can convincingly demonstrate that the Matthean and Lucan parables possess their present forms as a result of editorial modification of an earlier supposedly simpler parable. Far-reaching presuppositions concerning Jesus and the evangelists have clearly affected the issue here. One of these is that because of the recognition of the fact of interdependence the evangelists must be thought of as mere editors, confined to the use of written sources, and not as being also eyewitnesses and hearers, or persons in contact with them, who were able to hand down independent traditions. Or there may be the assumption that the variant form of similar teachings of Jesus must regularly be explained as due to modifications which have taken place in oral or written transmission rather than, at least in part, to the fact that because Jesus taught in many different places and over a considerable period of time there must have been almost constant repetition of themes and subject matter accompanied by substantial diversity of form.

1935), p. 121, admits that "the differences between the two versions of the parable make it unlikely that the evangelists depended upon a single proximate source." If the differences are so great that one may not fairly conjecture dependence upon "a single proximate source," is one on good ground in insisting upon a common ultimate origin? And J. Jeremias, *op. cit.*, p. 36, though also maintaining that there was only a single original parable, declares in connection with comment upon the common element that "we have here one of the numerous parables which, like the parables of the Laborers in the Vineyard and the Lost Sheep . . . , were applied by Jesus to his critics and opponents in order to vindicate the good news against them. You, he says, are like the guests who slighted the invitation; you would not receive it; hence God has called the publicans and sinners and has offered them the salvation which you have rejected." But if Jesus taught "numerous" parables with this thrust, why should it be insisted that the two parables under discussion here were necessarily one?

On the other hand, no doubt from time to time there have been orthodox interpreters who have also allowed that these parables are divergent accounts of the same discourse. Calvin, for example, treats them in that way in his Commentary *ad loc.* In reading Calvin, however, one receives the impression that he has not undertaken a careful comparison of the accounts. To say the least, there is no evidence in his exposition that he has made an adequate examination of them in relation to one another. Moreover, Calvin says that "Matthew and Luke differ in this respect, that Matthew details many circumstances while Luke states the matter summarily and in a general manner. . . . There is a remarkable agreement between them on the main point." This statement points up the fact that Calvin has not done justice to the distinctive features of Luke. And, apart from Lk. 14:23, he devotes very little attention to these elements in his exposition.

(3) Although Bornkamm does not precisely speak of *allegorization* of the allegedly original parable, it becomes obvious in connection with his comparison of Luke and Matthew that he regards various details in Matthew, and evidently in Luke as well, as betraying a process of allegorization, and that it is on this account that the parable cannot be held to be original with Jesus. At this point, however, he reflects a rigid and stereotyped conception of what a parable is and it may be that cannot be established scientifically, and least of all by way of appeal to the Bible, as, for example, Matthew Black's recent article on "The Parables as Allegory" emphasizes.[35] It is salutary that it is coming to be more widely recognized that the presence of so-called "allegorical traits" in a parable by no means establishes its secondary character. Moreover, in any case, there is no objective standard for judging that the Church might have allegorized parables but that Jesus could not have done so.

35. *Bulletin of the John Rylands Library*, XLII (March, 1960), 273-287. Another recent article that bears positively on this point is that of J. J. Vincent on "The Parables of Jesus as Self-Revelation" in *Studia Evangelica, TU* LXXIII (Berlin: Akademie, 1959), p. 79. Among older studies which avoided at least in part the absolute disjunction between parable and allegory mention may be made of A. M. Brouwer, *De Gelijkenissen* (Leiden, 1946). See also A. H. McNeile, *The Gospel according to St. Matthew* (London: Macmillan, 1938), p. 186 (quoted by Black). The flexibility of the term *mashal* and of παραβολή, as used in the Bible, together with a study of the "parables" themselves militates strongly against the rigid and over-simplified definition of a parable which, in reaction against the extremes of allegorization of parables, dogmatically and subjectively insists that a parable as such could not contain allegorical traits. This approach which has generally held sway since the monumental work of Jülicher is essentially maintained also by Dodd and Jeremias, though they are thoroughly cognizant of the flexibility of linguistic usage.
R. V. G. Tasker, *The Gospel according to St. Matthew, TC* (Grand Rapids: Eerdmans, 1961), on the basis of various subjective judgments as to what is proper to a parable, insists that Mt. 22:5, 6 "interrupt the story and are unnecessary for the exposition of the truth it enshrines." He then resorts to the radical expedient of explaining these verses as a textual gloss added after the fall of Jerusalem, which subsequently became embodied in the text. The presence of this "insertion," understood as "a reference to the destruction of Jerusalem which was by now a *fait accompli*" is, moreover, advanced in support of his thesis that the Greek Matthew, by an unknown author, was written considerably later than an original Aramaic Gospel of the apostle Matthew (*cf.* pp. 15, 206f.). This view of Matthew, as of the Synoptic problem as a whole (*cf.* pp. 11-16), is rather close to Wikenhauser's position. See below, pp. 52f., 89f.

And although the older allegorical method of interpretation of the parables, with its far-fetched endeavor to find some spiritual counterpart to every natural feature of the parable, should not be rejuvenated, the presence of a variety of fixed metaphors, such as father and son or king and kingdom, should compel greater caution in rendering judgments as to the marks of a genuine parable. Bornkamm's interpretations are clearly at fault in this regard.

(4) Another observable exegetical defect is that no proper distinction is made between the understanding of the fixed metaphors in a parable and the interpretation of other details which allegedly point to specific historical events. Under the former category may properly be placed Bornkamm's declarations that the king must have God in view, that the king's son is the Messiah and that the marriage feast is a picture of the messianic age. But the declaration that "in the military campaign we recognize the Jewish war, and in the destruction of the city, the catastrophe of A.D. 70," is of an utterly different character. The latter are not fixed metaphors, readily explained by way of reflection upon the history of revelation, but are bold assumptions without any specific exegetical support. This is particularly patent when one keeps in view that these details are presented *in a parable* rather than in a prophetic discourse. It is unscientific therefore to assume that these latter elements may be taken for granted as constituting the intended meaning of the declarations in Matthew 22:6, 7. Thus also the data of Matthew 22:8-14 do not possess that specificity of reference which would require one to understand that "a picture of Israel and the picture of the early Church" are definitely in view.

It is readily understandable, to be sure, that Matthew's parable, because of its setting near the end of the public ministry and following the Parable of the Wicked Husbandmen (21:33-44), might be interpreted by some expositors as reflecting on the rejection of the Jewish people. And on this approach it may seem to be but a short step to take Matthew 22:9 as referring to the mission to the Gentiles. In my judgment, however, more reserve and caution are in order than are commonly shown. Even the Parable of the Wicked Husbandmen, though clearly prophetic of the new order which would come to manifestation following the death of the Son, does not specify the components of the "nation" to which the kingdom of God would be given. The condemnation expressed in

THE SELF-WITNESS OF MATTHEW

41

the parable is that of the Jewish leaders, not of the Jewish
people as a whole; the Jewish leaders feared the multitudes
because they took Jesus for a prophet (21:46). The parable
of Chapter 21 accordingly provides no specific background of
reference to the calling of the Gentiles. And in view of the
far more general character of the language of the parable of
Chapter 22 one may hardly press the reference to "the partings
of the highways" in Matthew 22:9 as expressive of a prophecy
of the Gentile mission.

And even less plausible is the contention that the parable
of the great supper in Luke, in contrast to the teaching of the
Matthean parable, must be understood as having in mind "the
advance of the mission from Israel to the heathen world" merely
because of the change of scene from "the city" in Luke 14:21
to the area "outside" in verse 23.

One is astonished at the positiveness and even dogmatism
with which this interpretation is generally maintained. Jeremias is quite emphatic:

> Doubtless by the first invitation to the uninvited which takes
> place within the city, Luke is indicating the call of the publicans
> and sinners, while the invitation to those outside the city refers
> to the Gentiles. Since Matthew knows of only one invitation
> to the uninvited (Mt. xxii, 9), the repetition of the invitation
> is an expansion of the parable. This is not to suggest that the
> admission of the Gentiles to a share in the Kingdom of God
> lay beyond the horizon of Jesus' vision, but the possibility can
> only be hinted at here that Jesus envisaged the participation
> of the Gentiles in a different way, not in the form of the
> Christian mission, but as the inrush of the Gentiles in the
> eschatological hour, now so imminent (Mt. viii, 11ff.). It was
> the primitive Church, in a situation demanding missionary
> activity, which inserted a missionary command into our parable.
> Hence we conclude that the primitive Church interpreted and
> expanded the parable of Jesus in accordance with its own
> actual situation.[36]

36. Jeremias, op. cit., p. 37, and Dodd, op. cit., p. 122, speak of the interpretation as "probable." Cf. also ad loc. R. C. Trench, Notes on the Parables
of Our Lord (London: Macmillan, 14th ed., 1882), pp. 231f.; A. Plummer
(ICC); B. S. Easton, The Gospel according to St. Luke (Edinburgh: Clark,
1926); J. M. Creed, The Gospel according to St. Luke (London: Macmillan,
1930); S. Greijdanus (KNT and KV); N. Geldenhuys (NICNT); S. M.
Gilmour (IB); K. H. Rengstorf (NTD). T. Zahn, however, opposes this
interpretation in his discussion of the parable (ZKNT).

The most favorable estimate of this tendency toward an exegetical consensus is to be found in a laudatory desire for the discovery of exegetical relevance. It must not be forgotten however that the tendency is a highly dangerous one as it may easily lead to reading into a passage a teaching which was not actually present. This is no doubt part of the impetus behind the historic proclivity toward allegorical exegesis, and I fear that some conservative exegetes at this point disclose that they have not been successful in freeing themselves from this hermeneutical approach. On the other hand, it is somewhat ironical that many Liberal expositors, who insist that anything that suggests allegory in the record of the parables of Jesus must be forthrightly eliminated, at the same time, in reinterpreting the parables in their supposedly true life-situations in the Church, virtually apply the allegorical method and claim to discover many obvious concrete references and meanings in the general language of the parables.[37]

According to the Gospel records Jesus does indeed at times reflect prophetically upon the establishment of the Church, the future of Israel, and the salvation of the Gentiles. Wherever such prophecies appear, whether in a straightforward manner in utterances of prophetic form or indirectly and allusively, one must take pains to do full justice to their import for the understanding of the gospel message. Nevertheless the general restraint of prophetic discourse must be kept in view, and one must be sure never to run ahead of the evidence itself. And, finally, one's understanding of these prophecies will be bound up, to a greater or lesser extent, with the answer to the question whether they are in fact *vaticinia ex eventu* or are in truth genuine prophecies. Kilpatrick and Bornkamm are representatives of the former point of view; I join with many others in accepting the latter.

37. As an additional, specific point relating to the meaning of the Lucan parable it may be stressed that justice must be done to the setting provided for it in Lk. 14:12-14. Here the point made is that that kind of hospitality is approved which is offered without thought of recompense in the present life. The parable illustrates and reinforces this point by vividly emphasizing the unwearied persistence with which this hospitality must be manifested regardless of discouraging negative responses to it. The teaching, to be sure, is placed within the perspective of the coming of the kingdom of God (*cf.* 14:15) and the Lord who made the great supper is no doubt thought of as finding identification with God. But this is not to say that particular reference to the history of Israel and the Gentile mission is intended.

Conclusion Regarding Matthean Authorship

Who, then, wrote the Gospel according to Matthew? On the critical approach which has been under discussion, and for that matter frequently even on the basis of a somewhat higher estimate of the significance of Matthew as a witness to the life of Christ, one simply does not know the answer. The Gospel itself because of its contents is acknowledged on all sides as one of the greatest books ever written. And, as one recalls its history within the Christian Church and beyond its borders, it is also one of the most influential upon the life and thought of men.[38] Yet one would then have to be reconciled to the conclusion that its author's identity has been lost forever. He would simply be an unknown person though we might perhaps be constrained to call him The Great Unknown.

The agnosticism of such a conclusion is not essentially mitigated by theories which propose that this Gospel utilized a Matthean source and that Papias may be understood as referring to such a source. As the proponents of these theories would also admit, these hypothetical sources made a relatively meager contribution to the total contents of the Gospel, and the finished Gospel reflects such a high degree of integrity of thought and originality of arrangement that its author must be acknowledged to be a person and writer of great ability and stature. But, in any case, these theories are beset with very grave difficulties. As has been argued above, the appeal to Papias is especially implausible. And it is well nigh impossible to explain how a writing of the apostle Matthew, which was so honored as to be incorporated in a later Gospel or Gospels, should have completely disappeared. Moreover, because of the absence of supporting historical evidence, one is bound to resort to speculation to commend the conclusion that a non-apostolic gospel would easily and naturally come to be ascribed to an apostle who was the author merely of one of its sources.

On this last point it is particularly instructive to take account of Streeter's construction. Basic to his argument is the following perceptive observation:

38. On this point especially as it relates to the second century, see A. Wikenhauser, *New Testament Introduction* (New York: Herder & Herder, Third Impression, 1960), pp. 198f.

Now a poem or a pamphlet may lose little by being anonymous —
sometimes, indeed, it may gain in effect; but a record of events,
many of them of a marvellous description, purporting to give
an authentic account of one whose deeds, words, and divine
nature were a matter of acute controversy, would carry no
weight at all if by an unknown author.[39]

Because of Streeter's rejection of apostolic authorship, however,
he proceeds to the conclusion that this Gospel, in view of its
standing, must have originated in an important church and
have been backed by one of the great churches. And he concludes that it was

originally compiled for the use of some particular church which
accepted it at once as a reliable authority, simply because it
knew and had confidence in the person or committee who produced it.[40]

The evangelist himself, it is further contended, because he
knew that one of his sources was the work of the apostle
Matthew, gave a certain prominence to Matthew in his narrative by the introduction of that name in Matthew 9:9. And
then Streeter simply adds:

If, however, the Gospel incorporated a document which was
popularly ascribed to Matthew (I suggest Q), the book as a
whole would soon come to be regarded as his in the Church
for which it was first written.[41]

Even if one could assume the correctness of all that precedes
this last quotation, the conclusion that "the book as a whole
would soon come to be regarded as his" stands baldly alone
devoid of proof and incapable of proof.

The position of Kilpatrick, on the other hand, is marked by
a greater degree of simplicity. Not only, according to this
author, was the Gospel not written by the apostle Matthew
but we also possess no certain knowledge concerning the authorship of any of its sources. Papias must have been speaking
about this Gospel and regarded the apostle Matthew as its
author, but Papias was simply mistaken. Nevertheless, the
historian is faced with the necessity of accounting for the fact
that no later than A.D. 125 the Gospel was ascribed to Matthew.

At this point in his argument indeed Kilpatrick's simplicity
begins to desert him and he becomes no less speculative than

39. Streeter, *op. cit.*, p. 500.
40. *Ibid.*, pp. 500f.
41. *Ibid.*, p. 501.

those who hold to a somewhat more moderate but also more complex approach to the question of authorship. First of all, he conjectures that Matthew was probably known just as "The Gospel," but that it was found to be increasingly desirable to distinguish the Gospel from the other three by some name of apostolic weight.[42] Secondly, he seeks to face the question why the book was designated "According to Matthew" instead of, for example, "According to Peter." Even when one takes account of the information which this Gospel presents concerning the call of Matthew, it must be recognized, Kilpatrick declares, that "Matthew is a much less important figure than Peter and if an apostolic name was to be sought from the contents of the book, it would be expected that Peter would be chosen."[43] That it was ascribed to Matthew rather than Peter, he further contends, must be due to the evangelist himself. In short, the book from the beginning was "deliberately pseudonymous" and received "its pseudonymous heading" from its unknown author. The presence of the name Matthew in Matthew 9:9 is explained in terms of this same situation: the author changed the name Levi to Matthew and added the title as parts of the same action of false ascription of his book to the apostle.

Finally, Kilpatrick considers briefly the question of the plausibility and propriety of this false ascription in the light of the historical situation of that day. If one were to think of the publication of the Gospel as a private undertaking, he supposes, this might have created a problem: "A private production claiming apostolic authorship was, as we know of the later Acts of Paul, liable to severe scrutiny." If, on the other hand, it were an official production, Kilpatrick believes, no such difficulty would have been present:

An official work whose pseudonymity was approved by the authorities of the church would not have to meet the guardians of canonicity. Nor need the suggestion of deliberate pseudonymity on the part of the evangelist cause qualms. The ancient feelings and conventions about the practice were different from ours and we have an undoubted example in the New Testament in 2 Peter.[44]

42. Cf. Kilpatrick, op. cit., pp. 7, 138. Kilpatrick here appeals to B. W. Bacon, Studies in Matthew, p. 19, as having made the suggestion that at first Matthew was known just as "the Gospel."
43. Ibid., p. 138.
44. Ibid., p. 139.

The above construction of Kilpatrick is so replete with conjectural and speculative features that one does not need to engage in detailed analysis in order to assess its cogency and credibility. We ought to comment briefly, however, on the last point. Perhaps the most extraordinary feature of the statement is that it appears to allow for a kind of double morality: in dealing with individuals the church would feel the necessity of being quite scrupulous and circumspect in judging whether a work was truly of apostolic authorship. But in evaluating actions approved by the authorities of the church it would be under no such restraint or compunction! Perhaps, however, Kilpatrick's intent is to distinguish sharply between the standards of the church in the latter part of the second century and those which were in operation at the beginning. Can he possibly mean that the church strictly applied the test of apostolicity in judging canonicity at about the year A.D. 175 but that it followed different standards at about the end of the first century? It is perhaps difficult to make out this point with absolute certainty. In any case, he recognizes that the church at this earlier time had a keen interest in associating apostolic names with its authoritative teaching. And, in my judgment, there is not an iota of evidence that the church's profound interest in the apostolic message and its apostolic transmission, as that is reflected so fully in the New Testament and in such early post-apostolic writings as *I Clement* and the Epistles of Ignatius, could be met and satisfied by anything that was regarded as not being genuinely apostolic. As we have noted in commenting upon the tradition concerning Mark and Luke, even Gospels which were accepted as apostolic in content and associated in their origins with apostolic names, were not ascribed to apostles. Whatever might be said of the practice of pseudonymity in general, it is plain that it does not control the tradition of the fourfold gospel.

By way of summary, then, my position is that the tradition concerning the apostolic authorship of Matthew is strong, clear, and consistent and that the arguments advanced against its reliability are by no means decisive. One must take account indeed of the fact that the analysis of the self-witness of the Gospel is not a simple matter. One is involved in judgments concerning broad historical questions and profound theological issues. Nevertheless, it is my considered opinion that the apostolic authorship of Matthew is as strongly attested as any fact of ancient church history. In phrasing the matter in this way, however, it will be observed that I am maintaining a distinction here between the witness of the Gospel itself and the witness of tradition, which in the last analysis is the distinction between Scripture and tradition. Accordingly, however strong my conviction as to the apostolic authorship of Matthew, I maintain that one should not elevate this testimony of tradition to the level of the Scripture and so regard it as a dogma of the Christian faith. The understanding of the inspiration and authority of the Gospels must indeed not be abstracted from the historical situation in which they were composed and handed down to the Church. But the inspiration and authority of these anonymous writings ultimately do not depend upon the identification of their human authors but upon the activity of the Holy Spirit in the process of redemptive revelation.

CHAPTER THREE

THE QUESTION OF ORDER AND INTERDEPENDENCE

THE average Christian reader of the Gospels is likely, quite understandably and properly, to be absorbed in what the four documents, separately and in turn, witness to him concerning the glad tidings of salvation in Jesus Christ. His interest in their origins is apt to be minimal, though quite probably, if he is weighing their significance for himself and others, the matter of authorship will at least arouse his inquisitiveness. He may even eventually develop some curiosity concerning the dates of their composition and so also as to the sequence of their publication. Only if his reading is characterized by acute attention and his memory is keen, however, is he likely to take much notice of the basic ingredients of the Synoptic Problem as that emerges from observations concerning the extensive elements of agreement among the Synoptics along with substantial divergences. Not many readers of the Gospels presumably use a synopsis with parallel columns that might virtually compel attention to these elements and stimulate inquiries as to the likely explanation of them. Still, in some cases, reflection might develop to the point where one might ask whether the extensive agreements are possibly to be explained by the use which a later evangelist has made of a completed Gospel. Whatever may be true, however, of popular reading and inquiry, it is obvious that our approach here is oriented to the modern treatment of Synoptic origins and mutual relationships, a treatment which must be credited with a minute and thorough examination and comparison of the contents of the Gospels. And so the question of order is in the foreground of attention especially because of its bearing upon one's inquiry as to the possibility of interdependence. If direct dependence were to be established, and one could determine which evangelist or evangelists made use of a particular Gospel or Gospels, one would be making some substantial progress toward the solution of the Synoptic Problem.

The study upon which we have embarked here is therefore a broad one, so broad, in fact, that if I am to deal at all adequately with the more difficult aspects of the matter, it will be wise and necessary not to try to treat every phase of the subject. In particular, in view of the virtually unanimous agreement, even among scholars who hold to widely divergent theories concerning the origin of the Synoptics, that the evangelist Luke used the Gospel according to Mark, I shall pass over the study of that subject here.[1] This offers the hope that a measure of justice may be done to the incomparably more controversial and more difficult question as to the relationship between Matthew and Mark. Considering the question of order the issue is whether Matthew is prior to Mark or Mark to Matthew; evaluating the matter of possible interdependence it is whether Mark may have been used by Matthew or Matthew by Mark.

Opinions Concerning Priority

Before joining issue on these questions in terms of the pertinent evidence, it seems wise to try to clear the air with regard to the actual state of the question by way of brief reflection upon the development of the historical debate. Looked at in terms of history it might appear that the issue is rather simple, and so it is often thought to be. On the one hand, there is the traditional view which supports the priority of Matthew, a view which enjoys the advantage of support from the ancient fathers, was generally accepted in the Christian Church throughout the centuries until recent times, and still is stoutly defended by many able scholars in our day. On the other hand, in opposition to this so-called "conservative position," there is the position that maintains the priority of Mark, a view which

1. *Cf.* Zahn, *Einleitung*, II, 404ff. (Eng. trans., III, pp. 101ff.) ; H. J. Cadbury, *The Style and Literary Method of Luke* (Cambridge: Harvard University Press, 1920), pp. 73ff. Wikenhauser, *op. cit.*, p. 210 (*cf.* p. 250), makes the following brief summary statement: "There is almost universal agreement today that the Gospel of St. Mark was one of Luke's written sources. Not only did Luke take over more than half of Mark's material — about 350 out of 661 verses — with stylistic improvements and occasional trimming, but he also followed Mark's outline of the work of Jesus. With insignificant exceptions he did not rearrange the material which he took from Mark, and he fitted the material from other sources into Mark's framework." Quoted by permission.

originated only about 125 years ago and has found wide acceptance particularly among Liberal scholars during the past century. Such an assessment of the course of historical discussion,
especially if it is accompanied by the judgment that orthodox
Christians as a matter of course might be expected to accept
the traditional view, and Liberals the other, rests, in my opinion, upon an extraordinary oversimplification of the history
of the study of the Gospels.

On the one hand, to be sure, the view that Matthew was
written before Mark has been supported, as we presently shall
note in some detail, in a remarkably consistent manner from
ancient times onward. There is very little evidence, however,
that judgments concerning order were accompanied by reflection upon the possibility of interdependence, a fact easily explained from the observation that very few scholars addressed
themselves to a comparison of the Gospel contents. Augustine
was however an exception to this rule and he came to the definite conclusion that Mark was an abridgement of Matthew.
In his work on *The Harmony of the Gospels,* he says:

> For Matthew is understood to have taken it in hand to con-
> struct the record of the incarnation of the Lord according to
> the royal lineage, and to give an account of the most part of
> his deeds and words as they stood in relation to this present
> life of men. Mark follows him closely, and looks like his
> attendant and epitomizer. For in his narrative he gives nothing
> in concert with John apart from the others: by himself separately,
> he has little to record; in conjunction with Luke, as distinguished
> from the rest, he has still less; but in concord with Matthew,
> he has a very large number of passages. Much, too, he narrates in
> words almost numerically and identically the same as those
> used by Matthew, where the agreement is either with that
> evangelist alone, or with him in connection with the rest.[2]

In view of the place which the Roman Catholic Church
assigns to tradition, it is readily understandable that the priority of Matthew came to be clothed with authority. Thus,
for example, the Pontifical Biblical Commission on June 19,
1911, explicitly affirmed the view that "Matthew wrote before
the other evangelists."[3]   In accordance with this viewpoint,

2. Augustine, *De Consensu Evangelistarum* I ii:4 (PL 34, col. 1044):
"Marcus cum subsecutus, tanquam pedisequus et breviator ejus videtur."
Eng. trans. in *NPF*, 1st. Ser.
    3. For an English translation see John Chapman, *The Four Gospels*
(London: Sheed & Ward, 1944), p. 58.

Jacques M. Vosté, a member of the Pontifical Biblical Commission, in 1928 developed a theory of mutual or successive dependence in which an Aramaic Matthew was assigned priority.[4] Of considerable interest also is the learned work of the English Roman Catholic scholar, John Chapman, whose book entitled, *Matthew, Mark and Luke,* appeared in 1937.[5] Conservative Protestant scholars also, though they might not be expected to be so strongly under the influence of tradition as Roman Catholic ones, have, as has been noted above, generally maintained the priority of Matthew as a cornerstone of their position. At the same time, however, it may be well to remind ourselves that among non-Roman Catholic scholars there have been non-orthodox critics who have held to the traditional view for non-traditionalistic reasons. This is notably true of F. C. Baur and the Tübingen School who boldly assigned sequence and dates in accordance with a radical reconstruction of the history of early Christianity; a judgment concerning Matthew's allegedly Jewish-Christian *Tendenz* was basically determinative of its position as primary.

On the other hand, it is important to bear in mind that the conclusions that Mark was written before Matthew and that Matthew utilized Mark are not necessarily bound up with a single theory concerning the Synoptic Question. To be sure, it developed in connection with the evolution of the two-document theory, is part and parcel of it, and is associated most firmly with it in the minds of men. In taking account of the variety of viewpoints associated with the priority of Mark I shall of course not emphasize its acceptance by the proponents of the four-document hypothesis, for this is really only a variation of and expansion upon the two-document theory. It is of moment to observe, however, that a number of authors of scholarly standing including Ropes,[6] Enslin,[7] and Farrer[8] maintain the same position with regard to Mark and Matthew

4. *De synopticorum mutua relatione et dependentia* (Rome, 1928).
5. John Chapman, *Matthew, Mark and Luke* (London: Longmans, Green, 1937).
6. Ropes, *op. cit.*
7. Morton S. Enslin, *Christian Beginnings* (New York: Harper, 1938), pp. 426ff.
8. A. M. Farrer, *A Study in St. Mark* (Westminster: Dacre, 1951), pp. 186, 210; *St. Matthew and St. Mark* (Westminster: Dacre, 1954), pp. 7, 176; "On Dispensing with Q" in ed. D. E. Nineham, *Studies in the Gospels* (Oxford, 1955), pp. 55ff.

found in the two-document theory but have otherwise defended in general a quite different approach by insisting that the hypothetical document Q is dispensable. Of great interest in this context also is the observation that the Roman Catholic scholars Vosté[9] and Wikenhauser,[10] and Zahn,[11] a Protestant of eminent learning, while maintaining that strict priority must be assigned to an Aramaic form of Matthew, agree that the translator of Matthew from Aramaic into Greek utilized our Greek Mark! Particularly if one keeps in mind the fact that the Aramaic Matthew of Vosté, Wikenhauser and Zahn is at best a lost document and, if the testimony of Papias has gone astray at this point, it is moreover a purely hypothetical one, there is little or nothing to distinguish their views from the other theories regarding this narrow point of the relationship between Mark and Matthew.

Finally, brief attention must be drawn to the somewhat sensational development in the history of Synoptic criticism marked by the publication of the monumental work, *A Greek Synopsis of the Gospels,* by the Roman Catholic scholar Bruno de Solages.[12] The subtitle of this work, "A New Way of Solving the Synoptic Problem," has in view the fact that this elaborate work of 1128 pages applies the techniques of mathematical statistics particularly to the vocabulary of the Synoptic Gospels but also to various other aspects of the problem. And the arresting feature of the contribution is that its conclusions are virtually those of the proponents of the two-document hypothesis. It is somewhat premature to evaluate this new approach, not only because of the intrinsic difficulties of the method employed,[13] but also because there is a promise that this voluminous work is to be followed by another which will be devoted to the literary, exegetic and possibly the historical and theological aspects of the problem. As the author stresses, he "does not pretend to explain all Luke and all Matthew by the

9. Vosté, *op. cit.*

10. Wikenhauser, *op. cit.,* pp. 192, 250.

11. Zahn, *op. cit.,* II, 325; *cf.* pp. 265, 306 (Eng. trans., II, 602; *cf.* pp. 516f., 575f.) .

12. Bruno de Solages, *A Greek Synopsis of the Gospels* (Leiden: Brill, 1959) . The fact that the Cardinal Tisserant, President of the Pontifical Biblical Commission, speaks approvingly of it in the Preface is a fact of considerable historical interest.

13. See the favorable review of this book by K. Grayston and G. Herdan in *NTS,* 7 (Oct., 1960) , pp. 97f.

two sources Mark and X, but only their resemblances, which constitutes the whole of the synoptic phenomena."[14]

It would appear that Roman Catholic scholarship today gives evidence of not being as slavishly bound to tradition as was formerly the case. Since the time of the acute struggle with "modernism" half a century ago, a much freer attitude particularly toward questions of Introduction has developed. To the present observer it appears that a tension has been created by the definiteness of the commitment of the Pontifical Biblical Commission of 1911 to various positions, on the one hand, and the far more open attitude of the present day. Thus Wikenhauser, to cite an example, goes to extraordinary length to defend the decrees of the Commission as regards the originality of Matthew and the substantial identity of this Aramaic Matthew with our Greek Matthew even though the latter is understood as being, partly because of its considerable use of Mark, a thorough revision of the Aramaic original.[15] On the other hand, as recently as 1955, the Secretary and Assistant Secretary of the Biblical Commission, A. Miller and K. Kleinhans, have written articles in which they draw a sharp line of distinction between the decrees in so far as they are connected with truths of faith and morals and to the extent that they treat questions of a different character. In the latter area, which is clearly understood as including questions of authorship, date of composition, and integrity, it is said that "the scholar may pursue his research with complete freedom and may utilize the results of this research, provided always that it defers to the supreme teaching authority of the Church."[16] However one may interpret this shift of opinion and judge its historical validity, it should not be overlooked that the decrees of the Biblical Commission have never been thought of as irreformable or infallible.

If then Roman Catholic scholarship is moving away from a rigid commitment to tradition, and is insisting that "Sacred

14. de Solages, op. cit., p. 1085.

15. A somewhat fuller critical evaluation of Wikenhauser's position is presented below, pp. 89f.

16. Cf. E. F. Siegman, "The Decrees of the Pontifical Biblical Commission: A Recent Clarification," CBQ, XVIII (1956), 23f. For references to other recent literature the English reader may conveniently consult this article as well as A. Wikenhauser, op. cit., p. 9, n. 6. A gracious letter from Professor Joseph A. Fitzmyer of Woodstock College, in response to an inquiry of mine, has been very helpful on this point.

Scripture has always been the primary source and foundation of the truths of Catholic faith and of their progress and development,"[17] should not Protestant scholars by virtue of the qualitative distinction which has been drawn since the days of the Reformation between Scripture and tradition, adopt a less slavish attitude toward positions that have the support only of tradition and be ready to face questions of origin by making the testimony of the Scriptures themselves the ultimate arbiter?

The Testimony of Tradition

Irenaeus, as we have seen in connection with the treatment of his testimony concerning authorship, explicitly supports the order: Matthew, Mark, Luke and John. F. C. Grant, while presenting some pertinent evidence as to the lack of unanimity in the ancient Church in the matter of the sequence of the Gospels, hardly seems to be on good ground in his claim that Irenaeus himself reflects a different order in the statement, alluded to previously, concerning the four living beings of Revelation and the four evangelists.[18] Grant maintains that Revelation 4:7 with its reference to the lion, the ox, the man and the eagle, reflects a pre-Irenaean tradition, and that, in spite of the arbitrariness of the identification of these beings with the evangelists, the order Mark, Luke, Matthew and John is witness to authentic tradition concerning sequence. Irenaeus, on this view, in turn, though he himself is not interested at this point in the subject of sequence, but only in the fourfold form of the gospel, incidentally — and so all the more convincingly — adds to the evidence for this order which diverges from his own earlier statement.

With regard to Grant's conclusions, the following comments may be made. In the first place, there is a presumption that Irenaeus would not present two conflicting traditions, and especially not within such brief compass. Secondly, as Grant himself admits, in the context under discussion, the emphasis falls altogether upon the fourfold character of the Gospels, and

17. Siegman, op. cit., p. 24.
18. F. C. Grant, The Gospels: Their Origin and Their Growth (New York: Harper, 1957), pp. 64ff. Robert M. Grant, The Earliest Lives of Jesus New York: Harper, 1961), pp. 33f., mentions the Irenaean as being John, Luke, Matthew and Mark, but acknowledges that there is nothing to show that Irenaeus still has sequence in mind in this connection. For the previous comment on Irenaeus cf. above pp. 4ff.

not a word is said about order. That the identifications are forced and arbitrary does not fundamentally alter the situation. The same would be true with regard to any variation of identification such as we encounter, for example, in later authors. Thirdly, the appeal to Revelation 4:7 presents nothing positively in support of the conclusion that a tradition earlier than Irenaeus is reflected in his comments. Finally, it may be noted that Grant, though no doubt inadvertently, appears to ascribe to Irenaeus the order Mark, Luke, Matthew and John whereas actually the order of mention is John, Luke, Matthew and Mark.

As the discussion of the testimony of Tertullian in the first lecture has indicated, he also mentions Matthew first in his reflections upon the order of the Gospels. Nevertheless, as his discussion as a whole clearly points up, he does not base his conclusion so much upon the witness of history as upon dogmatic and polemical considerations. So powerfully is he affected by the development of his argument against Marcion that he comes to assign a place of lesser weight and later date to the writings of apostolic men — Luke and Mark — and a greater prestige and priority to the strictly apostolic Gospels — Matthew and John. The very fact that in this manner Tertullian determined the order as being that of Matthew, John, Luke and Mark, a sequence by the way found also in Codex Bezae, is indicative of the fact that the ecclesiastical tradition or traditions concerning order were not so fixed and authoritative as to command uniformity of judgment.

Clement of Alexandria may likewise be cited as supporting the view that Mark was written later than Matthew. But it is illuminating for our understanding of the larger question of the relative uniformity or flexibility of tradition that with regard to the four Gospels he agrees neither with Irenaeus nor with Tertullian. For he states that the tradition which came to him assigned priority to the Gospels which contained the genealogies.[19] Hence Luke as well as Matthew are regarded as prior to Mark, and there is nothing in his statement which excludes the possibility that Luke might have been written before Matthew.

When, accordingly, one examines this early evidence as a whole, and does not confine oneself to the bare question as to the order of Matthew, it is striking that tradition on this point

19. *Cf.* Eusebius, *HE* VI 14:5.

is far from being uniform. And is not this lack of a consensus with regard to order precisely what one might have been prepared to expect? In the very churches where the individual Gospels originated and were first received there would be, in the very nature of the case, because they purported, in Streeter's words, "to give an authentic account of one whose deeds, words, and divine nature were a matter of acute controversy,"[20] an inevitable concern with the identification of the author. While such an interest in authorship would continue to manifest itself in the ensuing history as they were circulated individually and as parts of the fourfold gospel collection, it would not emerge as a new factor within that history. The situation is quite otherwise, however, as regards the tradition concerning the order of the Gospels. While the use of one Gospel on the part of another presupposes a certain amount of circulation in the earliest times, probably they were generally known at first only in the different cities or areas to which they were addressed and considerable time elapsed before they were all brought together in such a way as to compel reflection on the question of sequence. The interest in authorship was of profound concern and apparently present from the very beginning; the interest in order was of more peripheral significance and presumably developed later on. A sound approach to the evaluation of tradition is therefore one in which the historian, forsaking the temptation either to accept it uncritically in its entirety or to repudiate it outrightly, seeks to sift it in the hope of distinguishing between that which commends itself as trustworthy and that which evidently has behind it merely conjecture or at best inferences not adequately grounded in fact.

Is Mark the First Gospel?

In view of the clarity and effectiveness with which Streeter has summed up the case for the priority of Mark, it seems advantageous to deal rather specifically and concretely with his presentation. One may seek thus to enter into a dialogue with him as well as others who have spoken on one side or the other of this and related issues, and hopefully deal with the most relevant facts and conclusions.

In the synopsis which prefaces the chapter dealing with "The Fundamental Solution," having indicated his general con-

20. Streeter, *op. cit.*, p. 500.

clusion that "Matthew may be regarded as an enlarged edition
of Mark; Luke is an independent work incorporating considerable portions of Mark," he sums up five reasons for maintaining
the priority of Mark. The first three (which may advantageously be discussed in advance of the last two) are as follows:

(1) Matthew reproduces 90 per cent of the subject matter
of Mark in language very largely identical with that of Mark;
Luke does the same for rather more than half of Mark.

(2) In any average section, which occurs in three gospels,
the majority of the actual words used by Mark are reproduced
by Matthew and Luke, either alternately or both together.

(3) The relative order of incidents and sections in Mark is
in general supported by both Matthew and Luke; where either
of them deserts Mark, the other is usually found supporting him.
This conjunction and alternation of Matthew and Luke in
their agreement with Mark as regards (a) content, (b) wording,
(c) order, is only explicable if they are incorporating a source
identical, or all but identical, with Mark.[21]

(1) *Agreement in Subject Matter.* Commencing with the
first point which centers attention on the extraordinary agreement in respect to subject matter in the Synoptics, and in particular in Matthew and Mark, one must weigh carefully the
fact that out of the total of 661 verses in Mark the substance of
only 55, that is less than ten per cent, is not paralleled in
Matthew. On the supposition that Matthew used Mark one
is confronted with the rather simple but nevertheless astonishing situation that it served the purpose of the evangelist Matthew to reproduce in substance virtually the whole of Mark;
his enlargement of Mark would on this view, however, be substantial since Matthew contains 1,068 verses, more than 400
representing materials not found in Mark. On the other hand,
on the view that Mark used Matthew the situation is not capable
of such simple analysis. For one would have to consider not
only Augustine's view that Mark is essentially an abridgment
of Matthew but other possibilities which might as well throw
light upon Mark's reasons for omitting large portions and many
details found in Matthew.

Although this way of stating the issue is one with which we
shall be very fully concerned in what follows, it is necessary to
remind ourselves that we must not leap ahead of the evidence.
The observation of agreement in subject matter by no means

21. *Ibid.,* pp. 151f.

establishes the conclusion of direct dependence, whether it be
of Mark upon Matthew or Matthew upon Mark.   Only when
the agreement in words and order of arrangement is assessed
will one be prepared to come to firm conclusions with regard
to the factor of interdependence.   On the basis of agreement in
subject matter one would have to allow seriously for the possibility that the dependence was merely of an indirect kind.   The
theory that our synoptic evangelists independently used an
original Aramaic gospel, held for example by Lessing[22] and
Abbott,[23] or an original Greek gospel, as such scholars as
Feine[24] and Bussmann[25] have maintained, or even an original
oral gospel in the form of stereotyped tradition, as developed
by Gieseler[26] and Westcott,[27] might quite plausibly explain the
extensive agreements in substance.   Moreover, even if the issue
of the nature of interdependence were narrowed down to one
between the view that Matthew used Mark or that Mark used
Matthew, the observations set forth merely in terms of statistics
and percentages could never provide an objective basis for a
decision between these two views.[28]

(2) *Agreement in Words.*   Streeter's second point concerns
the fact that where Matthew and Mark agree in substance the
actual words used are also remarkably identical.   Formulating
and developing the argument further from the point of view
expressed in his own synopsis, Streeter states:

> Mark's style is diffuse, Matthew's succinct; so that in adapting
> Mark's language Matthew compresses so much that the 600
> odd verses taken from Mark supply rather less than half of
> the material contained in the 1,068 verses of the longer Gospel.

22. G. E. Lessing, *Neue Hypothese über die Evangelisten als bloss
menschliche Geschichtsschreiber betrachtet* (1778).
23. E. A. Abbott, *The Fourfold Gospel* (Cambridge, 1913-1917).
24. P. Feine, *Eine vorkanonische Überlieferung des Lukas in Evangelium
und Apostelgeschichte* (1891).
25. W. Bussmann, *Synoptische Studien* (Halle, 1925, 1929, 1931).
26. J. C. L. Gieseler, *Historisch-kritischer Versuch über die Entstehung
und die frühesten Schicksale der schriftlichen Evangelien* (Leipzig, 1818).
27. B. F. Westcott, *An Introduction to the Study of the Gospels* (London:
Macmillan, 6th ed., 1881).
28. Nevertheless, in my judgment, even in the matter of agreement in
subject matter, when one turns from mere numbers to reflection upon
actual agreements and differences in contents, a very weighty argument in
favor of one view rather than the other may be developed. I shall postpone
the presentation of this argument until after we have had the opportunity
of reviewing Streeter's second and third points.

Yet, in spite of this abbreviation, it is found that Matthew employs 51 per cent of the actual words used by Mark.[29] Though this formulation is somewhat prejudicial because it more or less assumes the correctness of Streeter's final "solution," the estimate of the percentage of actual words of agreement apparently is unchallenged. To be sure, one cannot assess the force of this observation by way of summary statements in a brief discussion; in the last analysis one can do so only by taking account painstakingly of the minute agreements in language with which one is confronted as one compares the Gospel texts in a Greek Synopsis. In my judgment, these agreements are as a matter of fact so precise and so extensive that they provide a solid bulwark for the conclusion that there is actual interdependence between the Synoptic Gospels. The various theories of indirect dependence, which have just been referred to, however worthy of consideration and however plausible up to a point, are found seriously wanting at this juncture.

Nevertheless, in weighing this argument, one must again take care not to outrun the evidence. Interdependence is evidently established by the agreement in words. But is the interdependence one in which it has become clear that Mark has used Matthew rather than that Matthew has used Mark?

B. C. Butler, a Roman Catholic scholar, has recently vigorously challenged the validity of Streeter's arguments for the priority of Mark and has insisted that the argument as developed in terms of agreement in subject matter, words and order of materials does not seriously face the question whether these agreements may not be as well explained on the supposition that the order was Matthew, Mark and Luke.[30]

29. Streeter, op. cit., p. 159. Quoted by permission.
30 B. C. Butler, The Originality of St. Matthew (Cambridge: University Press, 1951), pp. 62ff. Cf. also J. Chapman, Matthew, Mark and Luke; John H. Ludlum, Jr., "More Light on the Synoptic Problem" in Christianity Today (Nov. 10 and 24, 1958) and "Are We Sure of Mark's Priority?" in Christianity Today (Sept. 14 and 28, 1959); W. R. Farmer, "A 'Skeleton in the Closet' of Gospel Research" (Reprinted from Biblical Research VI, 1961). A brief comment by the author on Ludlum's first two articles appeared in the same journal, April 13, 1959, pp. 23f. Farmer's essay is informative and valuable as a critical discussion of many phases of the history of modern evaluations of the Synoptic Problem including especially the two-document hypothesis as a whole and the significance of the Marcan hypothesis as well as the narrower question of priority. But there is very little that bears precisely on the arguments that pertain to the decision

It is well that this question should have been raised. As observed previously, Streeter's formulations of his arguments often presuppose the conclusions he is seeking to establish and so give the appearance of being somewhat partisan. Moreover, it must be acknowledged that at least some of his summary statements do not go beyond the inference of interdependence. Nevertheless, to do full justice to Streeter, one must not rest with the summary statements but take account of the further development of his argument. Germane to this point is the detail that, having commented upon the agreement in words in terms of percentages, he says:

> What is still more significant, if the collocation of words and the structure of sentences in Matthew and Luke be examined, it will be found that, while one or both of them are constantly in close agreement with Mark, they never (except as stated p. 179ff.) support one another against Mark. This is clear evidence of the greater originality of the Marcan version, and is exactly what we should expect to find if Matthew and Luke were *independently* reproducing Mark, adapting his language to their own individual style.[31]

If it were not for the fact that this statement refers to certain exceptions later described as "minor agreements of Matthew and Luke against Mark," this argument would be quite persuasive. For it presents a picture of disagreement in wording in areas of agreement of substance that is readily understandable on the supposition that Matthew and Luke independently used the same Marcan material. But such an estimate of disagreement in wording is hardly reconcilable with the view of Butler. For he, rejecting the position that Matthew and Luke were independent of one another, holds that Luke had access to Matthew (1) not only indirectly through Mark who had used Matthew but (2) also immediately through a direct dependence upon Matthew. It is inexplicable that Luke should have depended very substantially upon Matthew in the exten-

---

on the latter feature. My approach seeks to disentangle specific issues which have arisen within the ebb and flow of history and to re-examine certain questions, notably at this point that of priority, on their own merits. Farmer's unqualified praise of Hilgenfeld of the Tübingen School (*cf.* pp. 4, 14, 26, n. 55) and of Zahn (on whose view of Mark and Matthew see above, pp. 14f.) and his own low view of Mark (*cf.* p. 16, n. 33) seem to me to show that he is lacking in this respect.

31. Streeter, *op. cit.*, p. 161.

sive areas which the two-document theory assigns to Q and yet in the areas where the three Synoptics are dealing with common subject matter (the so-called triple tradition) quite consistently fail to disclose an acquaintance with Matthew. There remains, however, the fact that Streeter admits that there are exceptions to the rule. One is confronted therefore with the question whether the argument after all is a weighty one. This will depend upon decisions as to whether the exceptions are truly minor and may be satisfactorily explained on the supposition of the independence of Matthew and Luke.

Streeter first of all presents a brief evaluation of this question and later on devotes an entire chapter to it.[32] No thorough presentation of this discussion can be undertaken here; Streeter himself must be read with care and account should be taken of what others have had to say on this subject.[33] My own impression is that the exceptions noted are not of such a character as to set aside the considerable force of the argument as stated by Streeter. The agreements in view are properly termed "minor" for they consist largely of stylistic variations and for the most part affect only a word or two. What is in view is perhaps most clearly illustrated by the fact that Matthew and Luke very frequently employ an imperfect or aorist tense where Mark has the present tense. That the use of the historic present is a characteristic feature of the Marcan style is demonstrated by the list of 151 instances given by Hawkins; although the narratives in which these historic presents are found are for the most part paralleled in Matthew or Luke or both, in only 21 instances does Matthew agree with Mark in using this tense, and in only one case does Luke agree with Mark in its use. In the overwhelming majority of cases, therefore, where Mark has the historic present an aorist or imperfect form is found in Matthew and Luke. Matthew, to be sure, had no particular antipathy toward the use of the historic present for in addition to the 21 cases referred to there are 57 cases besides 15 in parables. On the other hand, Luke has only three clearly attested instances in addition to the single case where he agrees with Mark in its usage not including five cases

---

32. *Ibid.*, pp. 179ff., 295ff.
33. *Cf. e.g.*, Hawkins, *op. cit.*, pp. 143-153, on the use of the historic present in Mark and his paratactic style.

in parables.[34] Taking account of the more literary character of the style of Matthew and Luke as compared with that of Mark, it is plausible to maintain that these elements of agreement between Matthew and Luke against Mark arose simply as a result of coincidence and by no means offer proof that Luke reflects at these points a dependence upon Matthew.

The same reasoning applies to what Streeter calls the omission in Matthew "almost invariably of the unnecessary or unimportant words which are characteristic of Mark's somewhat verbose style." Streeter indeed believes that there are certain elements of agreement between Matthew and Mark in the contexts of the triple tradition which are difficult to explain as due simply to coincidence in stylistic improvement. But these, he holds, may be accounted for as due to assimilation in the transmission of the text of the Gospels.[35]

The judgment that the residue of Matthean and Lucan agreements against Mark are to be explained as the consequence of textual assimilation, while not without great force, is however somewhat dogmatic in view of the consideration that such alleged assimilation cannot be proved in detail or at least not in every instance. One may compare, for example, Matthew 21:39 and Luke 20:15 ("they cast him forth out of the vineyard and killed him") with Mark 12:8 ("they killed him and cast him forth out of the vineyard"), which is also in Matthew in D *et al.* This would allow for the possibility that Matthew originally agreed with Mark and that it was assimilated to Luke. But it is also possible, and at least as probable, that the D text of Matthew is an assimilation to Mark. Nevertheless the agreement of Matthew and Luke against Mark at this point does not prove their direct interdependence. For they may depend

---

34. *Ibid.,* pp. 144ff. It is also illuminating for the evaluation of Luke's style to note that there are thirteen uses of the historic present in Acts.

Another illustration of likely coincidence is to be found in the observation that Matthew and Luke agree characteristically in a preference for the particle δέ in contrast to Mark's strong proclivity toward the use of καί; in addition to the general evidence for these preferences Hawkins points out that there are at least twenty-six cases in which both Matthew and Luke have δέ where Mark has καί (pp. 150ff.) .

35. Streeter, *op. cit.,* pp. 180f., 306ff. J. P. Brown, "An Early Revision of the Gospel of Mark," *JBL,* LXXVIII (Sept., 1959) , 215ff., in disagreement with Streeter at this point, holds that Matthew and Luke's minor agreements against Mark are due to early textual revision of Mark, and that Matthew and Luke independently used this form of Mark.

here on a common written source or oral tradition. Even if some of these phenomena cannot be confidently explained as stylistic coincidences or textual assimilations, the fact remains that in the triple tradition the agreements of Matthew and Luke against Mark are so meager in extent and substance that strong support is lent the view that Matthew and Luke independently used Mark.

(3) *Agreements in Order.* The third point of Streeter is restated more fully in the following terms:

> The order of incidents in Mark is clearly the more original; for wherever Matthew departs from Mark's order Luke supports Mark, and whenever Luke departs from Mark, Matthew agrees with Mark. The section Mk. iii. 31-35 alone occurs in a different context in each gospel; and there is no case where Matthew and Luke agree together against Mark in a point of arrangement.[36]

This feature of the remarkable agreement in the arrangement of the gospel materials is of course not a fresh discovery of Streeter's. Lachmann's research on this point in his famous essay of 1835[37] drew attention to it and was one important factor in the subsequent development of the two-document hypothesis. Streeter is being quoted here, it will be remembered, because he so ably and succinctly sums up the argument for the priority of Mark. But it is important to add that apparently no one challenges the accuracy of the observations concerning order as such. B. C. Butler, for example, admits their accuracy; it is the inference relating to the dependence of Matthew upon Mark to which he objects.[38]

Before evaluating this crucial point we do well, I believe, to pause briefly to underscore this point of agreement. The extraordinarily extensive agreements in the order of the individual pericopes, no less inescapably than the agreement in words, compels one, in my opinion, to accept the judgment

---

36. *Ibid.,* p. 161.

37. "De ordine narrationum in evangeliis synopticis," in *Theologische Studien und Kritiken,* 8 (1835), 570ff. Lachmann himself, as Butler, *op. cit.,* pp. 62ff., stresses, did not however argue for the dependence of Matthew and Luke on Mark; rather he only went so far as to contend that Mark more consistently reflects the order common to the three Synoptics than the others, and that their source is closest to Mark with respect to order. See also Farmer, *op. cit.,* pp. 8ff.

38. Butler, *op. cit.,* pp. 62ff.

that there were relationships of direct dependence between the Synoptic Gospels. The theories which contend that the Synoptic Problem may be substantially solved by the thesis that the similarities may be adequately explained on the supposition that the three Synoptics made common but independent use of a single source — whether it be an original Aramaic gospel, an original Greek gospel or stereotyped tradition which had been handed down orally — fails to explain the phenomena satisfactorily. The conclusion that direct dependence is involved is reinforced especially as one relates the extensive agreements in the matter of order to the evidence that there is in our Gospels a relative unconcern to indicate the precise order in which the various events have taken place. The Gospels to be sure do contain many references to time and place which enable one to come to certain positive results with regard to itineraries of Jesus and many features of the framework of his public ministry. Nevertheless, none of the Gospels attempts to present a full and complete framework of the public ministry. On the contrary, so characteristic is this relative indifference to the exact sequence in which various events took place and teachings were delivered that the attentive reader of the Gospels will observe again and again the absence of particular evidence that would support firm decisions as to temporal order.[39]

Although then the evidence concerning the substantial agreement among the Synoptics with respect to the relative order of incidents and sections provides strong support of the fact of interdependence, the question remains whether it also serves to demonstrate the priority of Mark. On the premise that Matthew and Luke presuppose the Marcan order and that each utilized it independently as it suited his plan and purpose, one assuredly arrives at an easily understandable conception of the historical development: Matthew uses the Marcan framework and generally fuses the non-Marcan material into it. But Luke, when it is parallel with Mark, follows the Marcan order of events even more closely than Matthew because the evangelist has chosen to introduce the Marcan and non-Marcan material in alternate blocks.[40]

39. Cf. WMMC, pp. 127f., 132f., 146ff., 152 and WLC, pp. 60ff., 101ff., 125ff.

40. Cf. Streeter, op. cit., p. 152, who notes that the passion story is an exception since there "some interweaving of sources was inevitable."

Is it not nevertheless just conceivable that Mark could have derived his framework from Matthew *on a selective basis* and that Luke, without taking account of Matthew, could have followed Mark? Considered as a purely theoretical possibility this approach perhaps cannot be summarily dismissed. Nevertheless, we cannot be satisfied with weighing matters of this kind in purely theoretical and abstract terms. As in the case of the evaluation of agreement in words which was noted above, Butler at this point also seems to lose sight of various concrete aspects of the question. In the first place, while he appears to be stating the issue in terms of a choice between (1) the independent use of Mark by both Matthew and Luke over against (2) the possibility of the order Matthew, Mark and Luke, actually he maintains that Luke had direct knowledge of Matthew. Accordingly, he seems to be asking us to allow that Luke may have drawn very fully upon Matthew especially for reports of the teaching of Jesus but that in the matter of the order of incidents and sections he follows Mark alone. Secondly, while perhaps one can conceive of the possibility that Mark derived his framework from Matthew on a selective basis, it seems impossible to discover the criteria by which such a selection would have been made. At this point, it will be observed, however, that one is back with the question of subject matter, for one would have to account for Mark's reasons in omitting precisely the materials of Matthew which, on this approach, he did. And this, as we shall see presently, is so difficult to explain that it creates at least a presumption in favor of the simpler view that Matthew shared the high view of Mark reflected in Luke's substantial utilization of it and that in his own way he preserved the framework of Mark.

In an article on "The Priority of Mark," H. G. Wood has evaluated Butler's argument in similar terms. He says:

> So Dom Butler contends that Mark is a source only for Luke, and the knowledge of Matthew's order comes to Luke through Mark. This is very strange because Dom Butler claims to have proved that Luke is also dependent on Matthew. Why, having Matthew in his hands, Luke should follow Matthew's order only when it re-appears in Mark is difficult to understand and explain. If Dom Butler's thesis were true, there should be numerous agreements in order between Matthew and Luke against Mark, and admittedly there are none or next to none.[41]

41. *ExT* (October, 1953), pp. 17f.

While general considerations such as those which have been mentioned have their own particular pertinence and weight, in the last analysis one must be prepared to face the issue by way of a painstaking comparison of the order of events in the separate Gospels. It is hoped, however, that a fairly brief comparison of Mark 1:16-2:22 and Matthew 4:18-9:34 may suffice for our present purposes.[42] The call of the first disciples marks the beginning of this section (Mk. 1:16-20; Mt. 4:18-22). Mark next speaks of Jesus' entrance into the synagogue at Capernaum and of his activity there (1:21-28). No necessary temporal connection between the call of the disciples and the entrance into Capernaum is indicated, but it is clear that the events recorded in Mark 1:21-35 are all associated with Capernaum and closely joined in temporal sequence: (1) the healing of Simon's wife's mother is described as taking place directly after the departure from the synagogue (1:29-31); (2) the evening of that day is indicated as the time when the sick were healed (1:32-34); and (3) Jesus' departure from Capernaum is narrated as taking place "in the morning a great while before day" (1:35). The following sections, however, referring to (1) a general preaching activity in Galilee (1:39; cf. 1:36-38); (2) the healing of a leper (1:40-45); (3) the healing of a palsied man on the occasion of a later visit to Capernaum (2:1-12); (4) the call of Levi (2:13-17); and (5) the discussion of the question about fasting (2:18-22) — all these sections lack any specific reference to time or sequence. And so there is nothing to suggest that Mark has in view a fixed itinerary or that he intends to indicate that the events recorded happened in strict chronological succession.

In turning now to an examination of the Matthean framework, one is immediately impressed with the fact that Matthew, following the report of the call of the first disciples, has nothing comparable to the Marcan cycle of events connected with Capernaum but proceeds at once to speak generally of the preaching and healing activity in Galilee (4:23-25). Next Matthew goes on to illustrate the ministry of Jesus in considerable detail, introducing the Sermon on the Mount as an example of

---

42. Cf. WMMC, pp. 29f., 133-143, where, however, no particular evaluation of the question of priority is undertaken.

his preaching (Mt. 5:3-7:27) and many works of healing as instances of the manifestation of his power and mercy (8:1-9:34). The Sermon on the Mount, which contains almost no details that are parallel or similar to the Marcan references to the teaching of Jesus, is not assigned to a particular time nor to an exact place, and is evidently presented as typical of the teaching of Jesus on the subjects treated.[43] Nor does Matthew 8:1-9:34, in spite of the presence of various references to time and place, confront us with an orderly travel narrative. There are too few connecting links to permit this conclusion. Accordingly it becomes plain that in chapters 8 and 9 Matthew is mainly concerned to exemplify the miraculous activity of Jesus, as he has previously done with his ministry of teaching.[44] Pursuing this plan, Matthew follows the Sermon on the Mount with the story of the healing of a leper (8:1-4), thus returning to the Marcan framework at the exact point where he had left it to introduce the Sermon. There next follows in Matthew the non-Marcan story of the centurion's servant (8:5-13). Thereupon he introduces the healing of Peter's wife's mother (8:14-15) and the sick healed at evening (9:16-17), which correspond to two of the sections of Mark's Capernaum cycle (Mk. 1:29-31; 32-34). Continuing his concentration largely on miracle stories in chapters 8 and 9, Matthew introduces, following the references to two claimants to discipleship, the stories of the stilling of the tempest and of the Gadarene demoniacs (8:18-22, 23-27, 28-34), stories which Mark presents in a later context (4:35-41; 5:1-20). Thereafter the Marcan and Matthean orders agree in three sections as Matthew presents the healing of a palsied man (9:1-8), the calling of Levi (9:9-13), and the question about fasting (9:14-17), which are parallel with Mark 2:1-12, 13-17, 18-22. Four further miracle stories round out this Matthean section as he tells of Jairus' daughter and the woman with the issue of blood (9:18-26), which corresponds with Mark 5:21-43, the healing of two blind men (9:27-31), and of a dumb demoniac (9:32-34).

These phenomena may perhaps be examined to some advantage in the following index:

43. Cf. ibid., pp. 134f.
44. Cf. ibid., pp. 135-143.

	Mark	Matthew
Call of First Disciples	1:16-20	4:18-22
Christ at Capernaum	1:21-28	
Peter's Wife's Mother	1:29-31	(cf. 8:14-15)
Sick at Evening	1:32-34	(cf. 8:16-17)
Christ leaves Capernaum	1:35	
Preaching in Galilee	1:39 (36-38)	4:23-25
Sermon on the Mount		5:1-7:29
Healing of a Leper	1:40-45	8:1-4
The Centurion's Servant		8:5-13
Peter's Wife's Mother	(cf. 1:29-31)	8:14-15
Sick at Evening	(cf. 1:32-34)	8:16-17
Two Claimants to Discipleship		8:18-22
Stilling the Tempest	(cf. 4:35-41)	8:23-27
Gadarene Demoniacs	(cf. 5:1-20)	8:28-34
The Palsied Man	2:1-12	9:1-8
The Call of Levi	2:13-17	9:9-13
Question about Fasting	2:18-22	9:14-17
Jairus' Daughter and Woman		
with Issue of Blood	(cf. 5:21-43)	9:18-26
Two Blind Men		9:27-31
Dumb Demoniac		9:32-34

On the basis of this comparison of the Matthean arrangement of his subject matter in this section with the Marcan order the acceptance of Matthean priority hardly constitutes as live an option as that of the priority of Mark. In both Matthew and Mark, in spite of the presence of many temporal and geographical details, we note a relative unconcern to set forth the precise temporal sequence of the occurrence of various happenings. In this respect, however, Matthew manifests even less interest than Mark. This has been highlighted in the foregoing survey by the observation that Matthew does not present the Capernaum cycle of events found in Mark 1:21-35. On the other hand, as the manner in which the Sermon on the Mount is presented in chapters 5-7 and the long list of miracle stories in chapters 8 and 9 demonstrate, Matthew's approach is more topical and systematic. Thus Matthew is readily understood as having retained substantially the Marcan framework and as having inserted into this framework additional materials derived from various sources or known to him as personal reminiscences. To the extent that a selecting process is manifest it is clear that Matthew qualifies as the selector rather than Mark. On the other hand, if one should start hypothetically with the Matthean outline of events one would have to adopt the implausible supposition that Mark had chosen more or less at random various largely scattered elements of the Matthean framework and yet that he had introduced greater definiteness and concatenation of events into his outline.[45]

(4) *Agreements and Differences in Content.* The strength of the case for interdependence on the basis of agreements in subject matter, words and order of presentation is therefore manifest. On this background, I am now prepared, in accordance with an earlier promise, to ask more pointedly whether the subject matter of Matthew as a whole is not much more readily explained on the assumption of Marcan priority than on the reverse supposition.

In terms of statistics the following facts serve to introduce this discussion. Of the 661 verses in Mark only 55 are not substantially paralleled in Matthew. Of these 55, 31 are wholly distinctive of Mark; the other 24, while not in Matthew, are found in Luke. One must now proceed, however, beyond mere statistics to analysis of contents.

In the group of 31 verses there are only four pericopes: one parable, that of the seed growing secretly (4:26-29) ; two works of healing, of the deaf-mute (7:32-37) and of the blind man

---

45. H. G. Wood, in the article referred to, discusses some aspects of the data reviewed above as well as other contexts and concludes that if Butler had examined the question of order in detail, "he would almost certainly have been forced to recognize that again and again Mark's order is original and Matthew's secondary and derivative" (p. 18). Although Wood's evaluation of the implications of Mk. 1:21-35 for this subject is on the whole well taken, it seems at one point to be stated too strongly. Comparing the references to "at even" in Mk. 1:32 and Mt. 8:16 he says that in Matthew this reference "is pointless, and *the writer only retained it because he found it in his source*" (p. 18), basing this conclusion on the observation that in Mark the cures are indicated as having taken place on the Sabbath and that "only if the healing in Simon's house took place on the Sabbath would the people have waited till sunset before bringing their sick to be healed." Does it necessarily follow however that the reference to evening in Mt. 8:16 is "pointless" because Matthew does not specifically indicate that this cure took place on the Sabbath? The reference to evening in Mt. 8:16 may contribute to the conclusion that Matthew is dependent upon Mk. 1:32, but the evening might have been a particularly suitable time for bringing the sick to Jesus even if it was not the end of the Sabbath. And, of course, Matthew might conceivably have had the Sabbath in mind without being under the necessity of introducing this detail as a connecting link in a cycle of events.

at Bethsaida (8:22-26); and the singular story of the young man who fled naked at the time of the arrest of Jesus (14:51-52). Besides we have only a few scattered statements or sayings: (1) the reference to the beginning of the gospel (1:1); (2) the teaching that the Sabbath was made for man (2:27); (3) the declaration of the friends of Jesus that he was beside himself, and the setting in which this is found (3:20-21); (4) the parenthetical explanation of the ceremonial washings of the Pharisees (7:3-4); (5) the explanation as to why the disciples were not able to cure the epileptic child because "this kind can come out by nothing save by prayer" (9:29; cf. the text of Matt.); (6) the references to the fire that is not quenched and being salted with fire (9:48-49); and finally (7) a not altogether unparalleled exhortation to watch (13:33-37).

In the second group of passages, the 24 verses found in Luke but not in Matthew, there is the unique teaching concerning the right use of parables (4:21-24); the account of the exorcism at Capernaum (1:23-28); and the teaching concerning the strange exorcist (9:38-41). In addition there are only the references to the departure from Capernaum and the purpose to preach (1:35-38); the mention of the return of the Twelve (6:30); and the account of the warning against devouring widows' houses and the comments concerning the widow's two mites (12:40-44).

The distinctive materials of Matthew need not be reviewed in detail; it will suffice for our present purpose to be reminded that they include the altogether unique birth narrative of Matthew 1 and 2, the conspicuous, and largely unrepeated, features of the Sermon on the Mount (Mt. 5:3-7:27), the address to the disciples (10:5-42), the parabolic exposition of the kingdom (13:3-52), the teaching on the meaning of discipleship (18:3-35), the eschatological discourses (24:4-25:46); and the conclusion of the resurrection narrative (28:9-20). In addition there are many other striking incidents and teachings not found in Mark, including many miracles, of which some account has been taken above, comments on John the Baptist and other extraordinary teaching (11:2-30); and the declarations concerning the blessedness of Peter and the establishment of the Church (16:17-19).

Contemplating these differences we must now address ourselves to the question as to which of the two Gospels gives the impression of priority. As a principle of procedure, the analogy of the basic principle of textual criticism — of two contending readings that reading is to be preferred which better explains the origin of the other — appears to offer promise of genuine progress at this point. Which of these two Gospels — Matthew or Mark — better explains, on the supposition of interdependence, the origin of the other one? Taking account of the disposition of Matthew as a whole and relating it to that of Mark, it will be observed at once that Mark, in spite of the extensive agreement of this Gospel with Matthew, may not be regarded as essentially an abridgment or compendium of Matthew. On the supposition of Matthean priority there would be simply too many substantial sections of Matthew which are not abridged at all. And even if one might discover some other reason for Mark's supposed concern to produce a briefer gospel than that of Matthew, it remains quite baffling to explain his total omission of the birth narratives and the resurrection appearances and the substitution of the exceedingly abrupt introduction and conclusion of this Gospel.[46] And why should one who is not indifferent to the teaching of Jesus and acknowledges that it came with unique authority, have included so few traces of the long discourses which make up such impressive and fascinating features of Matthew? In fact, one might well ask whether it is not difficult on this approach to account at all for the origin of Mark in view of the fact that he presents so very little material that is not found in Matthew and leaves out so much that through the centuries has captivated its readers and gained unparalleled popularity. The relative obscurity of Mark in the history of textual transmission and exegetical study, moreover, offers at least a measure of support to this evaluation.

If, on the other hand, Mark is judged to be the original composition and Matthew is thought of as having utilized Mark, one is confronted with a quite explicable situation. For when the over-all disposition of Mark is observed and careful attention is given to its content, its *raison d'être* is eminently manifest. In publishing the gospel of Jesus Christ, the Son of God, Mark does not deal with historical backgrounds and historical beginnings as Matthew does, but omitting any reference to lineage or to birth in the bosom of a human family

---

46. *Cf. WMMC,* pp. 1-22, 86-118, for discussion of the preface and conclusion of Mark.

it introduces Jesus Christ in the most abrupt and mysterious manner imaginable. A connection with prophecy is indicated and there is mention of the preparatory word of John the Baptist, but the accent falls upon the fact that the Son of God is simply present in the world and is acknowledged to be so by a voice from heaven. As the Gospel narrative unfolds the same combination of revelation and mystery is conspicuously manifest. The human nature of Jesus is at times vividly in evidence. And the ethical teaching of Jesus is not passed over. Nevertheless, the reader is pervasively conscious of coming under the impact of overpowering acts of a stupendous person who, manifesting the divine power and authority, proclaims the coming of the kingdom of God and makes clear that its coming is bound up with his own person and ministry. And thus the elements of amazement and astonishment, of fear and trembling, tell of the reaction of men and demons in the presence of the Son of God.

But there is in Mark another ingredient of a quite different kind that comes to singular expression in this Gospel. All the Gospels deal so extensively and emphatically with the story and the theme of the passion and death of Christ that the somewhat provocative characterization of them as being passion Gospels with an extended introduction is not far astray.[47] And to the extent that this is apropos it must be acknowledged that Mark is the passion Gospel *par excellence*. The point is not that he has so much more to say concerning the passion than the others. It is rather that by virtue of his concentration on this theme, chiefly by means of restricting severely his reporting of the general teaching of Jesus, that the passion is set in bold relief. His is the Gospel which tells us with unparalleled emphasis that Jesus the Messiah, the supernatural, mysterious Son of God, the heavenly Son of Man, came not to be ministered unto but to minister and to give his life a ransom for many. There are intimations also that he is to come again on the clouds of heaven. And the overwhelming climactic fact of the resurrection is set forth. But the narrative ends as abruptly as it begins. All the Gospels except Luke, who is concerned to set forth the story on a broader canvas in two main acts divided

---

47. *Cf.* M. Kähler, *Der sogenannte historische Jesus und der geschichtliche, biblische Christus*, 2te Aufl. (Munich: Kaiser, 1956) , p. 59, n. 1: "Etwas herausfordernd könnte man sie Passionsgeschichten mit ausführlicher Einleitung nennen."

by the Ascension, end without, as it might appear, rounding off the narrative. But Mark's ending is so extraordinarily abrupt that many students of this Gospel find it difficult to believe that he concluded it as he did.

In sum, then, Mark is perfectly intelligible as an independent work when its remarkable disposition and message are envisioned.[48] The evaluation of it as an abridgment of Matthew is clearly very far from the truth. And on the supposition that it is merely, or at least very largely, a rather free selection of certain Matthean contents its origin seems quite inexplicable. But on the view that Mark was an original document and enjoyed the standing which Luke's use of it attests, and weighing the stupendous impact which Mark could have made and still is capable of making on us if we read and study it without particular reflection on the other Gospels, one may arrive at a quite satisfying estimate of the course of events in which Matthew and Luke to a remarkable degree left Mark intact and each in its own way supplemented it.

The View of Chapman

On this understanding of the course of events it may still be worth while to compare such a reconstruction as Chapman offers to explain Mark's supposed use of Matthew as well as the connection between Mark and Peter. In a chapter with the heading, "Mark Contains Only the Witness of Peter," Chapman begins by saying:

48. Inasmuch as Calvin, rejecting the thought of interdependence, attributes the agreements of the Synoptics to "the direction of the Divine Providence" so that under the diversity of their manner of writing as each followed the method which he reckoned best "the Holy Spirit suggested to them an astonishing harmony," he does not consider the possibility that Matthew might have used Mark. But it is interesting that, in rejecting the tradition that Mark is an abridgment of Matthew, he recognizes the distinctiveness of Mark as an independent Gospel. He says: "He [Mark] does not everywhere adhere to the order which Matthew observed, and from the very commencement handles the subjects in a different manner. Some things, too, are related by him which the other had omitted, and his narrative of the same event is sometimes more detailed. It is more probable, in my opinion — and the nature of the case warrants the conjecture — that he had not seen Matthew's book when he wrote his own; so far is he from having expressly intended to make an abridgement" (From the *Argumentum* of *Commentarius in Harmoniam Evangelicam, Opera Omnia* (Brunswick, 1891), XLV, 3 (Eng. trans., Grand Rapids: Eerdmans, 1949, I, xxxviii).

> If we compare Mk. with Mt. as the part with the whole, the chief characteristic of Mk. is seen to be this, that Mk. contains nothing but what St. Peter saw and heard, and might easily remember.
>
> Thus he omits all the long discourses save one, but preserves short and pithy sayings of the kind that would be easily remembered, and a few parables. He omits all incidents at which Peter could not have been eye-witness. He also omits all incidents which are to the honour of Peter.
>
> There is one important exception: he repeats the story of the death of St. John the Baptist, though Peter was not present at Herod's feast nor at the execution . . . .[49]

It is important to observe at once that Chapman here draws conclusions with regard to two quite distinct matters: (1) the understanding of the contents of Mark in terms of what Peter saw and heard, and (2) the explanation of the absence from Mark of the long discourses of Matthew by way of appeal to the inadequacy of Peter's memory. Although Chapman's formulation of and argument for the first point seems to me to be in some respects unsatisfactory, it is not necessary to enter here upon a thorough treatment of it. There are at any rate various features in Mark which require some qualification of the assertion in the title of the chapter — "Mark contains only the witness of Peter." But the conclusion regarding the dependence of Mark upon the preaching of Peter need not be challenged and, in any case, is not an issue in the present discussion.

Whether Chapman is even plausible, however, in his appeal to the vagueness of Peter's memory with regard to long discourses,[50] must be earnestly questioned. This contention can be properly evaluated only as one takes fuller account of his theory concerning the origin of Mark. On this subject his comments are as follows:

> It would seem that St. Peter is the real author, that he is addressing Gentile converts, that he gives only what he himself remembers, that he omits whatever he thinks unsuitable to Gentiles:
>
> That he uses our actual Greek Mt. as his textbook, that he reads out of it, in his own wording, whatever he has chosen, in conversational language, with much addition, with many verbal repetitions and all the vividness of personal recollection.

49. Chapman, op. cit., p. 38.
50. Ibid., p. 42.

Mk. is present and takes the lectures down as far as possible word for word, in shorthand . . . .[51]

Chapman's attempt to harmonize the phenomena with his own commitment to the priority of Matthew is, to say the least, highly imaginative.[52] Contrary to tradition he makes Peter himself the real author of Mark. And it is not the evangelist Mark but Peter himself who is conjectured to have used our Greek Matthew. And how surpassing strange is Peter's use of Matthew on this hypothesis! For he reads out of it, and evidently his dependence upon it must have been very close and extensive if one is to account for the broad areas of agreement between Matthew and Mark. On the other hand, Peter is regarded as having been so free in his use of his textbook Matthew that he immediately transposed its language into his own wording so that it gained the vividness of personal recollection but also acquired the redundancies, pleonasms and other features connected with his conversational presentation of his message. These in turn are explained as being found in Mark because this evangelist took down the lectures as far as possible word for word, in shorthand.

This conjecture as to how the redundancies, pleonasms and other non-literary features of Mark were produced by one who was reading from a document which lacked these features puts a great strain upon our credulity. But even if there were considerably greater plausibility at this point, we should still be left with the insuperable difficulty with which Chapman confronts us in laying as much weight as he does upon supposedly poor memory as the explanation for the omission in Mark of the longer discourses. For if Peter had Matthew in his hand and was reading from it, how could he have failed to read the long discourses and, on the assumption that his memory had become vague, had his memory refreshed? Manifestly, Peter's poor memory is a fiction devised to explain one feature of the theory of Matthean priority which is simply crying out for elucidation, i.e., Mark's failure to utilize the Sermon on the Mount and other discourses. For it is irreconcilable with

51. *Ibid.*, p. 90.
52. Chapman himself characterizes his reconstruction as an "effort of the imagination, which gives at least a possible explanation of some curious data" (p. 92). For Butler's similar, though perhaps somewhat refined conjecture concerning the relationship between Matthew and Mark and Peter's role, cf. *op. cit.*, pp. 166ff.

the central feature of Chapman's hypothesis that Peter was reading Matthew in his preaching.

The question whether Mark was written before Matthew and utilized by the latter has already been discussed at some length, and a brief summary of the progress made may be useful. First of all, the way was cleared for an explication of this subject in terms of the really pertinent data by observing that the history of critical discussion concerning divergent viewpoints by no means affords an *a priori* criterion for a decision. Moreover, the voices of tradition concerning the sequence of the Gospels are far from unanimous and so even less than in the case of authorship may it be appealed to as determinative or even as offering general guiding lines. What the Gospels themselves disclose concerning their own contents and form, as one minutely observes large elements of agreement in connection with substantial divergences, is to be the final court of appeal.

Considering the intrinsic difficulties involved in an investigation of this kind, and remembering the remarkably diverse theories which have developed in the course of time, one is warned in advance to show proper restraint. Facts must also be faced squarely, however, and even though one may still be baffled by many aspects of the Synoptic Problem, there is no merit in taking refuge in a position of complete agnosticism.

One conclusion growing out of the discussion above that appears unassailable is that there is actual interdependence among the Synoptics. And this conclusion serves a twofold purpose. It at once clears away as of little more than historic interest all theories which have sought to answer our problem on the supposition that there has been no dependence at all or that dependence is only of an indirect kind. Moreover, the acceptance of the fact of interdependence constrains one to seek earnestly for answers as to the nature of this interdependence, this being the principal reason why the order of the Gospels is important.

My own general position as to order and interdependence, as it applies to the most controversial feature of it, is that the evaluation of agreements and differences in contents, words and order of arrangement points to the priority of Mark and to the fact of Matthew's use of Mark. Not all of the arguments advanced for this conclusion appear to be decisive. However, especially reflection on order of arrangement and a broad comparison of the Gospel contents support the conclusion that Matthew utilized Mark rather than the reverse.

Are there, however, other arguments and considerations which need to be criticially evaluated before a mature decision may be registered? To the examination of certain other points summed up by Streeter I shall turn in the next chapter.

CHAPTER FOUR

THE FACTOR OF LANGUAGE

In our dialogue with Streeter — and with a number of other scholars who have supported or disagreed with his position concerning the priority of Mark — three of his arguments have been passed in review. In the interest of concreteness and definiteness, the two additional arguments, as summarized in his synopsis, may well be quoted. They are as follows:

> (4) The primitive character of Mark is further shown by (*a*) the use of phrases likely to cause offense, which are omitted or toned down in the other Gospels, (*b*) roughness of style and grammar, and the preservation of Aramaic words.
>
> (5) The way in which Marcan and non-Marcan material is distributed in Matthew and Luke respectively looks as if each had before him the Marcan material *in a single document,* and was faced with the problem of combining this with material from other sources.[1]

My impression is that the fifth point viewed as an independent argument for the priority of Mark is not of sufficient substantiality to require discussion here. The two points subsumed under (4), however, confront us with weighty issues which need to be evaluated with due care. For reasons that need not be delineated I shall reverse the order of these two topics, and so shall deal first of all with the language of Matthew and Mark.

General Appraisal

A point of contact with the immediately preceding discussion is to be found in the fact that Chapman's estimate of Mark's linguistic characteristics as noted above had been substantially set forth by Streeter previously. For Streeter stated:

> Mark reads like a shorthand account of a story by an impromptu speaker — with all the repetitions, redundancies, and digressions which are characteristic of living speech. And it seems

1. Streeter, *op. cit.,* pp. 151f.

to me most probable that his Gospel, like Paul's Epistles, was taken down from rapid dictation by word of mouth.[2] Butler specifically indicates his agreement with this formulation of Streeter. He moreover speaks of Streeter's fourth point as presenting "at last . . . an argument deserving serious attention," and in commenting in summary fashion on the details of Streeter's developed argument, says that if we "take it for all in all, it is an impressive case."[3]

Butler is disappointing however in that, though he promises to discuss these arguments in the later pages of his book,[4] he devotes almost no attention to them in detail but rather largely rests his case upon the supposed plausibility of his own reconstruction. Nevertheless, in the interest of doing justice to Butler, we must note that in reply to Streeter's conclusions regarding the evidence, he declares:

> We believe that the most formally relevant evidence is not that which appeals to any *a priori* theory of the evolution of the Christian attitude towards Christ, or of the relatively late intrusion or magnification of the miraculous element in the Christian tradition, but that which consists of the results of a direct comparison of parallel passages in their respective contexts and a determination on the basis of such comparison of the document which shows signs of the displacements, incoherences, etc. that are liable to be caused by the rearrangement and more or less loose reproduction of a written source.[5]

Butler believes that he has met this challenge by way of his elaborate evaluation of Matthew's great discourses and various miscellaneous passages.[6]

Although Butler's discussion of these materials is worthy of close attention, it does not seem to me to be necessary to enter upon a detailed treatment of it. In weighing the evidence which he presents one would have to keep in view that he is virtually presupposing the validity of his own theory of Gospel relationships, including such a rigid and exclusive conception of interdependence that, in comparing Matthew and Mark, he allows only for the possibilities that Matthew is making an excerpt of Mark or Mark of Matthew. Along with his elimination of Q as a source available to the later evangelists in addition to

2. *Ibid.*, p. 163.
3. Butler, *op. cit.*, pp. 68, 162, 164.
4. *Ibid.*, p. 68.
5. *Ibid.*, p. 163.
6. *Ibid.*, pp. 72-106.

their use of earlier Gospels, he appears never seriously to allow
for the possibility that the later evangelists had access to other
materials, including for example such as are found in the
hypothetical Q, by way either of personal reminiscence or
acquaintance with stereotyped oral tradition.

Thus, for example, observing that five verses of Mark 13:33-
37 are closely paralleled to certain scattered verses in Matthew
24 and 25, he insists that the issue with which the student of
Gospel relationships is confronted involves one in a decision
as to whether the five verses of Mark form the background for
the sixty-one verses of Matthew 24:37-25:46. Declaring that
"it would be preposterous to suggest that St. Matthew ac-
cidentally or deliberately worked practically the total contents
of Mark's five verses, in tiny fragments, into his own freely soar-
ing and monumental structure. . .", he concludes that "we are
driven to the alternative and natural supposition, that Mark has
hastily telescoped Matthew's sixty-one verses into the brief
finale of a chapter which no doubt was felt to be already too
long."[7]

This approach obviously does not allow seriously for two
other possibilities. One is that both Matthew and Mark had
independent and substantial knowledge of the eschatological
teaching of our Lord and that each followed his own plan in
presenting it, Matthew much more fully and Mark much more
briefly. The other possibility is that Matthew, still following
rather closely the Marcan outline, chose to supplement the
Marcan record of this teaching not only by the additional teaching of Matthew 24 but also and most conspicuously by the
largely distinctive contents of chapter 25. A further general
observation with regard to Butler's approach is that, in his
enthusiasm for Matthew, he is often severely critical of Mark,
ascribing to him on occasion bizarre and jejune language, and
attributing blemishes and mistakes to him.[8]   And as Austin
Farrer has pointed out, Butler tends to beg the very questions
which are at issue when, for example, he appeals to the Arama-
isms in Matthew as proof that he could not have been a Greek
writer using a Greek source; and declares that "perfection of
Semitic rhetorical or poetic form is equivalent to primitivity";
and that "limpidity of expression and clarity of logical order

7. *Ibid.*, pp. 83f.
8. *Cf. ibid.*, pp. 74, 80, 91f.

are Mark's originality. Obscure expression and broken verbal logic are signs of excerpting and artificial combination."[9] The approach taken by Butler, therefore, does not free one from the necessity of facing seriously the implications of the linguistic phenomena with which one is confronted as a result of a minute examination of the Synoptic Gospels. Nor will it suffice to be occupied only with Streeter's less than two pages of summary statement on this subject. For as he indicates he is mainly intending to recall the elaborate lists of data to be found in the *Horae Synopticae* of Sir John C. Hawkins (1909), the classic study to which every student of the Synoptic Question is highly indebted regardless of his final answer. No one can be satisfied that he has done justice to the question under discussion unless he has weighed carefully the statistics and observations presented by Hawkins under the following heads:

II. Enlargements of the narrative, which add nothing to the information conveyed by it, because they are expressed again, or are directly involved, in the context (pp. 125f.).

III. Minor additions to the narrative (pp. 127-131).

IV. Rude, harsh, obscure or unusual words or expressions, which may therefore have been omitted or replaced by others (pp. 131-138).

   (*a*) Various unusual words and construction (pp. 131-135).

   (*b*) Instances of anacoluthon, or broken or incomplete construction, in Mark, which are altered or avoided in Matthew or Luke or both (pp. 135-137).

   (*c*) Cases of 'asyndeton', or want of connection.

V. Duplicate expression in Mark, of which one or both of the other Synoptics use one part, or its equivalent (pp. 139-142).

VI. The historic present in Mark (pp. 143-149).

VII. The conjunction *kaí* preferred to *dé* in Mark (pp. 150-153).

In a previous connection, as the agreement of words in the Synoptics was being evaluated, some notice was taken of the last two sections, and no further discussion of them will be undertaken here.[10] But when they are examined together with Hawkins' statistics and observations concerning Matthew (pp. 154-173), one cannot seriously doubt that they support the conclusion, with regard to which Butler is in essential agreement with Streeter, that Matthew, like Luke, is characterized by a far more literary quality than Mark. Whereas Mark has

9. *JTS*, New Series, III (1952), 104f.
10. See pp. 61f. above.

frequent repetitions and redundancies and his language and style are relatively obscure and awkward or otherwise bear the marks of living speech, Matthew and Luke are more succinct, use more carefully chosen language and in general are more smooth and polished in their writing.[11] As Butler's study has served again to remind us, students of the Gospels are likely to continue to differ with regard to the implications of these linguistic data for the question of the order and the nature of the interdependence of the Gospels. On our part, however, we acknowledge that the linguistic phenomena which have been noted create a strong presumption in favor of the view that the less literary Gospel is the earlier.

So far no account has been taken of the appeal to the presence of Aramaic words in Mark as a further evidence of its primitiveness and priority. The retention in Mark of such words or phrases as *boanerges* (3:17), *talitha cumi* (5:41), *corban* (7:11) and *ephatha* (7:34) is, it would appear, more readily accountable on the supposition that they are original with Mark and were later omitted by Matthew and Luke rather than as Marcan additions.[12] These phenomena may be attributed in part to Mark's characteristic fulness and vividness which, as noted above, stand in contrast to Matthew and Luke's interest in succinctness and clarity. Moreover, Mark as the most Semitic of the Gospels may well retain various concrete details reflecting the Aramaic context of the ministry of Jesus, the proclamation of Peter, and the evangelist's own Palestinian background, whereas the other evangelists, Matthew as well as Luke, although still revealing to a greater or lesser degree the Semitic background, dispense with these details as not making a meaningful contribution to their own readers. This observation of differences between the language and style of Mark, Matthew and Luke, however, draw attention to the broader question which is most specifically before us, namely, that of the original languages of Matthew and Mark, and it is therefore expedient to proceed at once with a brief treatment of it.

---

11. On the succinctness of Matthew one should note, in addition to the materials of sections II, III and V above, the relative brevity of many narratives in Matthew as indicated in Hawkins' table on p. 159. In nine narratives or sections, including besides miracle stories the preparation for the passover, Mark employs 1,840 words, and Luke 1,476, while Matthew uses only 971. See also Mk. 14:36; 15:22 and 34.

12. *Cf.* Hawkins, *op. cit.*, p. 130; Streeter, *op. cit.*, p. 164.

Within the framework of our present discussion the question
of the original language of Mark is indeed of secondary importance. Whether Mark was originally composed in Aramaic,
as some scholars have contended, or owes its Aramaic coloring
to the tradition of narratives and sayings which influence the
author to write a kind of translation-Greek is in the nature
of the case very difficult to make out.[13] But inasmuch as our
own study centers upon order and interdependence, and it is
generally recognized that the interdependence of Matthew and
Mark involves an interdependence of Greek documents, we may
well concentrate upon the question of the original language of
Matthew.

The Original Language of Matthew

At this point the issue is rather sharply drawn among the
proponents for either side of our question. Those who hold
to the priority of Matthew seem quite consistently to maintain
that this Gospel was originally composed in Aramaic. The
priority assigned to it is that of the Aramaic original; it may
or may not apply to the Greek translation thereof as well. On
this view Mark may have utilized the Greek translation of
Matthew or the Greek translator of Matthew may have utilized
Mark. On the other hand, on the approach which maintains
the priority of Mark, Matthew is understood as having utilized
the Greek Mark so fully that it cannot be conceived of as an
originally Aramaic Gospel.

The presence of Semitic coloring in the language of Matthew
has naturally been emphasized by scholars who have defended
the hypothesis of an Aramaic original.[14] But its presence is
not denied by Kilpatrick[15] and others who hold to the priority
of Mark. My own judgment is that in a case like this, as in
the instance of the original language of Mark, it is impossible
to be dogmatic simply on the basis of a detection of the Semitic
coloring of the document. One possibility that must be kept
in view is that the Semitic cast of various New Testament writings comes about because they are rather slavish versions of
Semitic originals. It appears, however, to be equally possible

---

13. M. Black, *An Aramaic Approach to the Gospels and Acts* (Oxford:
Clarendon, 2nd ed., 1954), pp. 206ff.; V. Taylor, *op. cit.*, pp. 55ff.

14. *Cf.* Chapman, *op. cit.*, pp. 181ff.; 206ff.; Butler, *op. cit.*, pp. 147ff.;
Zahn, *Einleitung*, II, 306ff., 316f. (Eng. trans., II, 576ff., 591f.).

15. *Cf.* Kilpatrick, *op. cit.*, pp. 103f.

to explain such phenomena as due to the influence of Semitic sources or to the fact that the author's language and style had been largely fashioned by his Semitic background or the influence upon him of the Greek of the Septuagint. The reserve of Matthew Black on this point is noteworthy: "A survey of the results of this study in this connexion yield one conclusion only which can be regarded as in any degree established, that an Aramaic sayings-source or tradition lies behind the Synoptic Gospels."[16]

Two distinguishing features of the Marcan style which have previously been noted, namely asyndeton and paratactic construction, may be explained as due to Aramaic influence,[17] but the consideration that Matthew's style is less Semitic than Mark's does not prove that Matthew was originally written in Greek any more than that Mark was written in Aramaic. This observation, like that relating to the presence of Aramaic words in Mark, perhaps possesses some cumulative force when taken with other linguistic phenomena but it does not eliminate as such the possibility that Matthew was written in Aramaic.

In seeking to determine the language in which Matthew was originally composed, we are on stronger ground when we consider the quotations of the Old Testament in Matthew and observe that to a very large extent they reflect a dependence upon the Septuagint Version. The evaluation of this phenomenon is greatly complicated, however, by the fact that other quotations in Matthew are very free and at times disclose a knowledge of the Hebrew text. It is understandable therefore that those who posit an Aramaic original of Matthew have maintained that the Semitic elements in the quotations are to be explained as resulting from translation from the Aramaic while the quotations which conform rather fully to the LXX are to be accounted for by the consideration that the translator deliberately utilized this version when it suited his purpose. Thus Zahn appeals directly to the form of Matthew's citations from the Old Testament for proof that it is a translation. Our Greek Matthew, he maintains, "is the result of an effort to give a literal translation of a uniformly Aramaic original document."[18] Where no violence was done to the sense of his original, as in the case of many quotations, he found it practicable and convenient to

16. Black, *op. cit.*, p. 206.
17. *Ibid.*
18. Zahn, *op. cit.*, II, 580; *cf.* pp. 578ff.

follow the Septuagint. In other passages, however, "it must have seemed to him that the substitution of the text of the LXX would obscure the sense of his original and the purpose of the citation. In such cases he translated the O. T. quotations of his original in exactly the same way that he did the rest of the Aramaic book."[19] On this general approach, as represented by Zahn and other scholars, attention centers upon a supposed translator of the Aramaic Matthew into Greek rather than upon the activity of the evangelist.

Hawkins, drawing atention to an observation which had been made by Westcott and others, that "the quotations which are introduced by the Evangelist himself agree much less closely with the LXX than those which occur in the course of the common narrative," undertook a rather detailed classification of the quotations which led him to the conclusion that the divergences between the two main types of quotations are such as to suggest "prima facie that we have before us the work of more than one author or editor."[20] Since the time of Hawkins the conclusion that the work of more than one author or editor was involved has apparently enjoyed very little vogue. Nevertheless, the question of the principal divergences evident among Matthew's quotations has received a good deal of attention.

Most notable of all is the contribution of Krister Stendahl in his work on *The School of St. Matthew*.[21] Stendahl still recognizes the validity, broadly speaking, of the distinction between quotations with parallels in one or more of the Synoptics which have a rather pure LXX text and the so-called "formula quotations which are distinctive of Matthew and have a text differing noticeably from the LXX." Nevertheless, as he observes, this distinction is somewhat too simple. With regard to the first group of quotations it must be acknowledged that Semitic elements are sometimes present. However, the presence of such Semitic features does not require one to modify the classification of this group as essentially Septuagintal

19. *Ibid. Cf.* also pp. 610ff. See also Chapman, *op. cit.*, pp. 261-293, who holds that our Greek Mark was dependent upon the Greek Matthew, and M. J. Lagrange, *Évangile selon Saint Matthieu*, 8me ed. (Paris, 1948), pp. cxvii-cxxii, who maintains that the translator of the Greek Matthew to a significant extent utilized the Greek Mark. Butler does not discuss the quotations in Matthew.

20. Hawkins, *op. cit.*, pp. 154-157.

21. Krister Stendahl, *The School of St. Matthew* (Uppsala, 1954).

since they may be explained as due to the fact "that the Semitic background asserts itself and that it has not been completely harmonized with the LXX form." As a point of contact with our previous discussion of the language of the Synoptic Gospels it is interesting to observe that Mark's quotations have more such Semitic features than the other Synoptics, that Matthew's quotations which parallel Mark's have somewhat fewer such features than Mark and so are closer to the LXX, and that Luke retains the fewest Semitic traces. But these observations, it must be emphasized, leave substantially unimpaired the conclusion that Matthew generally followed the Septuagint as a matter of course.[22]

The characterization of the second category of quotations is now seen, however, to require considerable modification. It is not enough to call attention to the fact that these reflective quotations of Matthew present "a text differing noticeably from the LXX" and that at times they betray a knowledge of a Semitic original. In the first place, one must recognize that in this group of quotations evidence of familiarity with the LXX and even use of the LXX is not entirely lacking. Nevertheless, the degree of familiarity with or use of the LXX is relatively so meager as to justify the maintenance of the classification of the two main types of quotation. In the second place, however, it is now seen that the quotations of this second group, where they differ from the LXX, are not based simply on the Massoretic text. They disclose the influence not only of the Massoretic text but also of other readings which could be supported by examples from various LXX manuscripts, the later Greek versions, the Targums and even the O. T. Peshitta. In the area of the formula quotations, moreover, it must be recognized that the evangelist exhibits a remarkable freedom, a freedom which Stendahl regards as due to the adoption of the *pesher* method which has developed in the "School of St. Matthew" of which the evangelist was supposedly a member.[23] The

---

22. *Ibid.,* pp. 146-150.
23. *Cf. ibid.,* pp. 183ff. In a discussion of "Biblical Exegesis in the Qumran Texts and the New Testament" (*Biblical Exegesis in the Qumran Texts,* The Hague: van Keulen, 1959), pp. 66ff., F. F. Bruce concludes with the following pertinent observations: "Here, then, is the key to that distinctive interpretation of the Old Testament which we find in the New Testament. Jesus has fulfilled the ancient promises, and in fulfilling them He has given them a new meaning, in which their original meaning is not set aside but caught up into something more comprehensive and

evaluation of this larger question of the *Sitz im Leben* of Matthew need not detain us now.

Whether or not Stendahl has succeeded in making a convincing case for his precise thesis regarding the Matthean hermeneutics, including particularly the hypothesis of a *school* of St. Matthew, my judgment is that his conclusions regarding the original language of Matthew are sound. In the first place, the non-Septuagintal phenomena in the formula quotations involve such a distinctive reflection upon and use of the Old Testament, that they must be explained as due to the self-conscious approach of the evangelist rather than to a translator who was toiling with the peculiar problems of rendering an Aramaic original as accurately as possible into Greek.[24] Secondly, Stendahl presents one particular passage among the quotations as offering "the greatest obstacle to an original Aramaic Matthew," namely the Isaiah quotation in Matthew 15:8f. "Only in the LXX form," he observes, "has this quota-

---

far-reaching than was foreseen before He came. In His own perfect way He has accomplished a ministry which involves the finishing of transgression, putting an end to sin, atoning for iniquity, bringing in everlasting righteousness, setting the seal on vision and prophecy, and consecrating that spiritual sanctuary into which, by virtue of His self-offering, He has entered as His people's forerunner. And as we learn to interpret 'in all the scriptures the things concerning Himself' (Luke 24:27) we can best understand what He meant when He said of those scriptures: 'It is they that bear witness to me' (John 5:39)" (p. 77). See also my summary statement with regard to Matthew's perspective: "The fulfillment of the law and the prophets represents not a mere repetition or reiteration of the old revelation, but the announcement of the appearance of the age to which the old revelation looked forward. Accordingly, Matthew's witness to Christ finds its distinctiveness, or at least a highly important aspect of it, in its portrayal of the history of Jesus Christ in the perspective of the history of revelation. And this means far more that that he was the Messiah of the Old Testament Scriptures. The profound affirmation of Matthew is that *the coming of the Messiah of promise signifies the coming of one whose life and teaching were themselves a new epochal revelation that was the consummation of the old*" (*WMMC*, p. 198; cf. p. 253). For a treatment of *pesher* interpretation in relation to Paul's writings, cf. E. E. Ellis, *Paul's Use of the Old Testament* (Grand Rapids: Eerdmans, 1957), pp. 139ff.

24. To establish this conclusion fully one would have to present a minute study of all these quotations. It may suffice here, however, to mention Mt. 2:15, 2:23 and 27:9, 10 as among the most obvious instances of such understanding of the fulfillment of the O.T. in the new revelation concerning Jesus Christ. Stendahl's own treatment, *op. cit.*, pp. 96ff., is one of the most valuable discussions.

tion any meaning for Mark and Matthew."[25]   The quotation in view here is not one of Matthew's distinctive formula quotations, but is a part of the teaching of Jesus wherein a quotation of Isaiah 29:13 closely follows the LXX in syntax and wording rather than the Massoretic text. The agreement in wording relates particularly to the fact that where the Hebrew may be translated, "their fear of me is a commandment of men which hath been taught them" (ASV), the LXX and Matthew and Mark have: "But in vain do they worship me, teaching as their doctrines the precepts of men." In the New Testament context where Jesus charges the Pharisees and scribes with making void the Word of God because of their tradition (Mt. 15:6; Mk. 7:8) the reason for the introduction of the quotation is that it rather precisely presents this denunciation whereas the Hebrew text does not.

In passing it is interesting to notice that Stendahl does not exclude the possibility that the point made by the LXX was made by Jesus himself. "It is impossible to decide," he says, "whether Jesus referred to this passage in its Semitic form, or if the quotation is added in a church where the LXX Scriptures were used. In the former case we must suppose that the LXX form appeared to fit even better than the Semitic one, and thus influenced the Greek rendering; there is no direct way from the one to the other."[26]   Taylor, quoting Rawlinson to the effect that the form of the quotation shows that it was derived from the evangelist rather than from the Lord, concedes that this argument is probably sound so far as the form of text is concerned, but adds that "it is less certain that the Hebrew does not provide a basis for the charge."[27]

A further weighty consideration in support of Stendahl's conclusion regarding the original language of Matthew is to be found in his observation that Lagrange admits the far-reaching significance of the form of the quotation in Matthew 15:8f. But in order to maintain the basic features of his theory of Gospel relationships, it is necessary for Lagrange to modify it to the point where he enters the judgment that the Greek

25. *Ibid.,* p. 155; *cf.* pp. 56ff.
26. *Ibid.,* p. 58.
27. *Ad* Mk. 7:7. *Cf.* A. E. J. Rawlinson, *The Gospel according to St. Mark, WC* (London: Westminster, 7th ed., 1949), p. 94.

Matthew was not simply a translation but also an enlarged Greek edition of the Aramaic Matthew.[28]

Such an interpretation, if it is not actually a revision, of the position of the Pontifical Biblical Commission in 1911, which is reflected also in the theories of mutual successive dependence as developed, for example, by Vosté, Chapman and Wikenhauser, is not really a minor one. For it includes the view that for all practical purposes the Aramaic Matthew and the Greek Matthew are identical in contents. Once the uncontrollable factor of editorial revision of the original Aramaic Matthew is allowed to enter into this scheme of Synoptic origins, one cannot be at all confident with regard to its specific contents. Accordingly also the maintenance of the priority of the Aramaic Matthew loses at least something, and perhaps most, of its force as a principle of commitment to tradition. One is constrained to ask whether on such a view the commitment is not more nominal than real.

Wikenhauser's statement of the issue is especially illuminating. Having declared that most Roman Catholic scholars today "deny that Mark used Matthew, but say that whoever produced Greek Mt. made use of Mark; in either case, they say, the author of Greek Mt. was influenced by the style and vocabulary of Mark, while it must furthermore be remembered that he also took over some entire passages, and in parts followed Mark's order of events," he concludes as follows:

> It may be taken as certain that an Aramaic original of the Gospel of St. Matthew can be defended only if we regard Greek Mt. not as a literal translation of the Aramaic, but as a thorough revision made with frequent use of the Gospel of St. Mark. This is consistent with the decision of the Biblical Commission which declares explicitly that the tradition of the early Church is preserved if we uphold the substantial identity of Greek and Aramaic Matthew. Since there are no remains of Aramaic Matthew, and no one knows what it was like, we cannot make any more accurate or more definite statement about the relationship between the two forms of St. Matthew's Gospel.[29]

This summary appears to me to point up a deep tension within the position of many Roman Catholic scholars today. Tradition constrains them to accept the priority of Matthew, that is, of an Aramaic Matthew concerning which no one possesses

28. Lagrange, *op. cit.*, pp. xxxivff.; *cf.* Stendahl, *op. cit.*, p. 155.
29. Wikenhauser, *op. cit.*, pp. 194f. See p. 52 above.

any certain knowledge. On the other hand, the study of the Gospels themselves compels them to conclude that our Greek Matthew — the only form of the Gospel concerning which we have knowledge — was dependent on our Greek Mark, and the utilization of Mark by Matthew is so extensive that one would have to posit that our Greek Matthew must have been "a thorough revision" of the Aramaic Matthew. In spite of the extent of this revision, and clearly only in the interest of faith, the "substantial identity" of Greek and Aramaic Matthew is insisted upon. How Greek Matthew can be both a thoroughgoing revision of Aramaic Matthew and substantially identical with it is a mystery. What I wish to emphasize here, however, is that the extraordinary character of Lagrange's concession focuses attention on the fact that the theory of an original Aramaic Matthew does not nicely account for the phenomena of the quotations in the way that it has often been supposed to do.

My general conclusion is therefore that, while appropriate reserve must be exercised in forming firm decisions concerning the original language of such a document as Matthew, the theory of an Aramaic original, to say the very least, does not commend itself on the basis of the study of internal evidence. And there are some factors that point quite definitely to the conclusion that Matthew was originally written in Greek. When, moreover, one takes full account of the other arguments which have been advanced for the priority of Mark and Matthew's use of Mark, there is further confirmation of the conclusion that Greek was the original language of Matthew. His dependence upon the Greek Mark especially with respect to words and phrases would allow for no other conclusion. Nor should this be thought of as an argument in a circle. For the most striking evidences of Marcan priority are to be found, in my judgment, not so much in the areas of vocabulary and style, though these are not without force, as in the implications of the agreements and disagreements in subject matter and order of arrangement.

The Papian Declaration

Finally, it seems necessary to return briefly to Papias to inquire how his statement concerning the origin of Matthew is to be evaluated in relation to the conclusions reached above. Papias, it will be recalled, declared that Matthew arranged (or,

composed) the oracles in the Hebrew language and each translated (or, interpreted) as he was able. Because of the isolation of this passage from its original context and our uncer-
tainty as to the meaning of certain words, we cannot be absolutely dogmatic with regard to the main thrust of the statement. In any case, however, it is clear that Papias, evidently
speaking of our canonical Gospel Matthew (as has been argued
above), declares that it was originally composed in a Semitic
language. And he further seems to say that each translated
this document as he was able.[30]

On the view taken here of the basic evidence as to what
Matthew and Mark disclose concerning their own language,
the statement of Papias is obviously mistaken. But this need
not surprise us particularly. Just as there were explicable
uncertainties and divergences in the traditions regarding the
sequence in which the Gospels were written, so there could
easily have arisen erroneous judgments as to the original
language of the Gospels and in particular that of Matthew.
Contemplating the patent fact that Matthew manifests a particular interest in Judaism, and evidently was written first of
all for a church of Jewish-Christian character or perhaps even
to win Jews to an acceptance of Jesus Christ, one can readily
understand that in the course of time there arose a tradition
that it was originally composed in the Hebrew language. Chapman himself argues from his conclusion that Matthew was addressed to Palestinian Jews to the inference that it must have
been written in Aramaic, thus not giving sufficient recognition,
as quite possibly some ancient Christians did not, to the factor
that a large Jewish audience might also have been found in
various Greek-speaking centers such as Antioch in Syria.

In evaluating the tradition of Papias here one should also
take account of the possibility that there was confusion in the
minds of some of the ancients between our Greek Matthew
and another document. As a case in point one may recall the
fact that Jerome thought of the Gospel used by the Nazarenes
in his day — evidently the apocryphal Gospel according to the

---

30. In view of the reference to *language* in the prior clause, ἡρμήνευσεν
almost certainly refers to *translation* rather than to interpretation. And
that the statement relates to *oral* translation, rather than to the preparation of several versions as some scholars have held, is highly probable.
Cf. Zahn, *Einleitung*, II, 262ff. (Eng. trans., II, 511ff.); Bacon, *op. cit.*,
pp. 13f.

Hebrews — as being the original Hebrew Matthew.[31]   This case of mistaken identity must indeed be dated long after the time of Papias, but taking account of it one may not fairly exclude the possibility that even as early as his era there may have been some confusion with another document written in a Semitic language.   Perhaps even a Semitic translation of the Greek Matthew erroneously was judged to be the original Hebrew Matthew by some who did not possess a first-hand or accurate knowledge of conditions prevailing in the Jewish world within the first Christian century.

There are therefore a number of ways of explaining plausibly the origin of the Papian tradition concerning the original language of Matthew.   Since in any case the tradition is not binding, the feature of a non-extant Aramaic Matthew need not be retained as an essential ingredient of an acceptable solution of the Synoptic Problem, as it is for numerous Roman Catholic scholars and not a few Protestants.   A study of the linguistic phenomena of Matthew not only fails to produce any evidence that would disallow the conclusion that it was composed in Greek.   Positively, as the discussion above has demonstrated, especially the disclosures made by a study of the quotations offer persuasive support of the position that the evangelist Matthew wrote in Greek rather than Aramaic.

When now one recalls the striking differences in language and style between Mark and Matthew — such features as Mark's repetitions and redundancies and relative awkwardness and Matthew's more precise and literary language — which were discussed in the first half of this chapter, it appears that there is weighty confirmation of the conclusion reached tentatively in Chapter III.   The recognition of the priority of Mark to Matthew, and of the dependence of the latter on the former, constitutes a positive step toward the clarification of the Synoptic Problem.

31. *Vir. Ill.*, iii (PL XXIII, col. 643; E. T. *NPF*, 2nd Ser., III, p. 362) .

CHAPTER FIVE

THE RICH YOUNG RULER

THIS study of the Synoptic accounts concerning the rich young man who, according to Mark 10:18, asked Jesus, "Why callest thou me good?", is initiated because of its supposed bearing upon the subject of the priority of Mark. Since, however, the argument relating to priority takes the form that the apparently parallel passage in Matthew 19:17, "Why askest thou me concerning the good?", represents an alteration *from reverential motives*, there is involved alongside of and beyond the simple question of priority the deeper issue of harmony or discrepancy between Matthew and Mark. And thus in the modern debate concerning the historical Jesus, the Marcan form of the question has often been taken as being, as Paul Schmiedel put it, one of the few unassailable "foundation-pillars" upon which one might build with confidence "a truly scientific life of Jesus."[1]

My concern in this book as a whole comprehends this larger issue of the total witness of the Gospels, and so the exposition and evaluation that follow are by no means restricted to the question of sequence. Moreover, the rather detailed observations and judgments concerning the agreements and divergences in the three forms of the story serve not only to enhance our understanding of the passage as a whole and in detail and thus to put the issues of order and harmony in proper perspective, but also confront us with a case study of the nature and extent of actual differences in content and form which may appear in the transmission of a single story. It is this kind of minute evaluation which has been chiefly in view in our previous observations concerning Synoptic "agreement in words."

Before proceeding further with our study of this story as

---

1. *Cf.* the article on "Gospels" in *Encyclopaedia Biblica*, II (New York: Macmillan, 1901), col. 1881.

a whole, acknowledgment must be made that in limiting discussion to this single narrative a somewhat unfortunate restriction of treatment of the argument relating to the priority of Mark is entailed. It is true that it is this passage, along with Mark 6:5 as compared with Matthew 13:58, which Streeter singles out as a conspicuous illustration of his claim that Mark used "phrases likely to cause offense, which are omitted or toned down in the other Gospels."[2] Streeter's intent, however, is clearly not to rest his entire case upon these two passages. To say the least, he must have in mind the long list which, according to Hawkins, "may have been omitted or altered as being liable to be misunderstood, or to give offense, or to suggest difficulties," and especially the first main section which lists twenty-two "passages seeming (a) to limit the power of Jesus Christ, or (b) to be otherwise derogatory to, or unworthy, of Him."[3] The claim cannot be made accordingly that this line of reasoning for the priority of Mark is being adequately weighed here. Nevertheless, I believe that to an extent the argument as usually advanced may be rather fairly tested by the examination of this single passage. In being so selective there is at least the advantage of doing justice to the context in which the crucial supposedly discrepant words are found. My general impression is that in the treatment of such passages as these, as in the study of the harmony of the Gospels as a whole, there is a lamentable tendency to isolate them from their contexts and so oftentimes to draw drastic inferences from superficial comparisons. Hawkins' lists are well worth careful scrutiny, but it should be observed that his brief comments are hardly adequate to establish his general conclusions.

Introductory Considerations

Among commentators who have recently dealt rather fully with this passage mention may well be made of Vincent Taylor. In his learned and invaluable commentary on Mark he concludes that "the greater originality of the Markan narrative is manifest," stating that Matthew has recast it because he took exception to the Markan form "on doctrinal grounds."[4] Among the merits of Taylor's treatment is that he presents a brief

2. Streeter, *op. cit.*, pp. 151f.
3. *Ibid.*, pp. 117-125.
4. Taylor, *op. cit.*, pp. 424f., 427.

summary of various views that have been held in the history of interpretation before expounding his own position. Pursuant of this approach, it is interesting that he mentions in the first place the exegesis that the question of Jesus involved "an implicit acknowledgment of imperfection and sin," a view which Taylor rejects as "not only unnecessary in itself, but . . . at variance with the entire Synoptic portraiture of Jesus." Another viewpoint that receives comment is that of B. B. Warfield[5] which is epitomized as "maintaining that Christ's concern is not to glorify Himself but God, not to give any instruction concerning His own person, but to point to the will of God as the only prescription for pleasing Him." With regard to Warfield's interpretation Taylor declares that there is much to be said for it but that "it is open to the charge of over-simplification; it avoids the sense of contrast which pervades the saying." Still another position referred to is the ancient one which still has a good deal of influence, namely, that Jesus is repudiating the predicate "good" from "the questioner's point of view, and seeks to correct the man's flattery." This view, Taylor believes, likewise is good so far as it goes but also is an over-simplification. Finally, we note that Taylor indicates that he agrees with the explanations which recognize that "while the main interest of Jesus is the man himself and his facile appreciation of goodness, His question implies a tacit contrast between the absolute goodness of God and His own goodness as subject to growth and trial in the circumstances of the Incarnation."[6]

In approaching the issues raised in the light of the entire Marcan context of fifteen verses in Mark 10:17-31 together with the parallel passages, Luke 18:18-30 and Matthew 19:16-30, one does well to observe at the very beginning that the Marcan account is considerably longer than the others. He uses 279 words whereas Luke has only 202. Matthew is also

5. B. B. Warfield, *Christology and Criticism* (New York: Oxford, 1929, p. 139. Warfield's article, which was originally published in *The Princeton Theological Review*, XII, 1914, pp. 177-228, bears the title "Jesus' Alleged Confession of Sin" and thus treats the pericope from a somewhat different approach than that which is taken here.

6. Taylor here sums up the comment of H. R. Mackintosh, *The Doctrine of the Person of Jesus Christ* (Edinburgh: Clark, 1913), p. 37, evidently as agreeing with his own position, that "the words are not a veiled confession of moral delinquency, but a disclaimer of *God's* perfect goodness on the part of One who learned obedience by the things which He suffered, being tempted in all points like as we are (Heb. iv. 15, v. 8)."

shorter than Mark, using 270 words, and if one might quite
properly subtract the thirty-eight words used by Matthew in
the singular statement of 19:28, we would have only a little
more than 225 words in this account.

Although our interest continues to center upon the relationships between Matthew and Mark it is particularly illuminating
also to institute a comparison between Luke and Mark. If we
do so we shall observe an exceedingly close agreement in words,
phrases and sentences between them; there is almost nothing
that is distinctive in Luke's account. Of the 202 words used
in Luke, about 150, or approximately 75 percent, are identical
or almost so with Mark's words. And the unparalleled features
of Luke are very few indeed; he describes the young man as
a "ruler" (18:18); he uses a different Greek word for "needle"
(18:25); and he refers to "the kingdom of God" where Mark
has "for my sake and the gospel's sake" (18:29; Mk. 10:29; cf.
Mt. 19:29). Luke's differences from Mark are accordingly almost altogether in the area of omission. These omissions relate
especially to Luke's much briefer introduction of the rich man
(Lk. 18:18; Mk. 10:17); the non-inclusion of the largely repe-
titious declarations of Mark 10:24 and 30 and of various vivid
details in Mark 10:21 (Jesus loved him), 22 (his countenance
fell), 23 (Jesus looked round about), 24 and 26 (the wonder
and astonishment of the disciples).

These observations indicate that Luke has been concerned to
present a far more succinct account than Mark has done. For
he appears to omit nearly everything that is not essential for
the understanding of the narrative including graphic details as
well as longer statements that might seem superfluous. And
so an important basis of comparison with Matthew's account
is provided. And this comparison of Luke with Mark also
serves to confront us with an extraordinary fact that does not
seem generally to come to rightful recognition in discussions of
the present problem. This is the fact that Luke's modifications
do not touch Mark 10:18, and it would therefore appear that
the question of Jesus, "Why callest thou me good?", was unobjectionable doctrinally so far as he was concerned. To recognize this with regard to Luke is, to be sure, not tantamount to
saying that it could not have been a stumbling block to Matthew,
but it does point up the urgent necessity of exercising utmost
restraint in drawing conclusions as to what later evangelists
supposedly found offensive in Mark.

Matthew's narrative also agrees very closely with Mark as regards words, phrases and sentences. These correspondences are not quite as extensive as those of Luke with Mark, but they are nevertheless very substantial, extending as they do to more than half of Matthew's 270 words. And if one should omit Matthew's singular verse 28 from the total, the parallelism in words would be nearly 60 percent. To a noteworthy extent Matthew accords with Luke by omitting the longer statements of Mark 10:17, 24 and 30 and the vivid details of 10:21, 22 and 23. But these features, rather than pointing necessarily to interdependence between Matthew and Luke, appear to be adequately explained from the common concern of the evangelists to present far more succinct accounts than Mark has done. However that may be, inasmuch as our primary interest here is in a comparison of Matthew and Mark, it is more important to concentrate upon the unique elements of Matthew 19:17b, 19b, 21a and 28 in addition to the substantially different contents of 16, 17a which constitute the chief focus of concern in our present discussion.

If however we are to do justice to these details of Matthew's narrative, it will be necessary to compare the three accounts as a whole and observe their pervasive agreement with regard to the theme or themes which come to expression. It will be noted that in the three records there is a progression of development in two stages, the first centering in the young man (Mk. 10:17-22 and par.), and the second in the disciples (10:23-31 and par.). And in each of these, as we shall observe, there is likewise a double unfolding of Jesus' teaching.

The Young Man: Inquiry and Response

In the very foreground of interest then is the fact that Jesus responds to the young man's question concerning what he should do to obtain eternal life by centering attention upon *the requirement of obedience to God who has revealed his commandments* (Mk. 10:17-19 and par.). This God-centered character of Jesus' teaching, with its accent upon the necessity of the performance of the revealed will of God, is one of its foundational features. On another occasion, as reported by Luke, a lawyer, likewise concerned with the question of the inheritance of eternal life, was answered by Jesus, "What is written in the law? how readest thou?", and when he acknowledged that the law taught unqualified love of God and the love of one's neighbor as oneself, Jesus said, "Thou hast answered right; this do, and thou shalt live" (Lk. 10:25-28). Similarly, in the parable of the rich man and Lazarus, the call for a new revelation is answered by Abraham in the words, "They have Moses and the prophets; let them hear them" (Lk. 16:29; cf. 31).

This evaluation, it may be noted, is that which is emphatically set forth by Warfield who says that the purpose of Jesus was "to point the young man inquiring after a law of life to Him who had once for all proclaimed a perfect law of life." And the final statement in this theologian's elaborate study of "Jesus' Alleged Confession of Sin" is as follows:

> Jesus' concern here is not to glorify Himself but God: it is not to give any instruction concerning His own person whatever, but to indicate the published will of God as the sole and the perfect prescription for the pleasing of God. In proportion as we wander away from this central thought, we wander away from the real meaning of the passage and misunderstand and misinterpret it.[7]

In the second place, however, Jesus' teaching on the requirement of obedience to the law of God as the way to life eternal is supplemented by his sovereign declaration to the young man that, lacking yet one thing, he should *sell all that he had and give to the poor and follow Jesus* (Mk. 10:21 and par.). Much as Jesus was touched by the general uprightness of the young man he clearly detected in the altogether too facile claim that he had kept the whole law a quite superficial and inadequate estimate of what keeping the law meant in the concrete situation in which he lived. And so he demanded of the young man a decision and commitment which, because of his bondage to his own wealth, he was unwilling to make. Thus Jesus, in supplementing the teaching concerning obedience to the commandments of God, is not presenting a new and additional teaching but only indicating the implications of such obedience in the specific historical situation in which the young man encountered Jesus. Similarly, in the sequel of Jesus' reply to the lawyer as to the way to inherit eternal life, which has just been mentioned, Jesus exposes the glib readiness of the lawyer to justify himself by replying to his question regarding the identity of his neighbor in the lesson of the parable of the Good Samaritan (Lk. 10:29-37).

Up to this point I find myself in rather substantial agreement

7. Warfield, *op. cit.*, pp. 138, 139.

with Bornkamm's evaluation of this narrative. In his *Jesus of Nazareth*, having spoken of "Jesus' astounding sovereignty in dealing with situations according to the kind of people he encounters," and declaring that "a most illuminating illustration of Jesus' insight into the character of his interlocutors is the story of the rich man who asks him about eternal life," he says:

Jesus points him to the ten commandments (which shows that the right way has long since been made evident and does not need any specific new revelation), and the rich man professes that he has kept them all since his youth. The story ends, "And Jesus, looking upon him, loved him, and said to him: You lack one thing. Go sell what you have and give to the poor, and you will have treasure in heaven; and come, follow me." This is a demand on which the rich man founders (Mk. x. 17-22).[8]

And at a later point where he is discussing the meaning of discipleship according to Jesus, Bornkamm declares:

The kingdom of God is the sole foundation of Jesus' call to follow him. It imposes upon the disciples a special task, a special destiny, but also grants them a special promise. It is this task and this promise which are too much for the rich man who in Mark. x. 17-22 asks Jesus concerning the way to eternal life. Jesus' answer refers him back to God's commandments. Nothing indicates that this is not meant to be a clear and exhaustive answer. It is only when the rich man is not satisfied with it, and declares that he has from childhood kept all the commandments, that Jesus gives him the second reply: "If you would be perfect, go, sell what you possess, and give to the poor, and you will have treasure in heaven; and come, follow me." Surely this one thing that Jesus demands from him is not intended as an additional eleventh commandment. Nor should we suppose that there is any intention to shame the rich man and make him realise how poor his obedience to the first commandment, for example, has actually been. No, what makes the rich man fail is the call of the kingdom of God that now goes out to him in the call to follow Jesus. He thus fails when confronted with the unheard-of offer of "eternal" life, and turns again to the emptiness of his worldly possessions.[9]

It is useful also to recall here the viewpoint of Bornkamm in his significant essay on Matthew's eschatological and ecclesiastical outlook. Calling attention to some of the special features

8. G. Bornkamm, *Jesus of Nazareth*, pp. 58, 60.
9. *Ibid.*, p. 148.

of Matthew's account, he maintains that this pericope as found in Matthew reflects something of this evangelist's own perspective with regard to the law and the eschatological hope. Summing up, he says:

> In following Jesus therefore the perfection which the law demands finds fulfillment. To his disciples, who have left all and followed him, applies the promise that in the Regeneration at the appearance of the Son of man for judgment they would sit upon twelve thrones and judge the twelve tribes of Israel. Through the context and then again first by way of the saying which Matthew has added in 19:28 discipleship is firmly united with the law-concept and the promise which is valid for the true people of God.[10]

Although Bornkamm may be credited with a generally perceptive evaluation of the story of the rich young ruler, and notably of the first stage of the narrative, his position is open to a number of basic criticisms. That however on which I should like to center attention here concerns the question whether Matthew's account may be distinguished from the others in the way that Bornkamm claims it does. Postponing for the time being the consideration of his interpretation as it applies to the second stage of the narrative, it must be insisted that Matthew does not present anything particularly distinctive in his reflections upon the relationships between the keeping of the law and discipleship. The appeal which has been taken above to the teaching in Luke 10:25-37 is also pertinent here. And in the three accounts of the story of the rich young man the most that can be said is that Matthew has set forth this subject in somewhat sharper perspective. And this is due more to the feature of silence concerning Jesus' question, "Why callest thou me good?", than to anything really different in his positive declarations. Matthew's briefer and more abrupt form of introduction to the story serves to put in sharpest possible relief the very point which Bornkamm himself has declared to be central to Jesus' thought, namely, that Jesus refers the young man back to God's commandments.

Reflecting briefly on some of the details one may observe, in the first place, that Matthew's addition of the word "good" in the question, "Teacher, what good thing shall I do, that I may have eternal life?" and the formulation of the reply of Jesus in the words, "Why askest thou me concerning the good?"

---

10. P. 238. See footnote 11 in Chapter II above.

(Mt. 19:16, 17) do not serve to create a contrary impression with regard to the initial thrust of Jesus' teaching. In both the Old and New Testaments obedience to the divine commandments is characterized as doing good or doing the good. Thus Amos says, "Seek good, and not evil, that ye may live; and so the Lord, the God of hosts will be with you, as ye say. Hate the evil, and love the good, and establish justice in the gate . . ." (5:14f.). According to Paul, the law is holy, and the commandment holy and just and good (Rom. 7:12), and so he pronounces the blessings of glory and honor and peace to every man that worketh the good (2:10; cf. 12:2; 13:3; Gal. 6:10; Eph. 4:28). And in Mark 3:4 Jesus asks whether it is lawful to do good on the Sabbath (cf. Mt. 12:35; Lk. 6:45; Jn. 5:29).

In Mark 10:19, by way of reply to the question of the young man as to what he should do to inherit eternal life, Jesus introduces several of the commandments with the simple words, "You know the commandments." In Matthew 19:17b, on the other hand, the recital of the commandments is introduced with greater fullness in the words, "if you desire to enter into life, keep the commandments" (cf. also 18a). But it is by no means evident that Matthew says anything that is not implicit in the Marcan account.

Similarly, the Matthean form of the injunction to sell his possessions and to follow Jesus is somewhat unique. It includes in particular the words of 19:21a, "Jesus said to him, If you desire to be perfect. . . ." So far as the vocabulary of the Gospels is concerned, the word "perfect" is definitely Matthean, being found only here and in Matthew 5:48, "Ye shall therefore be perfect, as your heavenly father is perfect." But again the substance of the matter is not affected since the word "perfect" underscores the fulness of conformity to the will of God which constitutes the central thrust of Jesus' teaching in the three Synoptic accounts.

Followers of Jesus: Questions and Disclosures

The development of events and of Jesus' teaching in the second principal stage of our narrative also turns about the theme of discipleship. Now, however, by way of contrast with that which has been disclosed in connection with Jesus' contacts with the reluctant young man, those who are *genuine and faithful followers of Jesus are in view.*

The two stages are indeed not sharply marked off from one another. For by way of transition to the climactic teaching concerning the power of God unto salvation Jesus dwells at some length, though more fully in Mark than in Matthew and Luke, upon the perilous state of those who have many possessions. This peril is set forth in such solemn and discouraging terms that the disciples react first with amazement, as Mark reports, and later with even greater astonishment, as all three record. For Jesus not only speaks in general terms of the gravity of the spiritual situation with which the rich are perplexed but also, using a bold figure, expresses the practical impossibility of salvation when he declares that "it is easier for a camel to go through a needle's eye than for a rich man to enter into the kingdom of God." In these utterances Jesus is still no doubt reflecting upon the spiritual bankruptcy of the rich young man.

In view of what follows, however, it becomes clear that he arouses in the disciples the most heart-searching and confidence-shattering question as to whether then there can be salvation at all. The question of despair, "Who then can be saved?" becomes the occasion for one of the most revealing pronouncements of Jesus concerning the way of salvation. He reaches a majestic point of disclosure when he declares, "With men it is impossible, but not with God; for all things are possible with God" (Mk. 10:26, 27 and par.). Here the power and grace of God as offering the only hope of salvation shine forth in sublime splendor, and the disciples are reminded that for them, as well as for those who might have many possessions, salvation is wholly dependent upon the divine action of lovingkindness.

Warfield, though his discussion as a whole centers in the implications of the question of Jesus, "Why callest thou me good?", nevertheless more or less in passing recognizes this feature of salvation by grace when he says that "the disciples had had borne in upon them with tremendous force the fundamental fact that salvation in every case of its accomplishment is nothing less than an authentic miracle of divine grace; always and everywhere in the strictest sense impossible with man, and possible only with God, with whom all things are possible."[11] Bornkamm's treatment, though rather salutary in dealing with certain features of these narratives as we have seen,

11. Warfield, *op. cit.*, pp. 101f.

does not appear to recognize the indispensability of the sovereign action of divine grace for discipleship as one of the most foundational elements in this story as told in all three accounts. Following upon the teaching of Jesus concerned with the power of God unto salvation which offers the only hope for a genuine discipleship, there now appears a closing section declaring *the rewards of discipleship* (Mk. 10:28ff. and par.). Continuity with the entire preceding narrative is found in the fact that throughout there has been an occupation with the inheritance of eternal life and entrance into the kingdom of God. But in agreement with the contrast drawn between the rich young man and the loyal disciples of Jesus Peter now asks what they, as opposed to the one who refused to leave his possessions behind and follow Jesus, would receive for having left all and followed him. Peter's expectations of future blessings as an heir of eternal life and the kingdom of God have been well established in the teachings of Jesus as a whole, and they have now been given if possible an even firmer grounding in the declaration concerning the omnipotent power of God. And thus, rather than supposing that Peter has introduced an improper or unworthy feature into the situation,[12] we may recognize Jesus' final words as constituting a beautiful climax to the whole story. In brief, he indicates that the blessings in view encompass not only this age but the age to come. According to Mark, with its vividness and fullness of expression, Jesus said:

> Verily I say unto you, there is no man that hath left house, or brethren, or sisters, or mother, or father, or children, or lands, for my sake, and the gospel's sake, but he shall receive an hundredfold now in this time, houses, and brethren, and sisters, and mothers, and children, and lands, with persecutions; and in the world to come eternal life (10:29, 30).

At this point both Matthew and Luke manifest their characteristic succinctness. This appears especially in the observation that the second reference to houses and brethren and sisters, etc., is omitted. And with the dropping of these words the phrase "with persecutions" also disappears. Moreover, whereas Mark uses two expressions — "for my sake and for the gospel's sake" — to express the commitment of Jesus' disciples to

---

12. A. H. McNeile, *The Gospel according to St. Matthew* (London: Macmillan, 1938) maintains, ad 19:27, that Peter's words disclose "self-complacency" and "self-centredness."

himself that provides the basis for their forsaking the world, Matthew has more simply "for my name's sake" and Luke "for the sake of the kingdom of God."

The question remains whether Matthew's narrative presents an eschatological perspective at variance with that of the other accounts. It must be admitted that the contrast between the blessings of the two ages is not quite as sharply drawn in Matthew as in the other Gospels. Nevertheless, it would appear that the "manifold" blessings of 19:29 are viewed as being the portion of the disciples in the present life as distinguished from the inheritance of "eternal life" which follows. The fact cannot be contested, however, that the Matthean narrative gives greater prominence to the world to come particularly by way of its introduction of the saying of 19:28:

> Verily I say unto you, that ye who have followed me, in the regeneration when the Son of man shall sit on the throne of his glory, ye also shall sit upon twelve thrones, judging the twelve tribes of Israel.

Even if Matthew 19:29 is understood as being partially concerned with the blessings of this life, it cannot be doubted that the contents of verse 28, and even its place in the foreground of this section, assign the pre-eminent place to the blessings of the future age. Alluding to or utilizing language which recalls the divine action in creation and in fulfillment of the divine plan of redemption under the old covenant, Jesus depicts the new order as one that constitutes a radical transformation of the old and promises to the disciples places of unique pre-eminence and privilege in his kingdom.[13]

Having been concerned with a rather elaborate analysis of

---

13. The question whether the Matthean emphasis upon the future in this context is characteristic of this Gospel as a whole, and serves to distinguish it from the others with respect to eschatological perspective, is one that cannot be treated here. For some discussion of this subject cf. *WMMC*, pp. 233ff., 239ff.; *WLC*, pp. 154-158; and my review of Conzelmann's *The Theology of St. Luke* in *WTJ*, XXIV (Nov., 1961), pp. 65ff. In this review there is a discussion of Conzelmann's interpretation of Lk. 22:28-30, which is similar in its teaching to Mt. 19:28. Although this question is of the greatest possible intrinsic interest, the treatment of it would not be particularly germane here and would tend to distract attention from our concern at this point with the broad disposition of the story of the rich young man. The central point here has to do with the promise of rich rewards for the disciples who have left all and followed Jesus, and not with the subsidiary question whether the rewards are thought of as being wholly or chiefly bound up with the future age.

the ingredients of the story as a whole, and having observed
the themes which come under discussion within it, we are, I
believe, at long last prepared to undertake a comparison of
Mark and Matthew with regard to the question, "Why do you
call me good?". How shall we explain the absence of this
question from Matthew? Is the question which he presents,
"Why do you ask me concerning the good?" an alteration of
the Marcan question which Matthew found doctrinally objectionable?

The study of the teaching of Jesus in the story provides the
strongest possible ground for asserting that Jesus is not occupied here with questions of Christology. Questions about his
relationship to God as Son and Messiah are presented in the
Gospels. But taking the witness of the Synoptic Gospels as a
whole it may be observed that Jesus is so concerned and absorbed with the glory of God, the doing of God's will and the
coming of God's kingdom (as, for example, the Lord's Prayer
underscores) that his teaching concerning himself oftentimes
appears to be given a secondary place or at least to be presented
with remarkable reserve and restraint. Such reserve and restraint are explicable particularly when one takes account of
the fact that in the interpretation of his mission he centers
attention upon the fact that he is *the Lord's* Anointed who as
God's representative and servant has been called to be obedient
unto God. As the Lord's Anointed he speaks with divine authority and acts with divine power, and thus even in the exercise of his messianic office he sustains a unique relationship to
the Father which results in claims and acknowledgments of
divine dignity and honor. And this is pre-eminently true in
those historical situations where one is allowed to perceive
that the Lord's Anointed was also the Lord himself, that the
obedient and submissive Messiah was a divine person, that he
who lived the life of man in history was a pre-existent being
who became incarnate.[14]

These latter elements of the divine glory and authority are,
to say the least, not explicitly enunciated in the story of the
rich young ruler. In the foreground, as we have observed, there
is instead a concentration of concern with the necessity of a
whole-souled obedience to the divine commandments and with
the way in which alone through the gracious manifestation of

14. This point is developed more fully in the final chapter.

divine power it becomes possible for men to enter into the kingdom of God. In the narrative as a whole, therefore, there is no specific reflection upon the relationship which Jesus sustained to God. On the other hand, however, in keeping with the tenor of so much of the message of the Gospels, the relationship which men are to sustain to Jesus comes into view in an almost unobtrusive fashion. Without any elaboration of explanation the young man is told in one breath, and as involving really not two decisions but one, that he must not only sell all his possessions but also follow Jesus. Moreover, the promise of reward is indicated as directed to those who have faithfully followed Jesus and have left all for his sake (cf. Mk. 10:28, 29). And Matthew in his unparalleled eschatological saying in verse 28 precisely associates the prospective Regeneration with the session of the Son of Man upon the throne of his glory. These data as a whole, therefore, provide no adequate background for the supposition that Jesus, if only implicitly, is ascribing to himself a lower level of goodness than that which belongs to God.[15]

The form of words which Jesus employs in his question is fashioned by his reaction to the form of the young man's question, "Good teacher, what shall I do that I may inherit eternal life?" His question, evaluated on this background and in the light of all that follows, is far from requiring the interpretation that he implies that there is a significant contrast between himself and God with respect to nature or goodness. He does not say in effect, I am a sinner, or I am not good, or such goodness as I possess is on a lower level than the goodness of God, or my own goodness, in contrast to that of God's, is subject to growth and development. All such constructions must be regarded as quite far removed from the realm of possibility unless the question of Jesus is completely isolated from the context in which it appears. If, on the other hand, one does

---

15. The use of the enclitic $\mu\epsilon$ in the question of Mk. 10:18, indicating that no particular emphasis falls upon this pronoun, offers some support of this conclusion. More weighty, in my judgment, however, is the argument which has been adduced from the examination of what the passage as a whole really teaches. If nevertheless anyone should insist that Jesus is drawing a distinction between himself and God, the most that could fairly be said would be that, by way of asking the young man why he had called him good, he, at least for the moment, is diverting attention from himself and insisting that the primary concern must be with God and the keeping of his commandments.

take pains to interpret the question in the light of its setting, it is most reasonably understood as serving as a transition from the question of the rich young man to the central emphasis of Jesus' response to him that he must center his thoughts upon God and the keeping of his commandments. The approach which the young man took toward Jesus suggests that possibly he was concerned to flatter him. But in any case and at best his admiration is superficial and the apparent alacrity to take heed to the teaching of Jesus is soon shown to be a sham. Moreover, his approach to Jesus is shown to be wrong in that he does not really ask the right question, by-passing, as he does, the revelation of God already given in the interest of discovering whether Jesus might offer a fresh or novel answer as to how eternal life might be obtained. Jesus begins therefore by compelling his questioner to reflect, as he evidently had not previously done, on the implications of his reference to goodness. Jesus' purpose is accordingly to correct the wrong estimate of the situation envisioned in the young man's question. And so he says in effect, you are not conceiving of goodness in an adequate way when you so lightly address me as Good Teacher. If you wish to contemplate goodness, you should think of God who alone is good and of the keeping of his commandments.

In Matthew's account, on the other hand, the introductory references to the approach of the young man are conspicuous by their absence. Not only is Matthew distinguished by the simple vocative "Teacher" where Mark, followed by Luke, has "Good teacher," but also neither Matthew nor Luke contain the equivalent of Mark 10:17 with its reference to the eager obsequiousness of the young man: "And as he was going forth into the way, there ran one to him, and kneeled to him, and asked him . . ." Matthew has simply: "And behold, one came to him and said . . ." (19:16) whereas Luke reads: "And a certain ruler asked him . . ." (18:18). Remembering the characteristic interest of Matthew and Luke in succinctness, a mark that appears also at several points in the present story, one may quite properly urge that at least one factor that contributed to Matthew's simpler introduction of the young man was his interest to restrict his narrative to what he regarded as its essential features. He might therefore quite well have thought that the Marcan introduction was expendable. Stated

more positively, he may be understood as having chosen to concentrate at the very beginning upon the foundational theme of
obedience to the divine commandments. Recognizing these
factors, and keeping in view the broader aspects of interpretation which have been previously considered, one may render
the firm judgment that the absence from Matthew of the question, "Why callest thou me good?", has by no means been established as being due to the factor that Matthew would have
found it a stumbling block doctrinally. As has been emphasized above, the story is not concerned with Christological questions. There is rather a preoccupation with the theme of discipleship as that affects the ultimate issues of eternal life.
Moreover, the evangelist Matthew does not present an essentially different view of the relationship of Jesus to the Father
from that which appears in Mark.[16]

Some General Observations

The foregoing argument for the integrity of Matthew does
not however imply that the evangelist could not have exercised a measure of freedom in his literary composition of the
narrative. At other points this liberty appears. For example,
Mark and Luke report Jesus as saying to the young man, "One
thing thou lackest" (Mk. 10:21; Lk. 18:22), but Matthew records that it was the young man who said, "What do I still
lack?" As another example of such freedom one may recall
the differences of Matthew and Luke from Mark 10:29: "for
my sake and the gospel's sake." Here Matthew says nothing
of the gospel and has simply: "for my name's sake," while Luke,
omitting any specific reference to Christ himself, reads: "for
the sake of the kingdom of God." It is obvious therefore that
the evangelists are not concerned, at least not at all times, to
report the *ipsissima verba* of Jesus. And on this background
one must allow for the possibility that Matthew in his formulation of 19:16, 17 has not only been selective as regards subject matter but also that he used some freedom in the precise
language which he employed. The singular use of the adjective

---

16. Julius Schniewind, *Das Evangelium nach Matthäus*, NTD (1956),
agrees with those who hold that Matthew is troubled over the Marcan
account, but it is significant that he maintains that there is no fundamentally different view of Christ in the Marcan and Matthean contexts.

"good" might then be a particularly clear example of his use of that freedom.

A brief application to the larger question of the trustworthiness and harmony of the Gospels may perhaps be advantageously made here. Various tendencies in the history of the harmonization of the Gospels may be recalled. One tendency, that is both conservative and simple, has been to join divergent features and to seek to weave them together into a harmonious whole. Where, however, the divergent elements are excedingly difficult to combine in that way, it is insisted that the narratives must be regarded as reporting different events or different sayings. This approach is indeed one that I regard as fundamentally unobjectionable in principle; and at times its application leads to satisfactory results. And in general it certainly is to be preferred to the tendency, which seems to be characteristic of many modern writers, to cry "discrepancy!" at the presence of even minor linguistic differences. Or in the same spirit it may be declared dogmatically, without the benefit of any objective evidence, that two highly divergent narratives or records of teaching necessarily must be envisioned as the result of radical editorial modifications of a single source. Nevertheless, there is, in my judgment, a sounder attitude to most problems of harmonization than that which was characterized above as conservative and simple. It is marked by the exercise of greater care in determining what the Gospels as a whole and in detail actually say as well as greater restraint in arriving at conclusions where the available evidence does not justify ready answers. In particular, there is the possibility of genuine progress if one does not maintain that the trustworthiness of the Gospels allows the evangelists no liberty of composition whatsoever, and does not insist that in reporting the words of Jesus, for example, they must have been characterized by a kind of notarial exactitude or what Professor John Murray has called "pedantic precision." Inasmuch as this point seems constantly to be overlooked or disregarded in the modern situation it may be well to stress again that orthodox expositors and defenders of the infallibility of Scripture have consistently made the point that infallibility is not properly understood if it is supposed that it carries with it the implication that the words of Jesus as reported in the Gospels are necessarily the *ipsissima verba*. What is involved rather is that the Holy Spirit guided the human authors in such a way as to insure that their records give an accurate and trustworthy impression of the Lord's teachings.[17]

The bearing of our discussion of the story of the rich young man for the subject of priority still remains before us. The general thrust of our discussion, however, can only lead to the conclusion that the argument as presented by Hawkins, Streeter, Taylor and many others that a doctrinal modification has taken place is not established. If one studies such a passage as this one in its own setting and in the broader context of the Gospels it appears to be highly precarious to build a substantial argument for the priority of one Gospel or another upon it.

Nevertheless, the extensive study of this story as a whole

17. John Murray, *Calvin on Scripture and Divine Sovereignty* (Grand Rapids: Baker, 1960), p. 30, declares: "It must be emphatically stated that the doctrine of biblical inerrancy for which the church has contended throughout history, and for which a great many of us still contend, is not based on the assumption that the criterion of meticulous precision in every detail of record or history is the indispensable canon of biblical infallibility. To erect such a canon is utterly artificial and arbitrary and is not one by which the inerrancy of Scripture is to be judged . . . . The Scripture abounds in illustrations of the absence of the type of meticulous and pedantic precision which we might arbitrarily seek to impose as the criterion of infallibility. Every one should recognize that in accord with accepted forms of speech and custom a statement can be perfectly authentic and yet not pedantically precise. Scripture does not make itself absurd by furnishing us with pedantry." Quoted by permission.

The view presented here is that which has been maintained by leading Reformed theologians. *Cf. e.g.* Murray, *ibid.*, pp. 11ff., 29ff., 35ff.; B. B. Warfield, *Revelation and Inspiration* (New York: Oxford, 1927), pp. 205f., 420; *Christology and Criticism*, pp. 108f.; A. Kuyper, *Encyclopaedie der Heilige Godgeleerdheid*, 2nd ed. (Kampen: Kok, 1909), II, 505f. (Eng. trans., *Principles of Sacred Theology* (Grand Rapids: Eerdmans, 1954), p. 550; H. Bavinck, *Gereformeerde Dogmatiek*, 3rd ed. (Kampen: Kok, 1918), I, 469ff.; L. Berkhof, *Introduction to the New Testament* (Grand Rapids: Eerdmans-Sevensma, 1915), p. 42. Particular attention may also be directed to the statement of A. A. Hodge and B. B. Warfield, in their famous article on "Inspiration" in *The Presbyterian Review*, II (April, 1881): "There is a vast difference between exactness of statement, which includes an exhaustive rendering of details, an absolute literalness, which the Scriptures never profess, and accuracy, on the other hand, which secures a correct statement of facts or principles intended to be affirmed" (p. 238; *cf.* pp. 229ff., 237, 242, 244ff.). Cf. also A. Kuyper's conclusion, *loc. cit.*, "When in the four Gospels Jesus, on the same occasion, is made to say words that are different in form of expression, it is impossible that He should have used these four forms at once. The Holy Spirit, however, merely intends to make an impression on the Church which wholly corresponds to what Jesus said."

has, in my judgment, presented further support of the view that the Matthean account is more readily understood on the supposition that Matthew knew Mark and utilized his account than that Mark is for the most part an expansion upon Matthew. The latter then streamlines Mark in the interest of a more succinct and somewhat simpler narrative but also adds the saying of Matthew 19:28.

In conclusion, I wish to comment briefly on the point previously suggested that in the study of such a narrative as that of the rich young man two somewhat distinct, though interrelated, matters are involved. The question of the order of the Gospels may be considered as a relatively simple historical inquiry, though not without important implications for our understanding of the subject of Gospel origins. On this approach, and in particular comparing Matthew and Mark from several points of view, I have been concerned with the basic inquiry as to which Gospel, if the fact of interdependence be acknowledged, better explains the origin of the other. And, as has become clear in the foregoing, I have come to the judgment that Mark is evidently earlier than Matthew and has been utilized by Matthew.

We have seen also however that this specific question can hardly be answered without reflecting upon the broader questions which have been raised as to the nature of the total witness of the Gospels and in particular those regarding their historical trustworthiness judged in the light of differences of content and form. Consequently, one may well agree with this feature of Marcan priority and perhaps with others associated with the two-document theory and yet for sufficient reasons be under the necessity of rejecting other features of the hypothesis, perhaps even some of the most characteristic ones, as that hypothesis has been developed and found wide acceptance in the modern situation. What I have chiefly in view is that the two-document theory as it has been commonly developed and maintained involves certain radical implications with regard to the role of the evangelists themselves. Frequently in connection with a thoroughly negative or highly skeptical attitude toward the traditional views concerning authorship, there has been a tendency drastically to minimize the contribution of the evangelists to the point where they are thought of as mere scissors and paste editors. Or, if they are accorded freedom, they are charged with having substantially and tendentiously rewritten their sources in the interest of producing Gospels articulating their own individual historical and theological points of view as they had developed in the course of time. Still another approach, which is akin to the one just mentioned in its radical implications, but assigns a more inconspicuous function to the evangelists, is that which conceives of the Christian community, or various Christian communities, as the virtual creator of the Gospels. On this view the evangelists themselves are thought of merely as the persons who gave literary form to the contemporaneous witness of the communities.

This is not the place to survey or evaluate the history of Gospel criticism in detail, but to speak more concretely, at least for the moment, it obviously makes a world of difference whether one maintains the priority of Mark as an aspect, on the one hand, of the Liberal Marcan Hypothesis or Wrede's theory of the messianic secret or, on the other hand, recognizes it apart from the presuppositions and implications of such views and takes serious account of it in one's further study of the origins and contents of the Synoptic Gospels.

CHAPTER SIX

THE APOSTOLIC TRANSMISSION OF THE GOSPEL

HERETOFORE we have been occupied wholly with the Synoptic Gospels as they were originally published and as they have been handed down to us. As these Gospels are contemplated individually and one ponders their origins, the question of who their authors may have been inevitably is in the foreground of interest. But as one compares the Synoptic Gospels and reflects upon their extraordinary agreements in spite of their marked diversity, questions as to their possible interdependence arise. And if the phenomena appear to establish interdependence the further question as to their sequence and interrelations presses itself upon us. These questions to be sure have not been dealt with in a thoroughgoing or comprehensive manner in the foregoing discussion. The method of treatment has been a selective one. And thus the concentration upon the authorship of the Gospel according to Matthew has been justified. In like manner, although Luke has not been entirely neglected, the relations of Matthew and Mark have been chiefly in view.

In the following two chapters I turn to a quite different phase of our subject. We shall now be dealing with the history of events prior to the publication of the Synoptic Gospels so far as that history may illuminate the question of their origin. It is agreed on all sides that, however much one may learn by comparing the Synoptics with one another, the basic question of their origin is far from being explained simply in these terms. The earliest Gospel, whether it be Mark or not, did not drop miraculously from heaven nor did it spring into being as a kind of creation *ex nihilo* from the pen of a writer who was isolated from the history of his time. Even those critics who are the most skeptical concerning the historicity of the Gospel narratives acknowledge that there is a history of the Gospel tradition prior to the publication of the Gospels and that apart from genuine knowledge of that history of the pre-Gospel tradition the origin of the Synoptics would be inexplicable. As a matter of fact, the form critics, in spite of their radical presuppositions concerning the origin and development of Christianity and their generally negative appraisals of the historicity of the Gospel contents, must be credited with a salutary concern with this period. Those who find the method of form criticism as a whole quite erroneous and unscientific should be no less interested than these critics in the history of the Synoptic tradition, the formation of the Gospel tradition, the transition from tradition to Gospel and the gospel before the Gospels, to employ the terms used in the titles of several of the most influential books on this subject.

In establishing this point of contact with the form critics, however, it may be well to state at once that our interest in the tradition behind the Gospels is by no means restricted to its *oral* aspects. Once more, to be sure, I am happy to credit the form critics with the performance of a genuine service in this regard. Following upon the general abandonment of efforts to explain the Synoptic Problem by way of the hypothesis of an original oral gospel, Synoptic criticism tended to be exclusively occupied with questions of literary relationships and with the postulation of documentary sources. Considering the prominent and fundamental place which the New Testament accords to the oral preaching and teaching of Jesus Christ and of the apostles and their associates, one might well judge that the form critics, at least to a degree, were introducing a timely corrective to the one-sided development of literary criticism. It must be kept in mind, moreover, that the form critics appear largely to presuppose the general conclusions reached in that earlier phase of criticism.

Nevertheless, I cannot escape the impression that there is an evident tension between these two methods which has never been fully resolved. On the one hand, in my judgment, valid observations concerning the significance of oral tradition should compel a reassessment, in the direction of less rigidity, of the characteristic conceptions of literary relations and, on the other hand, observations concerning the fact and character of literary interrelations should constrain one to acknowledge that there is less fluidity in the transmission of the gospel than the form critics generally maintain. In any case, because we are interested in the history prior to the actual publication of the Gospels, while by no means neglecting its oral aspects, we must necessarily seek to do justice to the possibility that the evangelists used written sources. If as seems clear both Matthew and Luke have used Mark, there can be no objection in principle to the supposition that they as well as Mark have used other written sources. We may well be reminded in this connection that Luke in his Prologue refers, without any hint of disparagement, to the fact that "many" had previously undertaken the composition of accounts of Christian history. As we reflect upon the period prior to the publication of the Gospels, therefore, we are bound to search out all that may bear upon the direct understanding of those events and developments which constitute the background of the Gospels and serve to illuminate their origins.

The scope of our immediate inquiry is confined to the three decades or so following the death and resurrection of Jesus Christ when the apostles were the pre-eminent agents in the transmission of the gospel. On my view of the history of the gospel before the Gospels, however, it is quite impossible to restrict the inquiry to happenings and developments within the Christian community. This is so obviously because the apostles were appointed by Christ and acted as his representatives. It appears once again therefore, as I have been emphasizing in various ways in the preceding discussion, that the ultimate question with which the student of Synoptic origins is concerned is the question concerning Jesus Christ himself, including his relation to the apostles and to the church. Although then these various questions cannot be adequately considered, and much less settled, in isolation from one another, I shall reserve to the final two chapters, so far as possible, the foundational issue of the ultimate origin of the gospel in Jesus Christ.

Apostolic Transmission

That the apostles of Christ, chosen and endowed by him to act as his representatives and spokesmen, were pre-eminently responsible for the transmission of the Christian message is a conclusion which, as we shall be observing, is supported by a substantial body of evidence from the New Testament as a whole. In approaching this subject, however, it will hardly be contested that it would be most appropriate and meaningful to begin with the testimony of the Gospels themselves. All of the Gospels to be sure contain invaluable materials for the understanding of the role of the apostles. But in this regard Luke is surely in a class by itself. This is true especially because Luke alone of the Synoptics reflects specifically upon apostolic tradition as constituting the indispensable historical background and foundation for the production for such writings as his own. This dependence upon apostolic transmission or tradition comes to explicit expression in Luke 1:2 where in speaking of his predecessors he indicates that they wrote concerning the things which had been fulfilled "even as they delivered them unto us who from the beginning were eyewitnesses and ministers of the word." And with an eye upon the finely balanced structure of the stately period which constitutes the Lucan Prologue it becomes evident that what Luke has to say regarding his predecessors is by implication also applicable to himself.

One may not assume indeed the validity of these conclusions regarding the place which Luke assigns to apostolic tradition merely on the basis of a superficial reading of the Prologue. And if on another occasion I had not dealt rather minutely and extensively with the Prologue,[1] I feel that I should be under the necessity of doing so now. On the background of this earlier study I might perhaps content myself with a summary statement of the most pertinent observations.

Regarding the crucial point of the identification of those whom Luke acknowledges as responsible for the transmission of a knowledge of the foundational facts of Christianity there seems to me to be no serious doubt that he has the apostles in mind and at most would conceive of the apostolic company as being joined by a few of their associates in this action of transmission. Especially pertinent in this connection is the fact that he clearly has in view *a single company* of eyewitnesses-ministers of the Word rather than two groups of persons. The single predicate "handed down" with a compound subject, and the single article in the substantive participial construction "those . . . who were," require the conclusion that one close-knit company of persons is in view. The distinction between "eyewitnesses" and "ministers of the word" is accordingly to be explained from the fact that as eyewitnesses this company was qualified in a unique way to receive information and to bear witness to it whereas, as ministers of the Word, their function

1. *Cf. WLC*, pp. 24-45.

and activity in transmitting information are reflected upon. And since, moreover, the phrase "from the beginning" is best understood as qualifying the participle, and not merely the noun "eyewitnesses," the group is thought of as the original company of persons best qualified to perform the specified function.

The foundational role which Luke assigns to the twelve apostles, in both the Gospel and the Acts, in the proclamation of the Christian message and in general in the establishment of the Church offers overwhelming confirmation of this identification. In his Gospel Luke refers to the twelve as apostles with considerably greater frequency than the other Synoptists, but his witness concerning their appointment and commission to preach and to heal contains no really novel element (cf. Lk. 6:13; 9:1, 2, 10; 17:5; 22:14; 24:10).

It is the Book of the Acts, however, which by its very plan and contents highlights the significance of the apostles as those who were chosen to deliver over the Christian gospel to the Church. At the very beginning of the Acts attention is centered upon the fact that the ascension of Christ did not take place until "he had given commandment through the Holy Spirit unto the apostles whom he had chosen" (Acts 1:2). To this is immediately joined the statement that it was to the apostles that "he also showed himself alive after his passion by many proofs, appearing unto them by the space of forty days, and speaking the things concerning the kingdom of God" (1:3). And it was this same Christ who charged them that they should be his witnesses in the power of the Holy Spirit of Pentecost (1:8). Appropriately then, when the time came to fill the place of Judas, it was intimated that the selection should take place from among the company of those who had been associated with the apostles during "all the time that the Lord Jesus went in and went out among us beginning from the baptism of John, unto the day that he was received up from us" (1:21f.). At this point the apostolic witness centers in the resurrection of Christ as constituting the climax and crown of his life and ministry upon earth. But as the extensive records of the apostolic preaching in Acts consistently underscore, that climactic feature of the apostolic witness did not stand in isolation from testimony to the life and ministry of Jesus Christ prior to that event. Moreover, the large and conspicuous place given to the apostolic preaching in the Book of Acts,

quite apart from an analysis of its contents, serves to place in
bold relief the fundamental place which, according to Luke,
was recognized as belonging to the apostolic tradition.[2]
Considering the estimate which Luke-Acts provides of the
dependence of Christian believers generally upon the apostolic
tradition for their knowledge of the beginnings of Christianity
one might almost anticipate that Luke himself, if he were to
express his views on the matter, would likewise indicate his
dependence as a writer upon that tradition. In the Prologue
of his Gospel he stops just short of doing this in explicit terms
since, strictly speaking, the tradition of the eyewitnesses-ministers of the word is indicated as constituting the basis of the
literary undertakings *of his predecessors.* This conclusion
would indeed be of itself of far-reaching consequences for our
understanding of the position occupied by the apostolic tradition in the early church. But one may surely go on to observe
that, at least by way of implication, what Luke has to say
concerning his predecessors at this point applies essentially to
his own writing. This appears especially from the pervasive
parallelism and balanced structure of the protasis of Luke 1:1,
2 and the apodosis of vv. 3 and 4.[3] In the last analysis, to be
sure, it depends on judgments concerning the details of Luke's
language in the latter two verses. In particular, it depends upon
the conclusion that when Luke says that he "followed all things
accurately" he must have in view his dependence upon the
apostolic tradition at the foundation of Luke-Acts and that
he was "in the fortunate position of having been able to undertake a comprehensive and accurate inquiry into the course
of Christian history as that has been disclosed to the Church
by the original witnesses."[4]

Cadbury's View of the Lucan Prologue

One might be content with this summary statement as to
the place which Luke's Prologue ascribes to apostolic tradition
were it not for the fact that Henry J. Cadbury, who enjoys a
well-earned pre-eminence among scholars who have concentrated
upon Luke and Acts, has continued to insist upon a quite
different estimate of certain crucial features of the Prologue.

2. *Cf.* also Acts 2:42.
3. *Cf. WLC,* pp. 31f.
4. *Cf. ibid.,* p. 34.

Opposing especially the view that Luke in characterizing himself as "having followed all things accurately" has in view inquiry or investigation of sources of information, he argues that Luke must be referring to actual first-hand contact as an eyewitness. But if Luke is describing himself as an eyewitness in vs. 3 he can hardly be thought of, it is said, as sustaining a relationship of basic dependence upon the company of eyewitnesses referred to in verse 2. The general effect of Cadbury's exegesis at this point is, therefore, to assign a far less distinctive place to the eyewitnesses of verse 3. Rather than being thought of as essentially the apostolic circle they are regarded more vaguely as "those who had been at the start witnesses and helpers in the mission,"[5] and Luke would be judged in virtue of his claims in verse 3 to be including himself in this group. Since Cadbury has repeatedly made this point it may be well to add that he himself has on more than one occasion expressed surprise that "conservatives" have not accepted his conclusions with alacrity inasmuch as on his view the author of Luke-Acts would be making a broad claim of eyewitness-ship, and thus as having had first-hand contact with the events, rather than being dependent upon second-hand information in terms of the more usual exegesis.

In my study of the Prologue in *The Witness of Luke to Christ* the distinctive features of Cadbury's exegesis, as they had been presented in *The Beginnings of Christianity* and in *The Making of Luke-Acts,* were subjected to careful scrutiny and criticism and the judgment was rendered that his view was burdened with insuperable difficulties.[6] Believing as I do in the essential validity of the argumentation which I employed in my book published in 1951 I might possibly be content here with a general reference to what I wrote at that time. There has been another development however which constrains me to supplement my earlier treatment. At the annual meeting of the *Studiorum Novi Testamenti Societas* held in Utrecht in 1956, a meeting at which Professor Cadbury was elected president of the Society for the ensuing year, he gave a brief paper which was subsequently published in the journal of the Society

5. Henry J. Cadbury, *The Making of Luke-Acts* (New York: Macmillan, 1927), pp. 346f.
6. *WLC*, pp. 34ff. See *The Beginnings of Christianity* (London: Macmillan, 1922), I ii, pp. 489ff. and *The Making of Luke-Acts,* pp. 344ff.

under the title " 'We' and 'I' Passages in Luke-Acts."[7] He addressed himself again to this question and singled out my own
study for special comment. Chiding me for confining myself
to what he had had to say in his books and not having taken
account of an elaborate article which he published in *The
Expositor* in 1922, he concluded by saying:

> Nowhere however does Stonehouse bring forth any lexical
> evidence either in favour of his view that the verb means
> enquiry or against my view that it means observation or par-
> ticipation. In ignoring that well-attested meaning he has many
> predecessors and few exceptions. So continuous does a conven-
> tional critical review become when once it is promulgated.

Cadbury is not persuaded by my "elaborate criticism" of his
view, but no more am I of his position even after the benefit
I have gained from a study of his rather lengthy article of 1922
and his short study published in 1957. The sheer quantity of
the data that have been brought to bear upon the determination of these issues together with the intricacy often connected
with the argumentation would suggest the appropriateness of
a lengthy and detailed review of the whole matter. In this
context, however, in the nature of the case I must confine myself to a somewhat more simple and summary discussion.

(1) I shall begin this re-evaluation of Cadbury's position
by raising a question as to the validity of his approach in general. The entire thrust of Cadbury's contention is that the
issue must be determined by appeal to "lexical knowledge."
Thus he says, "The meaning of [having followed][8] is not a
matter of logical inference but of lexical knowledge."[9] I should
indeed be completely misunderstood at this point if I were
thought of as disparaging the fullest possible concern with
the usage of words with a view to determining their meaning.
Nevertheless, the statement quoted appears to me to be somewhat at fault because of the definiteness of the disjunction
which is set between "logical inference" and "lexical knowledge." Cadbury himself of course recognizes that lexical
knowledge is not arrived at apart from a careful study of the
usage of a term in the contexts where it is found, and he applies

7. *NTS* III (Jan., 1957), 128ff.

8. In this and other instances of "having followed" in brackets the
text quoted has the Greek παρηκολουθηκότι.

9. Henry J. Cadbury, "The Knowledge Claimed in Luke's Preface," *The
Expositor,* 1922, p. 400; *cf. NTS,* pp. 131, 132.

this method to advantage in his elaborate study of the use of this very term. Nevertheless, it is by way of his negative reflection in this connection upon "logical inference" that he appears to be minimizing or virtually setting aside contextual considerations which bear most pointedly upon the understanding of Luke's own usage.

(2) Moreover, the appeal which Cadbury makes to "lexical knowledge" at times at least gives the impression that the meaning of the word "follow" in the participial phrase "having followed all things" is quite firmly and inflexibly established by the usage outside of the New Testament, and that therefore one is guilty of a bit of theological obscurantism in laying as much emphasis as is commonly done upon the Lucan usage. Cadbury appears to make out a strong case for the possibility that the verb may mean: "to follow events through direct contemporary knowledge, especially as an eyewitness or participant."[10] But it is not insignificant that in connection with his plea for the adoption of the meaning, "to follow events through direct contemporary knowledge, especially as an eyewitness or participant" in Luke, he himself apparently feels the necessity of discounting somewhat the force of his own conclusion. For he states that "perhaps personal presence is more than the verb . . . actually claims. Possibly it was just the kind of verb that included both presence and indirect though contemporary information, and could be used by one who wished to suggest the utmost knowledge without defining too specifically how intimate that knowledge was."[11] Cadbury immediately adds the following: "The preface was peculiarly liable to exaggeration in antiquity, and claims of [eyewitnessship][12] were not always sincere. Even if no more than a continuous contemporary acquaintance with the events of Paul's missionary career is claimed, we may insist on taking even that with a grain of salt. We shall prefer to form our judgment

10. *Expositor*, p. 403; *cf. The Beginnings of Christianity* I ii, p. 501; *The Making of Luke-Acts*, p. 345; *NTS*, p. 130. But in his article in *The Expositor* he allows for no fewer than five definitions, and acknowledges that "unfortunately the verb is used in so many senses that absolute certainty is impossible" (p. 401; *cf. The Beginnings of Christianity*, pp. 501f., where three views are distinguished) .

11. *Expositor*, p. 419.

12. The word "eyewitness-ship" in brackets indicates that in the original text the Greek word αὐτοψία is used.

of the author's knowledge from the contents of his work rather than from any boastful claims of his own." In short, it is clear that the verb in question is used in a great variety of ways and therefore care must be taken in deciding upon its precise meaning in any given context. On the other hand, it must not be overlooked that there is nothing particularly obscure in the verb itself. For it simply means "to follow." Any obscurity connected with it is bound up only with the necessity of determining how in any particular context the verb "follow," with its great variety of possible applications, is to be understood.

(3) That from among all the possible meanings or applications of the word "follow" Cadbury should have singled out the meaning expressive of actual presence at, or even participation in, the events is the more remarkable when one observes that he himself acknowledges that his view is in conflict with the sentence structure of the Prologue as a whole. As he himself puts it: "Evidently we have to choose either a strict construction of the earlier clauses of the Preface, which would exclude Luke from the eyewitnesses, or the natural sense of [having followed] which would include him."[13] In the light of the foregoing point and Cadbury's treatment as a whole one may properly challenge his right to single out his interpretation of the verb as "the natural sense." Nor do I think that many students of Luke's language will be much persuaded by Cadbury's efforts to set aside what he calls the strict construction of the clauses, which exclude Luke from the category of eyewitnesses, in favor of his view that the structure may "perhaps" be "more artificial than real."[14]

In the first place, Cadbury argues against the strict construction of the clauses, which would support the thesis that the author was not among the eyewitnesses, by way of appeal to the differences in the uses of the pronoun "us" in verses 1 and 2. In the first instance the "us" contained in the phrase "matters which have been fulfilled among us" must have in view Christians of all time. In the second instance, where the reference is to transmission to "us" on the part of the eyewitnesses and ministers of the Word, the author would have to be understood, on the strict construction, as referring explicitly "to his own

13. *Ibid.*, p. 411.
14. *Ibid.*, p. 414.

generation to whom the information has been handed down." This change of reference in a single sentence Cadbury finds difficult. He maintains, moreover, that it would be particularly awkward to suppose that in the first instance the persons especially included with the author in "us" are "the contemporaries of the events narrated," while in the second instance these are the very persons excluded from the "us."[15]

Admittedly, in the double use of "us" there are somewhat different references in view. But this is far from allowing that there is any particular difficulty or awkwardness in this usage. For what needs to be recognized and stressed is that Luke does not have in mind two distinct groups of persons. On the contrary, his first reference is to a larger group, comprehending the Christians of all time, while the second reference is to a smaller group within this larger company of Christians. That in the former case the reference is to Christians of all time is clearly delineated by the mention of the occurrence of the events of Christian history ("the things fulfilled among us"). And the smaller group is marked off sharply as a segment within the Christian Church to whom a closely knit group of eyewitnesses handed down a knowledge of these events. The latter group consists accordingly of those who, like Luke, were not eyewitnesses but were dependent upon them. There is nothing awkward in the view that the members of the Christian community as a whole were contemporaries of the events fulfilled among them, and yet that those to whom the apostolic eyewitnesses handed down knowledge concerning these events formed a group within the whole company. They are not excluded from the larger company, as Cadbury affirms, but comprise a distinct group only in so far as their knowledge is dependent upon the tradition of the eyewitnesses. In evaluating this point it must not be overlooked that the company of persons included in the first "us," though, broadly speaking, contemporaries of the events narrated, are as a whole not themselves eyewitnesses. In the phrase "the things fulfilled among us" their relationship to the event is set forth in merely general terms; the fact that the events took place among them by no means qualifies them as first-hand witnesses regarding them. There is therefore no particular obscurity in the double use of the pronoun "us," and certainly nothing which sets aside

15. *Ibid.*, p. 413.

the force of the argument based upon the relationship of the several clauses.

In the second place, Cadbury states that "perhaps even more doubtful is the strictness of interpretation that excludes from the category of eyewitnesses all earlier writers mentioned."[16] Cadbury observes correctly that "the author does not say, 'Many have written as the eyewitnesses and ministers have transmitted *to them.*'" Nevertheless, the sentence structure really requires one to distinguish the many who have written from the company of qualified eyewitnesses; those who have written as a class from the qualified witnesses as a class. The dependence of the former upon the latter is unmistakable. Even if therefore with Cadbury one might allow for some overlapping between the many who wrote and the eyewitnesses, this would have to be by way of granting an exception to the rule. And in any case this would not provide a basis for the conclusion that Luke himself in verse 3 implies that he was an eyewitness. The structure of the sentence shows that Luke, when he speaks of himself, draws a parallel between the class who were dependent upon the tradition of the eyewitnesses and himself ("it seemed good to me also"). He certainly does not suggest that he is to be included among any conceivable exceptions that there might be to the general rule.

In the third place, on the understanding, which is also my own,[17] that the Preface applies to Acts as well as Luke, Cadbury appeals to the "we" passages in Acts as requiring the inclusion of the author among the eyewitnesses of 1:2.[18] And it is interesting that Cadbury expresses surprise that "conservatives" have not eagerly accepted his interpretation because it would involve the author in making a claim of being closer to the events than is ordinarily assumed and hence would be calculated to enhance the reputation of Luke-Acts for trustworthiness. With regard to this argument the following points may be noted.

(a) Beginning with the latter observation, it may be remarked that allowance ought to be given for the possibility that conservatives might be more deeply influenced by their understanding of what the Preface actually teaches than by supposed apologetic advantage bound up with an interpretation that does not otherwise commend itself. Moreover, it is in-

16. *Ibid.*
17. *Cf. WLC*, pp. 10ff.
18. *Cf. Expositor*, p. 414; *NTS*, pp. 130ff.

teresting that Cadbury himself does not want to be bound by
his own interpretation of the supposed bearing of the "we"
passages on the understanding of the author's claim in the
Preface. In the *Expositor* article, for example, in connection
with declarations of agnosticism regarding Lucan authorship,
he indicates various ways in which he thinks the force of the
argument may be weakened for he says:

> Perhaps personal presence is more than the verb [having fol-
> lowed] actually claims. Possibly it was just the kind of verb
> that included both presence and indirect though contemporary
> information, and could be used by one who wished to suggest
> the utmost knowledge without defining too specifically how
> intimate that knowledge was. The preface was peculiarly liable
> to exaggeration in antiquity, and claims of [eyewitness-ship] were
> not always sincere. Even if no more than a continuous con-
> temporary acquaintance with the events of Paul's missionary
> career is claimed, we may insist on taking even that with a
> grain of salt. We shall prefer to form our judgment of the
> author's knowledge from the contents of his work rather than
> from any boastful claims of his own.[19]

(b) More precisely to the point at issue is the evaluation of
the "we" passages in Acts. Cadbury himself indeed allows for
the possibility that "an earlier writing by an eyewitness is incorporated by the editor of Acts" as well as for the view that
the "editor himself was an eyewitness of the events which he
narrates in the first person."[20] Only the latter alternative would
seem to support the position that the author himself is claiming
to be an eyewitness, a position which commends itself to me.[21]
But I must most seriously question the pertinence of this conclusion for the understanding of Luke's claims in his Prologue.
Taken strictly, the eyewitness-ship claimed in these passages is
confined to a total of less than one hundred verses out of a
grand total of well over twenty-one hundred in Luke-Acts. And,
constituting as these sections do only a relatively small proportion of the narratives devoted to Paul in the latter half of Acts,
they do not for all of their interest focus attention upon the
eyewitness as a crucial figure for the understanding of Paul.
The very inobtrusiveness of the introduction of the "we" phenomena confirms this estimate. And even if one were justi-

19. *Expositor,* p. 419.
20. *Ibid.,* p. 414.
21. *Cf. WLC,* pp. 15ff.

fied in interpreting the claims of Luke 1:3 as meaning that "for a long time back"[22] the author had been in continuous contact with the events, thus stretching his supposed claims of eye-witness-ship to include more than the "we" sections, one would still be under the necessity of recognizing that the author's competence as an eyewitness was a highly restricted one. For evidently not only the monumental events associated with the beginnings of the life of the Christian Church in Jerusalem were not known through actual first-hand contact but also the great foundational facts of the Gospel including the birth, the public ministry, the death and resurrection of Jesus Christ.

One's evaluation of this point is, however, not confined to general considerations. For Cadbury's argument appears to founder in the face of the fact that the Prologue states that the author followed accurately "all things." And it is this relationship to "all things" which is made the basis of his claim to provide Theophilus with certainty concerning things where-in he had been instructed.[23]

Cadbury struggles with the problem created by the reference to "all things" but my impression is that a mere reading of what he has to say at this point betrays his failure to do justice to it. In the *Expositor* article he writes as follows:

> It is because of this close association with a considerable part of the story that he can commend to Theophilus his attempt to give authoritatively the facts concerning which the latter has been rather vaguely apprised. As the whole apologetic purpose expressed by Luke in verse 4 may be conjectured to apply especially to the closing of his two volume work, with their *apologia* for Christianity, so [having followed] in verse 3 perhaps was specially chosen in the light of the first-hand knowledge also embodied in the last part of Acts. It is no great exaggeration

---

22. Cadbury's rendering of ἄνωθεν.

23. Cadbury indeed also has his own distinctive interpretation of the final clause as it relates to Theophilus, maintaining as he does that Theophilus was an influential non-Christian, that the words are properly translated by "that you may gather the correctness as regards the accounts that you have been given to understand," and that the work was nominally "dedicated or addressed with the intention of meeting incriminating reports or impressions by the presentation of exonerating facts." I have endeavored to answer this evaluation in *WLC*, pp. 42ff. But even if Cadbury were correct with regard to his analysis in general, the reference to "all things" would still imply a claim of competence with regard to the entire contents of Luke-Acts rather than merely limited segments of it.

to say that the diarist has for some time . . . been an eyewitness of everything . . . .[24]

And in his recent article Cadbury has expressed himself as follows:

> The preface of Luke, however, is . . . a preface to the whole, and his suggestion that he begins with second-hand reports and continues with more immediate information suits the ancient practice of historians. The section of his writing to which [having followed] applies is therefore Acts as a whole or its later part. The only difficulty is that from [all things][25] one would expect the author's first-hand knowledge to apply to the whole section, whereas the 'we' passages are intermittent. There are reasons for thinking this part of Acts has more homogeneity than the alternating pronouns imply. Or the [all things] may be 'a pardonable exaggeration'.[26]

At this point Cadbury appeals to an article by James Hardy Ropes where the author comments: "that he writes [all things] is no more than to say that he has stood near the centre of things, and is at the most a pardonable exaggeration. No one would suppose that he meant it with absolute literalness."[27] Once again it must be insisted, however, that to reduce the meaning of a statement which supposedly says that the author had first-hand contact with all things to the point where he is thought of as merely standing near the center of things and as having been an eyewitness of exceedingly limited segments of the history which he records is to place in sharp relief the unacceptable character of the exegesis supported by these gentlemen from Harvard.

Having re-evaluated at some length Cadbury's principal conclusions with regard to the Lucan Prologue, I believe that it may be stated with even greater confidence that in the second verse a supreme and unique place is accorded to apostolic tradition. Expressed in more specific terms, the apostles, and perhaps a few others intimately associated with them, are recognized as having been responsible for the transmission to others of knowledge concerning the foundational events of Christian history. No doubt there were individuals here and

---

24. *Expositor*, p. 418.
25. The placing of "all things" in brackets indicates that in the original text the Greek word πᾶσιν is used.
26. *NTS*, p. 131.
27. James Hardy Ropes, "St. Luke's Preface: ἀσφάλεια, and παρακολουθεῖν" in *JTS*, XXV (1924), 71; *cf.* pp. 67ff.

there who were eyewitnesses of many separate events, and perhaps some who had considerable first-hand knowledge of many events. But the Lucan Prologue indicates that there was one close-knit group of persons who from the beginning were eyewitnesses of these basic happenings and who were recognized as responsible for their transmission by preaching and teaching to others. Evidently in the earliest stages of the transmission of this knowledge the tradition was oral in character. But the time came when there was an interest in setting it down in writing. And then those who wrote, and this applies to Luke too, recognized the need of basing their accounts upon that apostolic tradition.

Other New Testament Evidence

In the other Synoptic Gospels, in keeping with their strict anonymity, there is no comparable reflection upon Gospel origins and thus also no corresponding assessment of the significance of apostolic tradition. Luke's testimony on this point is however not an isolated one. The witness of the apostle Paul is specially instructive in this regard. And it is noteworthy that the very apostle who in Galatians passionately defends his ultimate independence of the other apostles against charges that he was inferior or subservient to them gladly acknowledges in I Corinthians, for example, that the action by which he received the gospel from the Lord evidently included the knowledge received through apostolic tradition. And it is moreover particularly illuminating for our understanding of this history that Paul describes his own activity in the proclamation or instruction of the Christian gospel in terms of handing down or delivering over that which he had received. It is quite understandable also therefore that those who received what Paul handed down to them were to hold it fast. The opening verses of I Corinthians 15 are most explicit:

> Now I make known unto you, brethren, the gospel which I preached unto you, which also you received, wherein also ye stand, by which also ye are saved, if ye hold fast the word which I preached unto you, except ye believed in vain. For I delivered unto you first of all that which also I received: that Christ died for our sins according to the scriptures; and that he was buried; and that he hath been raised on the third day according to the scriptures; and that he appeared to Cephas; then to the twelve; then he appeared to about five hundred brethren at once, of whom the greater part remain until now.

but some are fallen asleep; then he appeared to James; then to all the apostles; and last of all, as to the child untimely born, he appeared to me also.

Paul goes on to make abundantly clear that that which he received and delivered over in the proclamation of the gospel was not a message peculiar to himself but one that he shared with the other apostles. For though he acknowledges the lateness of his conversion and confesses that because he had persecuted the Church of God he was not meet to be called an apostle, yet by the grace of God he was one and as such proclaimed the common apostolic message: "whether then it be I or they, so we preach, and so ye believed" (I Cor. 15:11; cf. vv. 8-10).

Earlier in this same epistle Paul likewise underscores the basic significance of apostolic tradition. In I Corinthians 11:2 he declares: "Now I praise you that you remembered me in all things, and hold fast the traditions, even as I delivered them to you." And in I Corinthians 11:23, in speaking of the institution of the Lord's Supper, he says: "For I received of the Lord that which also I delivered unto you, that the Lord Jesus in the night in which he was betrayed took bread. . . ." And he had exhorted the Thessalonians: "So then, brethren, stand fast, and hold the traditions which ye were taught, whether by word, or by epistle of ours."[28]

A further specific point of contact with the Lucan Prologue is to be observed in I Corinthians 15:15. Having declared that "if there is no resurrection of the dead, neither hath Christ been raised: and if Christ hath not been raised, then is our preaching vain, your faith also is vain," he declares: "Yea, and we are found false witnesses of God; because we witnessed of God that he raised up Christ: whom he raised not up, if so be that the dead are not raised." In this verse, referring pre-eminently and perhaps exclusively to the apostles, and centering attention upon the place of the resurrection in the apostolic proclamation, he identifies their activity as that of witnessing. And in this case witnessing is clearly used in both the passive and active senses: they were eyewitnesses of the resurrection and they bore witness to the resurrection. In terms of the Lucan language, the apostles who were eyewitnesses of the resurrection, together with Paul who was singularly qualified as an eyewitness, transmitted to others, in their unique capacity as

28. II Thess. 2:15; cf. Rom. 6:17; Gal. 1:9; Phil. 4:9; I Thess. 4:1.

ministers of the Word, a knowledge of the resurrection of Christ
as constituting a central and climactic feature of the Christian message.

It is noteworthy, moreover, that Luke in the Acts again and
again characterizes the apostles as witnesses. And as he does
so he at times reflects upon their unique qualifications because
of that which they alone saw and heard including especially
the resurrection of Christ but also, and apparently with even
greater emphasis, upon their authoritative proclamation of the
gospel. In Acts 1:8 the emphasis in the words "ye shall be my
witnesses" appears to fall upon active witness-bearing, but even
in this case the pronoun "my" may well go beyond the thought
of their belonging intimately to Jesus to that of the object of
their testimony. Similarly, in connection with the appointment
of a twelfth apostle to take the place of Judas, there was in the
forefront of apostolic concern the necessity of choosing one
who with them would become a witness of the resurrection of
Christ. But there was also the insistence that to be qualified
for this task one had to belong to the company of those who
were associated with the apostles "all the time that the Lord
Jesus went in and went out among us, beginning from the
baptism of John, unto the day that he was received up from
us" (Acts 1:21, 22). This double aspect of apostolic witness
appears generally in the records of apostolic preaching but never
perhaps so explicitly as in the account of Peter's discourse to
Cornelius in Acts 10. Speaking of "the word"[29] which God sent
to Israel, preaching good tidings of peace by Jesus Christ,
which was published throughout all Judea, Peter particularizes
it as concerned with "Jesus of Nazareth, how God anointed
him with the Holy Spirit and with power: who went about
doing good, and healing all that were oppressed of the devil;
for God was with him," and he says:

> We are witnesses[30] of all things which he did both in the
> country of the Jews, and in Jerusalem; whom also they slew,
> hanging him on a tree. Him God raised up the third day,
> and gave him to be made manifest, not to all the people, but
> unto witnesses[31] that were chosen before of God, even to us,
> who ate and drank with him after he rose from the dead. And

29. τὸν λόγον.
30. Cadbury's quotation includes the Greek word μάρτυρες.
31. μάρτυσιν.

he charged us to preach unto the people, and to testify[32] that this is he who is ordained of God to be the Judge of the living and the dead. To him bear all the prophets witness, that through his name everyone that believeth on him shall receive remission of sins.

In the last verse in characteristic apostolic fashion the continuity and unity of the prophetic witness with that of the apostles is recognized. But this does not detract in any essential way from the total impact of the delineation of the apostolic proclamation as distinguishing between the apostles and the people generally as regards both the witnessing of what had occurred in the ministry of Jesus and witness-bearing bound up with their unique appointment and qualifications.[33]

32. διαμαρτύρασθαι.
33. Cf. also Acts 2:32; 3:15; 5:32; 13:31; 22:15; 26:16.

CHAPTER SEVEN

THE APOSTOLIC TRADITION: THE MESSAGE

OUR treatment of apostolic tradition in the sense of apostolic transmission of the Christian message, it will have been observed, has already involved us in some reflection upon apostolic tradition in the sense of that which the apostles were charged to transmit to those who came after. This latter aspect of apostolic tradition is assuredly of no less importance for our subject than the former. For only if there is a basic agreement between the apostolic proclamation and the contents of the Gospels, can the background of the Gospels be illuminated by attention to this central apostolic activity. In view of the intrinsic importance of this matter, accordingly, and also because of the elaborate attention which this theme has received especially during the last quarter of a century, one might well justify an extensive discussion of it. Nevertheless, for our present purposes I hope to do justice to this theme within a relatively brief compass.

Finding our starting-point again in the Lucan Prologue we observe that Luke is pointedly informative when he speaks of the contents of the apostolic tradition in terms of "those matters which have been fulfilled among us" (Lk. 1:1). The choice of the unusual Greek word translated by "have been fulfilled" stresses the fact that the evangelist is not interested in relating a number of rather ordinary events more or less isolated from one another. In the light of the perspective gained by a study of Luke-Acts as a whole they are understood as the events which were divinely ordered and came about to bring to realization the divine plan of redemption. In particular they are the events which, fulfilling the revelation of promise in the Old Testament, brought into being the new day of salvation. In accordance with this point of view, for example, Acts 1:1 sums up the Gospel as being concerned with what Jesus

132

began to do and teach, and for Luke Jesus was the divine Messiah and himself the Lord who through his presence upon earth and through the agency of the Holy Spirit accomplished this fulfillment of the divine plan.

In the choice of the word "fulfilled" it may be further noted that the accent appears to fall upon historical events. And thus, if I may restrict myself for the moment to the Gospel of Luke, the great foundational facts of the death and resurrection of Jesus Christ must be pre-eminently in view. But the Gospel also records other facts as enjoying a significant place within the redemptive events. The birth of the Saviour clearly belongs in this category. The miracles, moreover, form an integral part of the witness concerning Jesus Christ and what he brought to pass on behalf of men. But even the record of the teaching is a part of the organic whole. This is so, in the first place, because the very words of Jesus are conceived of as words of divine power by which, as well as through the miracles, the kingdom of God comes to manifestation. Thus the prophecy of the coming messianic age, as set forth in Isaiah 61, is fulfilled as Jesus preaches good tidings to the poor and proclaims release to the captives (Lk. 4:18, 19, 21; cf. 7:22; 16:16). And in the second place, it is evident that the events are not related as bare facts; they are rather surrounded in their telling by disclosures concerning their meaning within and for the understanding of the gospel. To a large extent these words of authoritative interpretation consist of the teachings of Jesus but on occasion they are also to be found in the record of the testimony of the disciples and of the evangelists themselves as well as heavenly voices and angelic messengers.[1]

Taking account further of the Lucan terminology in the Prologue it is worth noting that there is good reason to maintain that this evangelist also has the contents of the apostolic tradition in view when he refers to "the word" in his declaration concerning "those who from the beginning were eyewitnesses and ministers of the word." A true parallel for the use of the word "minister" as applied to an apostle in his responsibility toward that which he was privileged to see and hear is found in Acts 26:16. There the apostle Paul is reported as saying that the risen Lord declared that he had appeared

---

1. Cf. G. Vos, *Biblical Theology* (Grand Rapids: Eerdmans, 1948), p. 15, for a valuable treatment of the interrelationships of act-revelation and word-revelation.

unto Paul "to appoint thee a minister and a witness both of the things wherein thou hast seen me and of the things wherein I will appear unto thee." In this connection the combination of "witness" and "minister" is most striking.[2] In the Acts "the word" is repeatedly and characteristically employed, either without further qualification or in the form "the word of God," as a designation of the apostolic message.[3]

Another designation that serves well to sum up the contents of the apostolic message is "the kingdom of God." Thus Paul's activity in the synagogue at Corinth for a period of three months is spoken of as "reasoning and persuading as to the things concerning the kingdom of God" (Acts 19:8). Speaking to the Ephesian elders he refers to his ministry, in virtually one breath, as testifying "the gospel of the grace of God" and "preaching the kingdom" (20:24f.). Similarly in Rome his activity is described as "testifying the kingdom of God and persuading them concerning Jesus both from the law of Moses and from the prophets" (28:23) and as "preaching the kingdom of God and teaching the things concerning the Lord Jesus Christ" (28:31). During his public ministry Jesus had already charged his disciples to proclaim the kingdom of God (cf. e.g. Mt. 10:7; Lk. 9:2, 60), and his own message had been summed up in the same terms (cf. e.g. Mk. 1:15; Mt. 4:17, 23; 9:35; 13:19; Lk. 4:43; 9:11; 16:16). No detailed study of the New Testament doctrine of the kingdom of God can be undertaken here.[4] Nor is it really necessary from our present point of view if one will allow that Vos has defined its essential character with considerable aptness and precision in the following words: "to him [Jesus] the kingdom exists there, where not merely God is supreme, for that is true at all times and under all circumstances, but where God supernaturally carries through his supremacy against all opposing powers and brings man to the willing recognition of the same."[5] For this definition confronts us with the basic insight that, when the carrying through of the divine supremacy is recognized as taking place in and

2. Acts 13:5, as against Cadbury, is not a true parallel since John Mark is there spoken of as a minister or servant *of Barnabas and Paul.*

3. *Cf.* 4:4; 6:4; 8:4; 10:44; 11:19, etc.; 4:29, 31; 6:2; 8:14; 10:36; 11:1; 13:5, 7, 44, 46, etc.; 8:25; 13:26, 49.

4. *Cf. WMMC,* pp. 226ff.; *WLC,* pp. 152ff.

5. G. Vos, *The Teaching of Jesus concerning the Kingdom of God and the Church* (New York, 1903: Grand Rapids: Eerdmans, 1951), pp. 85f.

through Christ, the message concerning the kingdom of God
and its coming aptly epitomizes not only the message of Jesus
and the apostles, but also the comprehensive contents of the
Gospels themselves.

Dodd and the Kerygma

Of all the terms employed by the New Testament as a designation of the Christian message none has apparently been so
much in the foreground of attention as the term *kerygma*, a fact
in part attested by the observation that as a transliteration of
the Greek it has virtually become a part of our English vocabulary. Nearly everyone knows something of C. H. Dodd's
monumental work on *The Apostolic Preaching and Its Developments.*[6] Because of the general familiarity with this work
it may suffice for our present purposes to sum up his thesis
under the following heads. (1) By way of analysis of various
elements in the Pauline Epistles and a study of the record of
apostolic preaching in Acts he believes that one can recover
the essential features of the apostolic proclamation. I shall
not pause to list these features separately but only note that
Dodd defines the resultant *kerygma* as "a proclamation of the
death and resurrection of Jesus Christ, in an eschatological setting from which those facts derive their saving significance."[7]
(2) From the apostolic *kerygma* Dodd distinguishes sharply
the *didache* which is conceived of as the ethical teaching given
to those who were converted to Christianity by way of the
kerygma. Dodd tends to set the one so sharply over against
the other that he maintains that the incorporation of the
didache material in the Christian message had "the effect of
modifying in some degree the character in which Christianity is
presented. It is not so much a gospel of 'realized eschatology,'
as a new and higher code of ethics."[8] (3) Inasmuch as the
fountainhead of the tradition is to be found in the *kerygma*
Mark stands closest to the original proclamation. Matthew

6. C. H. Dodd, *The Apostolic Preaching and Its Developments* (London:
Hodder & Stoughton, 1936).
7. *Ibid.,* p. 47; *cf.* pp. 17f. For a recent evaluation of Dodd's position
cf. W. Baird, "What is the *Kerygma?* . . . ," *JBL* LXXVI (Sept., 1957),
pp. 181ff. Of particular interest also is the distinctive article of O. A. Piper,
"The Origin of the Gospel Pattern," *JBL* LXXVIII (June, 1959), pp. 115ff.,
which ascribes fundamental significance to the apostolic proclamation, but
in other respects is critical of Dodd.
8. *Ibid.,* pp. 120f.

and Luke still fall well within the general scheme of the *kerygma* but in various ways, and especially by the larger inclusion of the *didache* material, alter its perspective.[9] Nevertheless, all three Synoptic Gospels, Mark as well as the others, may be regarded "as an expanded form of what we may call the historical section of the *kerygma*."[10]   (4) Although Dodd's studies of the Gospels as a whole indicate that he regards much of the so-called expansion materials as deviations from the original *kerygma,* one is justified in assigning high historical worth to their *kerygmatic* elements.   He says on this point: "I believe that a sober and instructed criticism of the Gospels justifies the belief that in their central and dominant tradition they represent the testimony of those who stood nearest to the facts, and whose life and outlook had been moulded by them."[11]

It will be obvious from the stress which I have placed in the foregoing upon apostolic proclamation and witness, or if you please upon apostolic tradition, that I recognize that Dodd has made a notable contribution to the study of Gospel origins. In particular, to the extent that he has effectively exhibited a large core of continuity between the original apostolic preaching and the Gospels as we have them he has signally helped to illuminate our problem.

Nevertheless, Dodd's construction is vulnerable in several respects, and some of these need to receive at least brief mention here.   (1) Although Dodd's general characterization of the *kerygma* as centering in the saving significance of the death and resurrection of Christ is very much to the point, it is not possible to follow him all the way in the further details of his analysis of apostolic preaching.   There is more diversity in detail in the records of this preaching than would justify the rather rigid stereotype which Dodd formulates.   Accordingly many scholars who may even be broadly sympathetic with Dodd's main conclusions in this regard tend to disagree as to whether all the points listed are deserving of such recognition and whether perhaps other points should not be included.   In my own judgment there must be a larger recognition of flexibility as to the precise contents.   One of the principal reasons for exaggerating the stereotyped character of this preaching, in

9. *Cf. ibid.,* pp. 118ff.
10. *Ibid.,* pp. 104, 117ff.
11. *Ibid.,* pp. 128f.

my opinion, is that justice has not been done to the *occasional* character of the speeches in Acts as well as of the Pauline Epistles.

(2) The sharp distinction which Dodd draws between *kerygma* and *didache* cannot be maintained. This is borne out, first of all, by the consideration that the terminology of Acts, and for that matter of the Gospels, does not warrant it. The same message may from one point of view be regarded as proclamation and from another as teaching. The closing verse of Acts which speaks of "preaching the kingdom of God and teaching the things concerning the Lord Jesus Christ" is especially clear in this regard (*cf.* also Mt. 11:1). Some examples of Marcan usage also make the same point. In Mark 1:14 we encounter the general, programmatic reference, "Jesus came into Galilee preaching the gospel of God"; in 1:21f. reference is made to the fact that he entered into the synagogue and "taught," and that they were astonished at his teaching, for he taught them as having authority; and in 1:38f. his activity in the synagogues throughout all Galilee is described aas "preaching." A further confirmation of the conclusion that the *didache,* as understood by Dodd, may not be sharply distinguished from the *kerygma* is found in the observation made above that Paul includes both elements under the heading of tradition.[12] And, although this point cannot be developed in detail, it must be acknowledged over against Dodd's narrow conception of realized eschatology that the kingdom of God in the teaching of Jesus inextricably unites the redemptive and the ethical aspects of religion both by its evaluation of the kingdom as a kingdom of righteousness and by the call to repentance as the condition for entrance into it.

(3) Inasmuch as the *kerygma* cannot be isolated from the tradition of ethical teaching one is not justified in the conclusion that the Gospels are to be thought of as being in a more pure or less pure form *expansions* upon an original *kerygma.* And there is no positive evidence available to establish, on other grounds, Dodd's conception of the development beyond apostolic proclamation through the expansion of earlier materials. Accordingly, also, his far-reaching conclusions as to the supposed lateness of many elements of the Gospel tradition do not have a secure foundation.

12. *Cf.* above p. 128.

Riesenfeld's Hypothesis

From C. H. Dodd's approach to the question of Gospel origins, which seeks to establish their pre-history in the action and contents of the earliest apostolic preaching, it may be stimulating to consider briefly the recently enunciated views of Harald Riesenfeld which evaluate the foundational apostolic activity in rather different terms.[13] In passing, we shall be noting that Riesenfeld presents a vigorous attack upon form criticism as that method has been developed and applied in its more consistent forms. Thus, in terms of presuppositions and general approach, he distinguishes his position from that of Dodd which might fairly be characterized as a moderate example of form criticism. Dodd, as has been noted, assigns a significantly creative role to the communities in the development of *kerygma* and *didache* but arrives at relatively conservative conclusions as compared with most form critics because he accords to the apostles, and to Jesus himself, the unique place of the actual founders of Christianity. Riesenfeld, however, reduces the creative significance of the communities to a minimum and assigns the full weight of responsibility for the origins and transmission of the Gospel tradition to the apostles and ultimately to Jesus Christ himself.

The attractiveness of Riesenfeld's thesis, at least from the standpoint of the interest of Christian orthodoxy, may be partially gauged from his summary statement concerning his answer to the question as to the origin of the Gospel tradition.

> We must seek its origin ultimately in Jesus and his Messianic self-consciousness. Jesus is not only the object of a later faith, which on its side gave rise to the growth of oral and also written tradition, but, as Messiah and teacher, Jesus is the object and subject of a tradition of authoritative and holy words which he himself created and entrusted to his disciples for its later transmission in the epoch between his death and the parousia.[14]

13. Risenfeld's article, "The Gospel Tradition and Its Beginnings," was delivered as an address at the opening session of a Congress on "The Four Gospels in 1957" in Oxford, England, and it was originally published as a pamphlet in that same year (London: Mowbray). In 1959 it was incorporated in the volume *Studia Evangelica, TU* LXXIII (Berlin: Akademie), a collection of the papers presented at this Congress, pp. 43ff. The pagination followed here is that of the pamphlet. For a learned presentation and development of the main features of Riesenfeld's position, cf. B. Gerhardsson, *Memory and Manuscript, Oral Tradition and Written Transmission in Rabbinic Judaism and Early Christianity* (Uppsala, 1961).

14. *Ibid.*, p. 30.

Nevertheless, to set this conclusion in its proper perspective, one must take note of further elements.

(1) First of all, he clears the ground for the presentation of his positive view by his critique of form criticism. The view that "a considerable part of the material which is contained in the Gospels was freely invented and then given definite shape" presupposes, he says, "an extraordinary creative capacity in the first Christian generations."[15] And he adds, "The very existence of such an anonymous creative generation in primitive Christianity presupposes, in view of what we know from the New Testament about the apostles and the other members of the early Christian community, a truly miraculous and incredible factor in the history of the Gospel tradition."[16] Another strong point in his critique relates to the influence of purely *a priori* conclusions concerning Jesus which decisively control the method of form criticism. Modern judgments essentially inapplicable to the material under consideration, Riesenfeld observes, are introduced into these analyses. And he goes on to say:

> Scholars have set out from a conception of Jesus which has been constructed *a priori* and have then asked what portions of the Gospel material accord with this conception. They have more or less unconsciously used as the measure of their inquiry what Jesus can or cannot have done, without taking account of the fact that from the very first the tradition understood the deeds no less than the words of Jesus as something wholly unique which can be understood only in an eschatological setting.[17]

(2) Besides such general evaluations of form criticism Riesenfeld draws the specific and distinctive conclusion that the *Sitz im Leben,* or life-situation, and the original source of the Gospel tradition, was neither the preaching in the Christian mission nor the catechetical and other instruction of the primitive communities. With regard to the former activity, namely that of missionary preaching, Riesenfeld admits that with the help of Acts and the Epistles we can come into possession of "fragments of kerygmatic formulae about the saving work of Christ" but he goes on to contend that there is nothing which establishes the connection between these elements of the proclamation and the materials from which our Gospels were con-

15. *Ibid.,* p. 8.
16. *Ibid.,* p. 9.
17. *Ibid.,* pp. 9f.

structed. And he likewise maintains that there is no evidence of a definite connection of the instruction of catechumens and the general edification of the members of the community with the Gospel tradition concerning the words of Jesus. This latter argument is the more remarkable since he admits that in the Epistles of Paul and of James, for example, there are clear evidences of the remembrance of sayings of Jesus. At this point his argument seems to rest upon the absence of express citations of the words of Jesus. And he adds that "there can be only one explanation of the strange fact, namely, that the primitive Christian letter-writers, and among them Paul, took express pains to avoid citing the sayings of Jesus in the context of their original utterance."[18] It should be noted here that Riesenfeld at this juncture is not merely dissociating himself from the more radical conclusions of the form critics regarding the life-situations in which the origin of the contents of the Gospel tradition must to a substantial extent be supposedly envisioned. But he is isolating the Gospel tradition from the *public* preaching and teaching activity of the apostles.

(3) But if the life-situation in which the Gospel tradition originated and was handed down is not to be conceived of in these terms, how is it to be understood? "The gospel tradition," he says, "belongs to a category which is *sui generis* and, to put the matter concisely, it has its own *Sitz im Leben*." A genuine analogy is to be found, however, in the *milieu* in which the Gospel tradition arose, and in particular it may be discovered in the pattern given by Jewish oral tradition and its ultimate reduction to writing. Here Riesenfeld to be sure is not breaking wholly new ground, for his position has much in common with the hypothesis of oral tradition as developed originally by Gieseler and as it found able exposition in Westcott.[19] Nevertheless, Riesenfeld's view is not simply to be identified with this older theory. For, in the first place, he allows that it may "be possible to establish points of interdependence in the existing Gospels."[20] Moreover, he is concessive to the modern point of view in affirming that "it is self-evident that the moulding of the tradition — *e.g.* by the collecting and grouping of individual pericopes, through its transformations and also through its additions — came about grad-

18. *Ibid.*, p. 14; *cf.* pp. 10-16.
19. Westcott, *op. cit.*, p. 16. See footnotes 26 and 27 in Chapter III.
20. Riesenfeld, *op. cit.*, p. 6.

ually in the life of the primitive Church."[21]   And, finally, there
are clearly elements of freshness and originality in the statement of his view.

To fill in some of the details, we may begin by noting his
formulation of the analogy which he finds in the Jewish
milieu:

> This was the so-called 'Sayings of the Fathers', that comprehen-
> sive exposition and elaboration of the Law which was carefully
> handed on from generation to generation and finally found its
> literary embodiment in the Mishnah *c.* A.D. 200. In this case
> we have indeed an authoritative 'holy' tradition which it was
> sought ultimately to derive from the revelation of Jahweh to
> Moses at Mount Sinai.[22]

On the background of this conception of the pattern of the
Gospel tradition, Riesenfeld declares that "the situation as
here conceived is not the vague diffusion of narratives, sagas,
or anecdotes, as we find it in folk-lore, but the rigidly controlled
transmission of matter from one who has the mastery of it to
another who has been specially chosen to learn it."[23]   The result
was a fixed body of material, learned by heart.   Moreover, "the
oral tradition was esoteric, and this not in the sense that it
was treasured as a dark secret, but that it was not entrusted to
everyone nor was it at everyone's disposal to use as he wished."[24]
It must be assumed moreover, he maintains, that those who
performed the task of receiving and handing down the tradition were "an exactly defined group within the community."[25]

All of these features then are thought of as applying to the
New Testament situation.   In agreement with the position
which I have taken above in speaking of the subject of apostolic
tradition in terms of the data of the New Testament, and by
way of appeal to many of the same passages in Luke-Acts and
Paul, Riesenfeld concludes that Paul and the other apostles
were the bearers of the Gospel tradition, and that their "safe-
keeping and committal to trustworthy persons of the words and
deeds of Jesus, that is of the Gospel tradition" was an obligation
that fell upon them *in addition* to that of preaching and the
oversight of the communities.[26]   On this understanding of the

21. *Ibid.*, p. 27.
22. *Ibid.*, p. 17.
23. *Ibid.*, pp. 17f.
24. *Ibid.*, p. 18; *cf.* p. 24.
25. *Ibid.*, p. 18.
26. *Cf. Ibid.*, p. 20.

background of the preservation of the Gospel tradition, Riesenfeld feels that he finds support for his sharp distinction between (1) this Gospel tradition and (2) the public preaching and the community instruction of the early church.

Here we have the reason why the words and deeds of Jesus were probably never quoted verbally in the missionary preaching and only on rare occasions in the community instruction. The tradition which was recited was holy and hence, in contrast to present-day practice, was not readily mentioned by word of mouth. Mission preaching, indeed, pointed and led to it. The instruction in the community presupposed it and linked itself up with it. But in its verbal form and in its *Sitz im Leben* in the community it was *sui generis*.[27]

As an additional point in Riesenfeld's construction it may be noted that the Jewish pattern of oral tradition eventually committed to writing is thought to help us to understand why, as the need for authorized transmitters of this tradition became greater — as the Christian Church itself grew and its communities increased in number — there would have been "the written fixation of the text at a comparatively early date."[28]

Critical Evaluation

Riesenfeld's hypothesis as a whole has many attractive features and may be said to have even a large measure of plausibility. His critique of the "romantic picture" drawn by the form critics and his appeal for realism by way of reflection upon the history of tradition in Judaism are in general praiseworthy. And the unique place which he assigns to Christ and the apostles in this history is most salutary. Nevertheless, there appear to be at least three important respects in which Riesenfeld's view does not carry conviction. In the first place, one must question whether the Gospel tradition ever possessed such a *fixed* character as the Jewish tradition. It is true that Riesenfeld allows at least for a slight measure of variation here even in the learning and transmission process and for some modification of the tradition in the life of the primitive Church.[29] But does even this much change accord with the presupposition that what was involved was "an authoritative *holy* tradition" which would have been viewed as sacrosanct? And is it not more

27. *Ibid.*, p. 23.
28. *Ibid.*
29. *Cf. ibid.*, pp 18, 27.

satisfactory to explain the elements of diversity within the Gospels as envisioning a quite different situation from that which obtained in the case of the rabbis? Jesus addressed many audiences in different places over a considerable period of time. The apostles similarly, though basically concerned to transmit what they had seen and heard, evidently enjoyed the freedom to adapt their message to a variety of historical situations.

In the second place, the conclusion that "the oral tradition was esoteric" is not, at least as it is supposed to apply to Christian history, supported by any definite evidence. The total impression given by the New Testament regarding the propagation of the Christian faith is that there was a sense of urgency to make it known as far and wide as possible, and it is inexplicable that the *kerygma* should have been sounded abroad and the Christian communities in general nurtured while there was a hedging about of the contents of the Gospel tradition. There may not be an easy answer to the question why our Gospels, or at least the body of tradition which they include, are not quoted in the records that we possess of apostolic preaching and teaching. The generally held conclusion that such a record of apostolic preaching as we have in Acts 10:36-39, for example, may be an epitome of the Gospel tradition, and that it does not refer more particularly to the teaching of Jesus because of its summary character, is in any case not so easily set aside, in my judgment, as Riesenfeld supposes.[30]

Finally, and this point is the most important of all, Riesenfeld's construction breaks down because the Gospel pattern is truly *sui generis,* and does not find a genuine parallel in the authoritative "holy" tradition thought of as given by the Lord to Moses on Mount Sinai. Riesenfeld seems to me to tip his hand in this respect in that he frequently speaks of the Gospel tradition as consisting of "the words and deeds of Jesus."[31] But far from justice is being done to the distinctiveness of the Gospels when they are characterized as consisting essentially of the words and deeds of Jesus. Considering the framework of the Gospels and taking account especially of the disposition of their contents as they relate to the ministry of Jesus Christ there is much truth, as was observed above, in the characterization of them as "passion-narratives with an extensive intro-

30. Cf. *ibid.,* pp. 12f.
31. Cf. *ibid.,* pp. 20, 21, 22, 23.

duction."[32]   From this perspective it is evident that Riesenfeld's evaluation of the Gospel tradition as consisting of the words and deeds of Jesus is faulty and inadequate.   And this is emphasized the more if account is taken of the place of *the resurrection* of Jesus Christ, as the great supernatural action which brings the gospel to its climax.   For it is the resurrection joined to the passion and the passion to the resurrection that put the *sui generis* character of the Gospels in sharpest relief.

Riesenfeld recognizes indeed that his formulation of the tradition does not include, for example, the Passion narratives. At this point he appeals to the institution of the Lord's Supper as evidence that Jesus reckoned with an intervening epoch between his death and the parousia, that is, with the epoch of the Church, and that the intention of Jesus in this regard must have been complemented with the element of teaching.[33]   But even if one might thus account for the presence within "the holy words and deeds of Jesus" of his teaching and action in connection with the institution of the Supper, this would still be in the nature of a preparatory disclosure, and would not explain the emphasis of the gospel upon the death and resurrection of Jesus Christ as *saving events which had been accomplished.*

The examination of the contents and disposition of the Gospel tradition, therefore, points up a certain basic incongruity within Riesenfeld's construction.   For it is impossible to carry through consistently the broad distinction which he draws between (1) the proclamation and instruction reported in the Epistles and Acts and (2) the tradition of the holy words and deeds of Jesus which supposedly constitutes the pre-history of the Gospels.

Further questions concerning the history of the apostolic tradition behind the Gospels cannot be pursued here.   In particular, I shall not enter upon a discussion of the contents and form of the sources, whether oral or written, which may have been drawn upon by the evangelists.[34]   I am content to leave

32. *Cf.* footnote 47 in Chapter III.

33. *Cf.* Riesenfeld, *op. cit.,* pp. 26f.

34. This involves passing over in this study many of the questions, and a vast amount of literature, relating to the Synoptic Problem. No evaluation can be undertaken *e.g.* of such an approach as is represented by W. L. Knox's *The Sources of the Synoptic Gospels* (Cambridge: University Press, Vol. I, 1953; Vol. II, 1957) . Moreover, the Four-document Hypothesis, origi-

these questions open at least for the present, not so much because of lack of space although that is also a factor, but especially because of the intrinsic difficulty, if not impossibility, of
reaching firm and final conclusions on these questions. In the
nature of the case decisions in this area must be largely hypothetical in character. Positive conclusions on these matters, in
my judgment, must come, and in any case must be sought,
within the framework provided by the principal positive observations which have been made concerning the earliest history
of Christianity and the place occupied by the apostles within
that history, as set forth in the New Testament as a whole.

---

nated by Streeter and developed by many able scholars as a modification
of the Two-document Hypothesis, must be left undiscussed. And even
the Q-hypothesis, a fixed ingredient of the generally held view, cannot be
assessed here.

It may not be superfluous, however, to make the observation that one
must not try to settle questions raised by such theories on the basis merely
of generalities. Simple solutions are attractive, and so it might appear to
be well to insist that there is a presumption against conjectural documents.
So B. C. Butler, *op. cit.*, p. 1, who quotes C. H. Turner as saying, "I have
an incurable preference for the simple solution of literary problems." On
the other hand, W. L. Knox, *op. cit.*, I, p. 7, in connection with the
development of his position that many written sources were used by Mark
and the other Synoptists, asserts: "Here I can only record my conviction
that in dealing with the primitive Church we must recognize that everything we know of its history and outlook suggests that the single and
simple explanation is likely to be furthest from the truth." Shunning such
axioms one must seek to discover where the facts lead, always, however,
taking great pains not to settle questions which do not admit of clear-cut
solutions. The question of Q appears to me to be one of extreme difficulty.
The problem which the Q-hypothesis seeks to answer must in any case
be faced. And while one may not be convinced that the existence of Q
has been proved, there is nothing within the so-called "conservative" position on the Bible which rules it out of court. Although perhaps oral
witnesses have at times had difficulty in getting a hearing, it by no means
follows that written sources are to be discounted or eliminated from
consideration as one endeavors to understand the history leading up to the
publication of the Gospels.

CHAPTER EIGHT

MODERN DEBATE CONCERNING ULTIMATE ORIGIN

THE question of ultimate origin is that of the relationship of Jesus Christ himself to the Gospels. It is concerned with the inquiry whether in the last analysis they owe their very existence to him and whether they are what they are because of what he was and did. No one will dispute that this question, so understood and formulated, is the profoundest question with which we can be concerned in our present study. For to a very large extent our final evaluation of the very nature of Christianity will depend crucially upon it.

Although we shall be concentrating upon this subject in the final two chapters it will be recognized that it has engaged our attention more or less explicitly at many points of our previous discussions. Even when we have devoted our attention to the Gospels as literary documents and have dealt with such subjects as order, interdependence and sources, we have found ourselves substantially involved time and again in assessing positive and negative arguments and considerations in terms of one's ultimate conception of Jesus Christ. And naturally enough this has been even more true when attention has been centered upon the fact that (though literary interdependence has been established as a positive factor and the use of oral and written sources is regarded as, to say the least, highly probable) the leading members of the Christian Church, including especially the apostles but not overlooking the evangelists themselves, have decisively affected and even determined the final result.

To restrict ourselves for the moment to the significance of the apostles, as that was dwelt upon in the previous chapters, I would simply call attention to the fact that that which makes apostolic tradition, in both the active and passive senses, truly meaningful for our study is that the apostles were apostles *of Jesus Christ.* They did not speak and act as possessing authority in their own right but only with an authority derived from Christ. Nor were they qualified for the performance of their functions by their innate wisdom or their subjective religious experience but by the knowledge and power which sprang wholly from their relationship to him. They were the servants of Jesus Christ with no rights of their own, and hence they acknowledged him as Lord and Master. But in view of their appointment and endowment to act as representatives of him, who were to act in his stead and with his plenipotentiary power, they possessed and exercised among men unique functions bound up with their peculiar office. In a word, the apostles were nothing in themselves. But in virtue of the fact that they were chosen and commissioned by Christ to act in his place they were to be acknowledged as possessing singular authority and were even to be received as Christ himself. As Jesus said, "He that receiveth you receiveth me, and he that receiveth me receiveth him that sent me" (Mt. 10:40). And again, "A servant is not greater than his lord; neither an apostle [namely, one that is sent] greater than he that sent him . . . verily, verily, I say unto you, he that receiveth whosoever I send receiveth me; and he that receiveth me receiveth him that sent me" (Jn. 13:16, 20).[1]

If therefore the factor of apostolic tradition must, in accordance with our previous discussion, be assigned a place of central meaning for the understanding of the pre-history of the Gospels, the consideration that the apostles were acknowledged as speaking and acting in the place of Christ would demand the recognition that they stood on a qualitatively different and higher level than that of ordinary human tradition. In agreement with this perspective Paul says, for example, that the tradition which he delivered over to the Corinthian Church concerning the Lord's Supper was one that he had received of the Lord (I Cor. 11:23). One of the merits of Oscar Cullmann's important study on "The Tradition" is that he stresses the unique-

---

1. See especially the article by K. H. Rengstorf in *TWNT*, I, pp. 406ff., now available in an English translation by J. R. Coates, *Bible Key Words*, II (London: Black, 1952). *Cf.* also my study, "The Authority of the New Testament," in *The Infallible Word* (Philadelphia, 1946; Grand Rapids, 1953), pp. 110ff.; Norval Geldenhuys, *Supreme Authority* (Grand Rapids: Eerdmans, 1953); Herman Ridderbos, "De Apostoliciteit van de Kerk volgens het Nieuwe Testament," in *De Apostolische Kerk* (Kampen: Kok, 1954), pp. 39ff.

ness of the apostolate and apostolic tradition.[2]   It is also noteworthy that Harald Riesenfeld in his paper, "The Gospel Tradition and Its Beginnings," which has been subjected to some
major criticisms above, draws the conclusion that in view of
the relationship which the apostles sustained to Jesus the
Messiah, Jesus "is the founder of the gospel tradition."[3]   Or,
to put the matter more specifically in terms of his own hypothesis, "Jesus is the object and subject of a tradition of authoritative and holy words which he himself created and entrusted
to his disciples for its later transmission in the epoch between
his death and the parousia."[4]   In the modern approach to the
subject of Christian origins, however, as everyone who has read
even a little in this area will agree, the accent is upon discontinuity between Jesus and the Gospels.

Allow me now to press forward to a somewhat deeper prob-
ing of this question of ultimate origin.   On the one hand,
there is the position which, stressing continuity, affirms that
Jesus was the real creator of Christianity and thus was also
ultimately responsible for the origin of the Gospels.   On the
other hand, discontinuity is the emphasis of those who discover
a profound gulf between (1) what Jesus was and said and
purposed and (2) the faith of the primitive Christian church
which, following the rise of faith in Christ's resurrection, developed distinctively first in Palestine and then beyond its
borders.   For it is the latter which supposedly produced the
Gospels as expressions, at least as regards their most dominant
features, of their faith in him.

The final decision on the issue of continuity or discontinuity
rests basically, it will be generally acknowledged, upon one's
estimate of Jesus Christ himself.   This in turn depends upon
one's assessment of the witness of the Scriptures to Jesus Christ
and the response that one is constrained to make to that witness.   As those who are committed to take a consistent Christian stand at this point of inquiry as well as every other, we
must address ourselves vigorously and earnestly to an ever deeper
and more responsible evaluation of the testimony concerning

---

2. Oscar Cullmann, *Die Tradition, als exegetisches, historisches und
theologisches Problem* (Zürich: Zwingli, 1954) ; Eng. trans., in *The Early
Church* (London: SCM, 1956), pp. 54ff.   It is evaluated more fully and
critically in my review in *WTJ* XIX (Nov., 1956), pp. 78ff.

3. Riesenfeld, *op. cit.*, p. 64.

4. *Ibid.*, p. 65.

Jesus Christ. And my own goal in this brief series of studies cannot be attained apart from an effort to set down the principal guiding lines especially by way of appeal to Jesus' own self-revelation.

In the conviction, however, that our powers of discrimination may be sharpened by a review of the modern situation in which a divergent point of view, or a variety of them, has emerged, I propose to submit a sketch of some of the leading aspects of the historical development in which the accent upon discontinuity has come to expression.

Adolf Harnack

In such a study one may begin to advantage with the classic Liberal point of view of the Ritschlian theological movement. And because of the brilliance and lucidity which were distinguishing features of Harnack's presentation of Liberalism we can well afford here to restrict our exposition to his formulation of it.

And as one thinks about Harnack's conception of Jesus Christ and the gospel, there are surely no words which so immediately and perspicuously introduce one to an understanding of his fundamental position as the following:

> The gospel, as Jesus proclaimed it, has to do with the Father only and not with the Son.[5]

It is doubtful that anyone could have expressed more precisely in a single sentence the heart of the Liberal message as it concentrates upon the fatherhood of God but does not allow to Jesus himself a place within the original proclamation to which the Liberal would make his basic commitment. It would be irresponsible, however, to neglect to observe that for Harnack Jesus is not merely the teacher and proclaimer of this message but that also, in a sense, he is involved in the message itself. For Harnack goes on to say:

> He is the way to the Father, and as he is the appointed of the Father, so he is the judge as well . . . It is not as a mere factor that he is connected with the gospel; he was its personal realization and its strength and this he is felt to be still.[6]

Nevertheless, even this noteworthy qualification does not imply

5. Adolf Harnack, *Das Wesen des Christentums* (Leipzig: Hinrichs, 1901), p. 91; Eng. trans., *What Is Christianity?* (London: Williams and Norgate, 1901), p. 144.

6. *Ibid.* (Eng. trans., pp. 145f.).

that after all Jesus is thought of as an essential component of
the gospel as he proclaimed it. The history of Jesus is, however,
definitely meaningful for the understanding of that message.
To recognize that Jesus is thought of as the example as regards
religion and ethics hardly does full justice to what Harnack
has in view. When he says that Jesus was the personal realization and the strength of the gospel he has in mind that, in a
fashion that borders on the unique, the understanding of the
gospel continues to depend upon the impact which his personality is capable of making upon us. As he says in another
place, "Words effect nothing; it is the power of the personality
that stands behind them."[7]

In agreement with this Liberal understanding of the message
of Jesus and of his own person and work in relation to it Harnack judges that the ultimate thing that may be said about
Jesus Christ is his originality in acquiring a profound sense
of sonship in relation to God the Father. And hardly less ultimate was the ensuing conviction that it was his peculiar mission to bring others to essentially the same experience and
calling.

He allows then that Jesus was both Son of God and Messiah.
But he leaves us in no doubt that the connotations of these titles
are for him quite divergent from those which they enjoyed in
historical orthodoxy. In keeping with his neo-Kantian philosophical presuppositions, and reinterpreting the biblical data
in the framework of Liberalism, he repudiates the metaphysics
involved in traditional views of God and Jesus Christ and insists that Jesus' experience of God, however extraordinary, was
after all that of a mere man. Even Matthew 11:27, by way of
a radical reconstruction of the text, is made to support this
understanding of a merely ethico-religious sonship which originated in the course of Jesus' historical life. And the messianic
consciousness, reduced as it is to the bare sense of mission,
retains only formal significance for Jesus, and thus in affirming
its historicity Harnack takes pains to reject its specific biblical
and historical content. In using the concept of messiahship
Jesus was in the distressing position of accommodating himself
to something that was utterly uncongenial to him. As Harnack
says:

7. *Ibid.,* p. 31 (Eng. trans., p. 48).

But however we may conceive the "Messiah," it was an assumption that was simply necessary if the man who felt the inward call was to gain an absolute recognition within the lines of Jewish religious history — the profoundest and maturest history that any nation ever possessed, nay, as the future was to show, the true religious history for all mankind. The idea of the Messiah became the means — in the first instance for the devout of his own nation — of effectively setting the man who knew that he was the Son of God, and was doing the work of God, on the throne of history. But when it had accomplished this, its mission was exhausted. Jesus was the "Messiah," and was not the Messiah; and he was not the Messiah, because he left the idea far behind him; because he put a meaning into it which was too much for it to bear.[8]

Much more might be said that would round out our understanding of Harnack's essential Liberalism. These include his distinction between the Easter faith and the Easter message with its implication that faith may be valid altogether apart from the historicity of the resurrection of Christ's body; the low view of sin joined to a merely moral influence theory of the atonement which is in keeping with an essential moralism or reduction of religion to ethics; the basically non-eschatological conception of the kingdom of God; the minimizing and essential repudiation of miracles. But enough has been said to demonstrate that for Harnack the gospel about Jesus Christ, and particularly concerning the redemptive effect of his death and resurrection, have no place in the evangel which Jesus proclaimed.

How all of this bears on the discussion concerning the continuity of Jesus Christ and the gospel is highlighted by the observation that Harnack has no hesitation whatsoever — when he comes to express himself regarding the gospel of Jesus Christ as that was enunciated, for example, by the apostle Paul — in admitting that Christ "belongs pre-eminently to the content of the gospel." In the same connection he says, moreover, that the preaching of the crucified and risen Christ was for Paul "the gospel in a nutshell." The conclusion of Harnack that the gospel, as Paul proclaimed it, has to do with Christ and his saving work through the cross and resurrection is the more striking because in the context in which these quotations appear he is developing at considerable length an argument for the

8. *Ibid.*, p. 89 (Eng. trans. p. 141).

view that in the phrase "the gospel of Christ" the relationship of Jesus Christ to the gospel intended to be brought to mind is that he was "the author who gives it forth in teaching and preaching."[9] There have, to be sure, been differences of opinion among New Testament scholars with regard to the force of the genitive in this phrase "the gospel of Christ" but there does not appear to be any serious dispute today with regard to the proposition that the Pauline *kerygma* centered in him "who was delivered up for our trespasses and who was raised for our justification" (Rom. 4:25). Obviously those who hold that the genitive is objective differ from Harnack at this specific point only in maintaining that Paul's terminology even more consistently and precisely supports this conclusion.

As one considers accordingly the antithesis which Harnack discovers between the place assigned to Jesus Christ within the gospel as Jesus proclaimed it and the gospel as Paul proclaimed it, one is confronted abruptly with the fathomless gulf which, on the Liberal reconstruction, separates Jesus from the preaching and teaching of the Christian Church. In keeping with this estimate the Christianity of the New Testament writings as a whole, in spite of persistent claims to the contrary, constitutes a fall or a falling away from the pristine state represented by Jesus' own teaching. As Harnack himself develops the matter in his provocative work on the origin of the New Testament canon, "the New Testament itself, when compared with what Jesus purposed, said, and was, is already a tradition which overlies and obscures."[10] This estimate of the development of the New Testament canon is spelled out by Harnack in a variety of ways. Among them none is more pertinent to and illuminating for the subject presently under discussion than that in which he addresses himself to the question, "What motives led to the creation of the New Testament?"[11] Harnack's conclusion is that "the embryonic history of the New Testament" may be sketched in four leading motives. Only two of these will however concern us here. The contrast which he draws between

---

9. Adolf Harnack, *The Constitution and Law of the Church in the First Two Centuries* (London: Williams and Norgate, 1910), pp. 297, 298, 296. Translation of *Entstehung und Entwickelung der Kirchenverfassung und des Kirchenrechts in den zwei ersten Jahrhunderten* (Leipzig, 1910).

10. Adolf Harnack, *The Origin of the New Testament* (London: Williams and Norgate, 1925), pp. 43f. Translation of *Die Entstehung des Neuen Testaments* (Leipzig, 1914).

11. *Ibid.*, p. 6.

the second motive and the first again sharply underscores the
fact of discontinuity in Harnack's reconstruction of the history
of the beginnings of Christianity. For he says:

> The second motive, manifested with peculiar force in St.
> Paul, but by no means exclusively in him, is the interest in
> the death and resurrection of the Messiah Jesus, an interest
> which necessarily led to the assigning of supreme importance
> to, and to the crystallization of the tradition of, the critical
> moments of his history. Under the influence of this motive
> "the Gospel" came to mean the good news of the Divine plan
> of Salvation, proclaimed by the prophets, and now accomplished
> through the death and resurrection of Christ; and it would be
> felt that an account of the critical moments of the life of
> Christ must take its place side by side with the Old Testament
> history regarded as prophetic . . . With this stage of develop-
> ment correspond our Gospels, or rather the many Gospels, of
> which St. Luke still speaks.[12]

The earliest motive for us, on the other hand, was, according
to Harnack, "the supreme reverence in which the words and
teaching of Christ Jesus were held." This motive, which is
judged to have been present in the circle of Jesus' disciples
from the beginning of the apostolic age, is regarded by Harnack
as finding its ultimate foundation in the authority with which
Jesus set forth his message. Here then, according to him, we
encounter the nucleus of the New Testament. But he is quick
to add that "if the motive here described could have had free
course, undisturbed by other motives, we should have expected
that a collection of authoritative sayings of Jesus . . . would
have taken its place beside the Old Testament," a development
which indeed he feels to have taken place in the compilation
of Q.[13]

No thorough criticism of Liberalism can be undertaken here.
If one were to embark upon it it would be necessary to ex-
amine with care the philosophical presuppositions; this would
require one to center attention upon the essential naturalism
and rationalism which it shares with the Deism of the En-
lightenment and which still found eloquent expression in
Kant's *Religion within the Limits of Reason Alone;*[14] and

---

12. *Ibid.,* pp. 9f.
13. *Cf. ibid.,* pp. 7f. and p. 8, n. 3.
14. Immanuel Kant, *Religion within the Limits of Reason Alone* (Chicago: Open Court, 1934), translated from *Religion innerhalb der Grenzen
der blossen Vernunft,* 2te Aufl., 1794.

notice would have to be taken of basic features of Kant's critical philosophy as well as of Lotze's theory of value-judgments.
And in the area of interpretation of the New Testament one
might demonstrate that Harnack, for all the poignancy of his
search for the Jesus of history and for all the scintillation of his
prose as he seeks to capture the spirit of Jesus, is so arbitrary
and imaginative and speculative in his approach to the data
that one cannot seriously allow for the possibility that his Jesus
ever lived. And it is emphatically plain that this Jesus is utterly
incapable of accounting for the origin of Christianity with its
faith in the crucified and risen Saviour. By the same token the
origin of our Gospels cannot be traced in any basic fashion to
this hypothetical religious personality who is supposed to have
thought of himself in terms that are quite at variance with
those which are employed by the evangelists in witnessing to
Jesus Christ.

From some points of view no doubt this Liberalism of Harnack and his associates stands apart from other aspects of modern
criticism as a distinctive movement born of fresh and vigorous
new impulses and which gradually subsided after reaching its
crest about the beginning of the present century. An interesting case might indeed be made for the thesis that one
school of criticism after another has arisen, and that each in
its turn has shown the deficiencies of earlier points of view. It
would be more accurate, however, in my judgment, in the
midst of all this change to discern a far greater degree of unity
in the critical perspectives of our modern times and to observe
that the divergences are to a greater or lesser extent essentially
vacillations between more moderate and more radical points
of view which flow from the unresolved and unresolvable tensions within these reconstructions. But I am inclined to say
that even this latter evaluation hardly does full justice to the
factor of continuity in modern thought. Considerable diverg-
ence in detail there certainly is among the various schools of
criticism. But there is also present, as I see it, what may with
very little exaggeration be characterized as the persistence of
Liberalism.

Strauss and Baur

Thus even Ferdinand Christian Baur and David Friedrich
Strauss may from certain points of view be regarded as Liberals
before the rise of Liberalism. Because Strauss' theory places in

the foreground of attention the creative role of the Christian community as responsible for the largely mythical content of the Gospels, it involves an even greater emphasis upon discontinuity and might appear to be radically at variance with the Liberal who centers our thought upon the Jesus of history. Nevertheless, Strauss, feeling that he cannot allow himself the luxury of maintaining that the creative activity of the Christian community was carried on *ex nihilo*, seeks to support his conclusions as to the possibility and the probability of the creation of myths by way of reflection upon historical backgrounds. And in this connection he appeals not only to prevailing ideas of the times but quite specifically to the history of Jesus. And then it turns out that his Jesus is after all somewhat like the Liberal Jesus of later times, for he has in common with him a number of elements. His words and works made an overwhelming impression upon his associates. And since he not only regarded himself as the Messiah but was thought of by his disciples as being the Messiah Strauss believes that the necessary ingredient has been provided to explain how, even after the death of Christ had annihilated belief in his messiahship, the earlier impression began to revive and eventually the whole resurrection story came into being. There are indeed intolerable tensions and conflicts within Strauss' construction. There is far too much discontinuity within it to justify his historical affirmations and too much continuity to account for the creative role that he assigns to the Christian community.

Strauss' construction lacks the apparently face-saving feature which Liberalism found in its historicism which, by way of absolutizing the relative to which the Christian revelation had been reduced, seemed to maintain the permanent religious significance of Jesus. But Strauss had something which from his own point of view more or less served the same purpose. For in his Hegelian distinction between idea (*Begriff*) and representation (*Vorstellung*) he claimed that the idea or the ideal was all that really counted and that therefore one could be basically indifferent with regard to the criticism that might be leveled against the historical representations of religious concepts. But in any case a particularly weak point in Strauss' construction, as is widely admitted, is his total effort to account for the origin of the Gospels on his philosophical presuppositions and by way of the development of the details of the sup-

posed course of the history of Christianity beginning with the
life of Jesus.

It is ironical that F. C. Baur, whose views of the Gospels were
in many basic respects as negative and radical as those of
Strauss, should have been able to carry on a long and honored
career as a professor in Tübingen while the publication of
Strauss' *Life of Jesus* called forth such a storm that his academic
career came to an end before it had fairly begun. To be sure,
Baur avoided the major offense created by the mythical theory
of his disciple and evidently seemed to deal more responsibly
with the historical documents as he developed on a grand scale
his reconstruction of early Christian history by way of application of the Hegelian dialectic. Nevertheless, as time eventually
showed this grand scheme was grandly wrong. And his *Tendenz* criticism, with its basic espousal of conscious fiction (as
distinguished from the unconscious fiction attributed to the
community by Strauss) also virtually isolated the Gospels from
Jesus Christ.

In spite of the radical character of Baur's criticism as a
whole, however, he interpreted Jesus in essentially Liberal
terms. Basing his conclusions largely upon the Sermon on
the Mount he sets forth a "moral" interpretation of Jesus which
is close to that of Kant, a factor which would help to explain
Baur's general acceptance in his own day as well as his continuity with the later theology of his disciple Ritschl. On the
one hand, the Sermon on the Mount appeals to Baur because
the discourses there, in his judgment, do not turn on the person of Jesus and a super-human dignity. The personal element, he thinks, remains as it were in the background of the
theme. For Baur, it is rather the profound and weighty discourse that reveals to us the true character and greatness of
the speaker. It is the thing itself that speaks here; it is the
inner force of truth making its way straight to men's hearts,
which here announces itself in all its significance for the history
of the world.[15] Summing up he says:

> It is in the beatitudes of the Sermon on the Mount that we
> obtain the deepest and most comprehensive insight into the
> fundamental way of looking at things, the fundamental mood,
> out of which Christianity proceeded. What is it that finds ex-
> pression in all those utterances in which blessedness is said

15. *Cf.* F. C. Baur, *The Church History of the First Three Centuries*
(1853; Eng. trans., 1878), I, 26f.

to belong to the poor in spirit, to those who mourn, to the meek, to those who hunger and thirst after righteousness, to the pure in heart, to the peacemakers, to those who are persecuted for righteousness' sake? It is religious consciousness which is penetrated by the deepest sense of the pressure of the finite and of all the contradictions of the present, and yet is infinitely exalted, and knows itself, in spite of this, to be far superior to everything finite and limited.[16]

Somewhat later Baur says:

The beatitudes of the Sermon on the Mount express, in an absolute manner, what constitutes the inmost self-consciousness of the Christian, as it is in itself, and apart from external relations. The original and radical element of Christianity appears further in a form of absolute moral command in the controversial part of the discourse which is directed against the Pharisees, and in other parts of it.[17]

Among other points of contact with the later Liberalism one may note the stress which he places upon human ability to attain righteousness[18] and his man-centered and this-worldly conception of the kingdom of God. With regard to the latter he says:

In the kingdom of God the will of God is, in the first place, what every individual feels himself required, with the force of an absolute moral command, to fulfill; and, in the second place, the common task of a certain definite association. All the members of this association are to cooperate to realize the object which the will of God sets before them, and the more closely they are united with each other the more will that object be realized among them. The social element, which is an essential part of religion, is also the leading and essential feature of the kingdom of God.[19]

One further quotation serves effectively to sum up what Baur regarded as the essence of the teaching of Jesus and of Christianity itself:

If the ideas on which we have been enlarging are the earliest and most essential element of the teaching of Jesus, it appears to be purely and entirely moral in its tendency, and what it aims at is simply to throw men back on their own moral and religious consciousness. A man has only to become clearly aware of that which announces itself in his own consciousness as his

16. *Ibid.*, p. 27.
17. *Ibid.*, p. 29; *cf.* p. 33.
18. *Cf. ibid.*, p. 34.
19. *Ibid.*, p. 35.

highest moral end, and can realize it by his own efforts. When
we thus look back to its earliest elements, Christianity appears
as a purely moral religion; its highest and most peculiar distinction is that it bears an essentially moral character, and is
rooted in the moral consciousness of man.[20]

It is also interesting, as one ponders the persistence of Liberalism, that Baur, with only a slightly different emphasis from
that of Harnack, affirms the historicity of the messianic consciousness of Jesus. For he seeks to explain how in the messianic
idea "the spiritual contents of Christianity was clothed on with
a concrete form in which it could enter on the path of historical
development."[21]

Wilhelm Wrede

The views of Wilhelm Wrede constitute such a thoroughgoing repudiation of the Liberalism represented, for example,
by Harnack, that one might wonder whether it would not be
necessary in his case at least to allow for an exception to the
generalization here being made with regard to the continuity
of an essential Liberalism in modern criticism of Jesus and the
Gospels. His rejection of the Marcan Hypothesis, his castigation of the psychologism of the Liberal lives of Jesus, his critique
of the Liberal exegesis as atomistic in character and as involving without support of objective evidence the application to
the gospel narrative of evolutionary concepts, and other features, are so generally known that no detailed exposition of
them is necessary at this point. One must recall briefly, however, that his own positive theory of the messianic secret, proceeding as it does on the background of utter agnosticism with
respect to the historicity of the messianic consciousness (which
for all practical purposes amounts to denial thereof), involves
a radical reconstruction of the history of primitive Christianity.[22]

On his view Mark, still judged to be the earliest Gospel, is
regarded as being fundamentally the product of the theologiz-
ing of the early Church at a certain phase of its development
rather than as in any basic sense a report of historical events.

20. *Ibid.*, p. 37.

21. *Ibid.*, pp. 38f.

22. See especially Wilhelm Wrede's influential work *Das Messiasgeheimnis
in den Evangelien* (Göttingen: Vandenhoeck & Ruprecht, 1901). On Wrede's
views *cf.* my discussion in the article entitled, "Rudolf Bultmann's Jesus"
(*WTJ*, I, Nov. 1938, pp. 9ff.); republished in *PBA* (Grand Rapids: Eerdmans, 1957), pp. 117ff.; and *WMMC*, pp. 53ff.

The other Gospels on this approach are thought of as representing to a greater or lesser extent more advanced stages of this development. His general attitude toward them finds expression in the following statement:

> Our testimonies to Jesus are only later accounts, which were not put together by eyewitnesses. The amount of true information which they unquestionably contain is overlaid with thick layers of legendary adornments and historical fancies, prompted by the faith of the later community; it is only after a weary labor of discrimination, beset on all sides by many uncertainties, that we can hope to come near to the core.[23]

The radicalness of his position is also to be observed in his evaluation of Paul as "the second founder of Christianity." Paul is credited with the innovation of having "laid the foundation of religion in these acts of salvation, in the incarnation, death, and resurrection of Christ." And this is a view of Christianity to which Wrede believes credence cannot be given because it is "necessarily, in its own essence, a mythological conception."[24]

On Wrede's understanding of the origin and development of Christianity, and reflecting upon his estimate of the essentially non-historical character of the Gospels, it will be obvious that the accent falls with peculiar force upon discontinuity as regards any ultimate responsibility which Jesus might have for the origin of the Gospels. Nevertheless, even Wrede, for all of his agnosticism and skepticism, and his complete lack of sympathy with the gospel of salvation as accomplished by the death and resurrection of Christ, still affirms the historicity of Jesus. And when he does so he likewise speaks with the voice of a Liberal. Thus, in an essay on the subject of biblical theology, he declares that Jesus' whole concern was with "an ethical imperative born out of the highest religious individualism."[25] This same point of view is set forth somewhat more fully in his book on Paul:

> In Jesus everything aims at the personal character of the individual. Man shall yield his soul whole and undivided to God and God's will. Most of Jesus' preaching has, for this reason, the imperative form, or at least an imperative character. True,

23. Wilhelm Wrede, *Paulus* (Halle: Gebauer-Schwetschke, 1904), p. 1; Eng. trans. *Paul* (Boston: Unitarian Press, 1908), pp. xi f.

24. *Cf. ibid.*, pp. 103f. (Eng. trans., pp. 178f.).

25. *Über Aufgabe und Methode der sogenannten ntl. Theologie* (1897), p. 67.

the moral appeal is everywhere backed by reward and punishment, and these are to Jesus by no means superfluous ideas; but their chief end is to make men feel the stern earnestness of the will of God, and the greatness of human responsibility. The preaching of Jesus certainly exhibits other features, but its heart is to be found, if anywhere, in these things.

In Paul the central point is a divine act, in history, but transcending history, or a complex of such acts, which impart to all mankind a ready-made salvation. Whoever believes in these divine acts — the incarnation, death, and resurrection of a celestial being — receives salvation.

And this, which to Paul is the sum of religion — the skeleton of the fabric of his piety, without which it would collapse — can this be a continuation or a remoulding of the gospel of Jesus? Where, in all this, is that gospel to be found, which Paul is said to have understood? Of that which is to Paul all and everything, how much does Jesus know? Nothing whatever. Let people point as often as they will to his claim to have been chosen as Messiah; it must still be doubted — in spite of a few places in the Gospels which assert as much — that he ever made himself an object of faith or doctrine. It is as improbable as anything could be that he ever assigned to his death a saving power, although this thought also has once or twice made its way into the Gospels.[26]

Once again therefore one is confronted with a profound tension within a single point of view which discloses its basic lack of coherence and intelligibility. For on the one hand there is a radicalism and skepticism that goes beyond that of Strauss but on the other a virtually Liberal effort to make the Jesus of history understandable and meaningful. And one may observe how hopeless is the effort on this approach to give satisfactory answers to the question of ultimate origin.

Albert Schweitzer

When one turns from Wrede to Albert Schweitzer it might appear that the latter has every advantage so far as the question of the final responsibility of Jesus Christ for the contents of the Gospels is concerned. In contrast with the devastating skepticism and the negative conclusions of Wrede regarding the

26. Wilhelm Wrede, *Paul*, pp. 93f. (Eng. trans., pp. 162ff.). On Wrede's view of Paul and Jesus see especially J. Gresham Machen, *The Origin of Paul's Religion* (New York: Macmillan, 1925; Grand Rapids: Eerdmans, 1947), pp. 173-199. The recent comment by James M. Robinson in *A New Quest of the Historical Jesus* (London: SCM, 1959), p. 109, is of interest.

historicity of the gospel message there stands Schweitzer's remarkably positive attitude toward the narratives as a whole, an
attitude which results in the utilization of large segments and
numerous details in his own construction. In brief, for Schweitzer the contents of the Gospels are accepted as being so largely
historical that a major shift toward the continuity of Jesus and
the Gospels results.

Before we reflect further upon the crucial differences between Wrede and Schweitzer, however, it will prove advantageous to recall that Schweitzer's work, as well as that of Wrede,
constituted a powerful critique of the Liberal construction regarding the so-called historical Jesus. The double-barreled nature of this attack is the more remarkable when one notes the
coincidence that Schweitzer's brief work, *The Secret of the
Messiahship and the Passion* (which presented the main thesis
he was to develop in his more famous *The Quest of the Historical Jesus,* first published in 1906) appeared in 1901 on the
very day of the publication of Wrede's *The Messianic Secret in
the Gospels.*[27] There is no particular advantage in dwelling
here upon the manner in which "thoroughgoing skepticism"
and "thoroughgoing eschatology" unwittingly joined forces in
exposing the untenability of the Liberal view; this has been
done by Schweitzer himself in a chapter extending to nearly
seventy pages.[28] But the summary of results as formulated by
him is still interesting:

> The Jesus of Nazareth who came forward publicly as the
> Messiah, who preached the ethic of the kingdom of God, who
> founded the Kingdom of Heaven upon earth, and died to give
> His work its final consecration, never had any existence. He
> is a figure designed by rationalism, endowed with life by liberal-
> ism, and clothed by a modern theology in an historical garb.[29]

27. A. Schweitzer, *Das Messianitäts- und Leidensgeheimnis* (Tübingen,
1901); Eng. trans., *The Mystery of the Kingdom of God* (New York:
Dodd, Mead, 1914); *Von Reimarus zu Wrede* (Tübingen: Mohr, 1906);
Eng. trans., *The Quest of the Historical Jesus* (Edinburgh: Black, 1910).
28. *Cf.* Schweitzer *The Quest of the Historical Jesus,* pp. 328-395.
29. *Ibid.,* p. 396. Schweitzer also stated: "The so-called historical Jesus
of the nineteenth century biographies is really a modernization, in which
Jesus is painted in the colours of modern bourgeois respectability and neo-
Kantian moralism." *Cf.* James M. Robinson, *op. cit.,* p. 32. See also *The
Quest,* pp. 310f., where Schweitzer charges that it is especially the Germanic
spirit which has been responsible for an act of historical violence which
in the end injures both religion and history: "A time will come when our
theology, with its pride in its historical character, will get rid of its

In drawing attention now to the more positively historical character of Schweitzer's own view of the witness of the Gospels we may well begin by taking advantage of his own forceful contrast of his position and that of Wrede. In a word, he says, the difference is that what the latter regarded as Mark's dogma, the dogma of the messianic secret, he himself recognized as being precisely and centrally historical. Considering that the atmosphere of the time "was saturated with eschatology" he asks whether the eschatological messianic teaching attributed to Jesus in the Gospels should not be precisely the historical element.

> For, after all, why should not Jesus think in terms of doctrine, and make history in action, just as well as a poor Evangelist can do it on paper, under the pressure of the theological interests of the primitive community.[30]
> Eschatology is simply "dogmatic history" — history as moulded by theological beliefs — which breaks in upon the natural course of history and abrogates it. Is it not even *a priori* the only conceivable view that the conduct of one who looked forward to His Messianic "Parousia" in the near future should be determined, not by the natural course of events, but by that expectation? The chaotic confusion of the narratives ought to have suggested the thought that the events had been thrown into this confusion by the volcanic force of an incalculable personality, not by some kind of carelessness or freak of the tradition.[31]

I should not leave the impression that Schweitzer accepts more of the historical data at face value than he actually does.

---

rationalistic bias. This bias leads it to project back into history what belongs to our own time, the eager struggle of the modern religious spirit with the Spirit of Jesus, and seek in history justification and authority for its beginning. The consequence is that it creates the historical Jesus in its own image, so that it is not the modern spirit influenced by the Spirit of Jesus, but the Jesus of Nazareth constructed by modern historical theology, that is set to work upon our race . . . . Any one who, admiring the force and authority of genuine rationalism, has got rid of the naive self-satisfaction of modern theology, which is in essence only the degenerate offspring of rationalism with a tincture of history, rejoices in the feebleness and smallness of its professedly historical Jesus, rejoices in all those who are beginning to doubt the truth of this portrait, rejoices in the over-severity with which it is attacked, rejoices to take a share in its destruction."

30. Schweitzer, *The Quest of the Historical Jesus*, p. 348.
31. *Ibid.*, p. 349.

Consider, for example, his consistent rejection of the miracles and his judgment that as a result of the work of Strauss "supernaturalism practically separated itself from the serious study of history" and "miracle no longer concerns the historian either positively or negatively."[32] Moreover, and this is central, his view of the kingdom of God and of the messiahship of Jesus as wholly future involves a grave distortion and even a perversion of the message of Jesus. The defect which is present in this prospective view goes far beyond being one of omission. For Schweitzer's error is not merely that he does not look upon the ministry of Jesus and the coming of the kingdom in sufficiently comprehensive terms. It is poignant and even tragic that at this very point where Schweitzer has made his most telling contribution, namely, in compelling the recognition of the eschatological as essential and even central to the teaching of Jesus, nearly every detail of the gospel narrative is forced tortuously into the framework of his distinctive scheme. His assessment of the ethics of Jesus as an *Interimsethik* and his interpretation of the meaning of the death of Jesus in terms of messianic tribulations constitute conspicuous examples of the way in which Schweitzer, as he seeks to force the narrative as a whole into conformity with his dogma of the so-called consistent eschatology, treats the data of Scripture in an extraordinarily inadequate, and frequently indeed in a quite arbitrary and highly fanciful, manner.

Another feature of Schweitzer's outlook that bears pointedly upon our evaluation of his total estimate of Jesus is concerned with his own basic attitude toward eschatology. It is ironic that the very man who did more than any other to expose the untenability of the Liberal view of Jesus because of its virtual rejection of the eschatological element should himself find this very feature just as uncongenial to his own way of thinking as it was to the Liberal himself. And what is even more revealing than the fact that Schweitzer can find no genuine place for eschatology within his own modern philosophical and religious outlook upon history is the consideration that, in the last analysis, his reconstruction of the earliest Christian history itself devaluates the eschatological. This devaluation, it may be noted in the first place, finds expression in the history

32. *Ibid.*, p. 111; *cf.* p. 95.

of the church from the beginning.   For he sums up that history as follows:

> The whole history of "Christianity" down to the present day, that is to say, the real inner history of it, is based on the delay of the Parousia, the non-occurrence of the Parousia, the abandonment of eschatology, the progress and completion of the "de-eschatologising" of religion which has been connected therewith.[33]

But secondly, and this is most illuminating of all, the situation is not merely that the church could not live with eschatology but that even Jesus himself could not at long last live with it. For at the time of his death he in effect repudiated it.   Although Jesus, as depicted by Schweitzer, deliberately went up to Jerusalem in order to die, and although every step and aspect of that climactic phase of his life was controlled by the conviction that his death would bring to realization the expected kingdom of God, even he could not hold on to this conviction to the very end.   For his dying experience was one of despair rather than of joyful and confident expectation.

> The tragedy does not consist in the modification of primitive Christianity by eschatology, but in the fate of eschatology itself, which has preserved for us all that is most precious in Jesus, but must itself wither, because He died upon the cross with a loud cry, despairing of bringing in the new heaven and the new earth — that is the real tragedy.   And not a tragedy to be dismissed with the theologian's sigh, but a liberating and life-giving influence, like every great tragedy.   For in its death-pangs eschatology bore to the Greek genius a wonder-child, the mystic, sensuous, Early-Christian doctrine of immortality, and consecrated Christianity as the religion of immortality to take the place of the slowly dying civilisation of the ancient world.[34]

With these observations in view one is prepared for the conclusion that for all of his apparent "conservatism" in treating the historicity of the Gospel narratives Schweitzer is basically a radical, radical not only in the thoroughness of his historical reconstruction but also and especially in his total estimate of Jesus as being dominated from beginning to end, or one should say almost to the very end, by a fantastic illusion concerning himself and the meaning of his life.

The fact that Schweitzer wrote a dissertation for his medical

33. *Ibid.*, p. 358.
34. *Ibid.*, p. 254.

degree on the subject, *The Psychiatric Estimate of Jesus*,[35] may indicate that he himself perhaps felt that it might be difficult for many to reconcile his own reconstruction with the sanity of Jesus. Whatever his motive may have been, I do not believe that the question which is naturally raised as to the normality of Jesus' self-consciousness, on Schweitzer's construction, is adequately answered by way of reference to the apocalyptic hopes and expectations of the time. But even if a panel of experts could agree in pronouncing Schweitzer's Jesus sane he would still have to be regarded as one of the most preposterous and deluded men of all history in view of the role which he claimed for himself. Schweitzer may believe that his historical Jesus must take the place of the non-existent Liberal Jesus. But this supposedly prospective Messiah who himself was at last completely disillusioned, and whose central teaching concerning the future had to be abandoned by the Christian Church, offers no better explanation of the origin of the church than does the Liberal Jesus. And this eschatological Jesus, as he is portrayed in detail by Schweitzer, is so uncongenial that one might not have been surprised if he had come to the conclusion that Jesus had no permanent significance for religion and that at most he was worthy of a place among the curious and bizarre religious fanatics of the past. In spite of some appearances to the contrary, accordingly, the accent in Schweitzer's construction falls upon discontinuity rather than continuity in assessing Jesus' responsibility for the future.

Having made all these observations regarding Schweitzer's view of Jesus Christ we are likely to suppose that, in his case at least, there can be no talk of a persistence of Liberalism. He has joined forces with Wrede in showing that the Liberal Jesus was non-existent. Moreover, the eschatological hope which, according to his estimate, contains all that is most precious in Jesus, has for the modern man withered away. Nevertheless, as one proceeds with the reading of Schweitzer one comes upon the astonishing discovery that even he is really a Liberal at heart and boldly claims the authority of Jesus for this Liberalism.

His approach to be sure is not the historicism of the Ritschlian

---

35. Albert Schweitzer, *Die psychiatrische Beurteilung Jesu* (Tübingen: Mohr, 1913) ; Eng. trans., *The Psychiatric Study of Jesus* (Boston: Beacon, 1948) ; *cf.* Albert Schweitzer, *My Life and Thought* (London: Allen & Unwin, 1933) , pp. 131ff.

School. There is rather a fundamental indifference to the results of historical criticism which is akin to that of the Hegelian Strauss, and which, it is claimed (quite erroneously, I believe), finds expression in the word of Paul in II Corinthians 5:16: "Even though we have known Christ after the flesh, yet now we know him so no more." Understandably, therefore, his teaching about morality as summed up in his "ethical mysticism" differs from classical Liberalism. But there is no mistaking the fact that it is a form of Liberalism after all. Having confessed that he himself had suffered because he had come to feel that he had to join in the work of destroying the portrait of Jesus on which Liberal Christianity based its appeal, he declared:

> At the same time I was convinced that this liberal Christianity was not reduced to living on an historical illusion, but could equally appeal to the Jesus of history, and further that it carried its justification in itself.
>
> For even if that liberal Christianity has to give up identifying its belief with the teachings of Jesus in the way it used to think possible, it still has the spirit of Jesus not against it but on its side. Jesus no doubt fits His teaching into the late-Jewish Messianic dogma. But He does not think dogmatically. He formulates no doctrine. He is far from judging any man's belief by reference to any standard of dogmatic correctness. Nowhere does He demand of His hearers that they shall sacrifice thinking to believing. Quite the contrary! He bids them meditate upon religion. In the Sermon on the Mount He lets ethics, as the essence of religion, flood their hearts, leading them to judge the value of piety for what it makes of a man from the ethical point of view. Within the Messianic hopes which His hearers carry in their hearts, He kindles the fire of an ethical faith. Thus the Sermon on the Mount becomes the incontestable charter of liberal Christianity. The truth that the ethical is the essence of religion is firmly established on the authority of Jesus.[36]

This quotation from his autobiography of 1931 simply re-echoes what he had already said in the *Quest* of 1906:

> Jesus means something to our world because a mighty spiritual force streams forth from Him and flows through our time also. This fact can neither be shaken nor confirmed by any historical discovery. It is the solid foundation of Christianity.[37]

We are experiencing what Paul experienced. In the very

36. Schweitzer, *My Life and Thought*, pp. 73f.
37. Schweitzer, *The Quest of the Historical Jesus*, p. 397.

moment when we were coming nearer to the historical Jesus than men had ever come before, and were already stretching out our hands to draw Him into our own time, we have been obliged to give up the attempt and acknowledge our failure in that paradoxical saying: "If we have known Christ after the flesh yet henceforth know we Him no more." And further we must be prepared to find that the historical knowledge of the personality and life of Jesus will not be a help, but perhaps even an offence to religion.

But the truth is, it is not Jesus as historically known, but Jesus as spiritually arisen within men, who is significant for our time and can help it. Not the historical Jesus, but the spirit which goes forth from Him and in the spirits of men strives for new influence and rule, is that which overcomes the world. . . .

The abiding and the eternal in Jesus is absolutely independent of historical knowledge and can only be understood by contact with His spirit which is still at work in the world. In proportion as we have the Spirit of Jesus we have the true knowledge of Jesus.

Jesus as a concrete historical personality remains a stranger to our time, but His spirit which lies hidden in His words, is known in simplicity, and its influence is direct. Every saying contains in its own way the whole Jesus.[38]

There is a profound inner inconsistency in this effort to clothe modern Liberal views of religion and ethics with the authority of Jesus as he spoke in the Sermon on the Mount — or at least with that of his "spirit" as it supposedly lies hidden in his words — and yet to insist on the thoroughgoing and radical indifference to the history of Jesus which is so unambiguously formulated by Schweitzer. To put the matter in somewhat different words, the consistently eschatological Jesus who is dominated from beginning to end in every thought and action by an apocalyptic dogma is not truly identifiable with the person whom Schweitzer has de-eschatologized so as to allow him, or his "spirit," to speak forth with the voice of a Liberal Jesus. That Schweitzer supposes that he can effect a harmony or synthesis between these contradictory elements does to be sure demonstrate once again that Liberalism, even under the most adverse conditions possible, somehow manages to survive. Even in Schweitzer there is a remarkable element of continuity with Liberalism. Neither in this aspect of agreement nor in

38. *Ibid.*, p. 399.

that of his fundamental difference is there any progress toward a satisfying answer to the question of the ultimate origins of Christianity, of the gospel and the Gospels.

Rudolf Bultmann

In pursuing further this line of inquiry as to whether various modern views of Jesus truly explain the origin of the Gospels it is necessary now to take what may appear to be a great leap forward in order to say something about the present situation. Regrettably it is impossible now to undertake an analysis of such leading New Testament specialists as Dodd, Jeremias, Cullmann, and other influential scholars both at home and abroad. It would be important to take note of the substantial differences which exist among these men. In particular, the older Liberalism and the so-called neo-orthodoxy would have to be distinguished. My own impression is, however, that for all of such variations and differences, the elements of unity and continuity are even more conspicuous. I am not happy in confining myself to such generalities here but hope that at least some slight amendment in the direction of specificity may be made by undertaking a brief assessment of Bultmann's place in this development.

Considering how complex and controversial a figure Bultmann is, it may seem foolhardy to say anything at all about his position without undertaking a rather comprehensive exposition of it. The latter however is not a genuine option. And I believe moreover that one may hopefully engage in an appraisal of his position only if one first does some justice to elements of basic continuity with various predecessors including Wrede and Schweitzer.

Bultmann's agreement with and indebtedness to Wrede are particularly noteworthy. Writing in 1930 Bultmann stated that Wrede's book on *The Messianic Secret* was "the most important work in the field of gospel research in the generation now past."[39] What Bultmann has chiefly in mind is evidently that Wrede must be given a major share of credit for developing the view that the Gospels are products of the faith and life of the early communities rather than authentic sources for the

---

39. Rudolf Bultmann, *Die Erforschung der synoptischen Evangelien*, 2te Aufl. (Giessen: Töpelmann, 1930), pp. 10f.; Eng. trans., by F. C. Grant in *Form Criticism* (Chicago: Willett, Clark, 1934), p. 22.

study of, or witnesses to, the life of Jesus upon earth. As a corollary of this view that the Gospels are theological rather than historical there was a common negativism and skepticism so far as the trustworthiness of the witness of the Gospels to Jesus Christ is concerned. And this finds most pointed expression in their fundamental agreement with regard to the question of the historicity of the messianic consciousness. Although, as we have seen, Wrede appears to stop just short of an absolute denial of its historicity, and identifies his position as that of essential agnosticism, Bultmann leaves us in no doubt whatsoever that he regards this element of the tradition as distinctly mythological.[40]

The part which Bultmann played in the development and application of the method of form criticism required, to be sure, in some respects a modification and refinement of Wrede's general position. This method was advanced by its supporters, it may be recalled, as constituting a more scientific and objective critical approach than had been previously developed to isolate the various strata of tradition and to recover the supposedly original bedrock of tradition represented by the life of Jesus. Nevertheless, as Bultmann applied the method, rather than enlarging substantially upon the tradition which was thought to afford authentic witness to Jesus, it was judged to confirm the radically skeptical view. Thus in his book *Jesus* there is a picture merely of one who, as rabbi and prophet, was simply the bearer of a religious and ethical message. As the bearer of that message Jesus had no place whatsoever within it. And when pressed by those who asked whether on his approach there remained any substantial argument for the historicity of Jesus himself, Bultmann answered that, while he himself held to such historicity, he had no quarrel with any who might wish to take "Jesus" as an abbreviated designation for the historical phenomenon.[41] At this crucial point therefore Bultmann's accent upon discontinuity between Jesus, on

---

40. *Cf.* Rudolf Bultmann, *Jesus* (Berlin: Deutsche Bibliothek, 1926) ; Eng. trans., *Jesus and the Word* by Louise P. Smith and Erminie H. Lantero (New York: Scribner's, 1934) , pp. 9, 12ff.; *The Theology of the New Testament* (New York: Scribner's, 1951) , I, 26ff.; *Jesus Christ and Mythology* (London: SCM, 1958) , p. 16.

41. Bultmann, *Jesus*, p. 17 (Eng. trans., p. 14) ; *cf.* Bultmann, *Die Erforschung der synoptischen Evangelien*, pp. 32f., 38ff. (Eng. trans., pp. 60ff., 71ff.) .

the one hand, and the church, the Christian message, and the Christian documents, on the other hand, appears to go beyond that of Wrede, not to speak of Strauss, and approaches the radicalism of Bruno Bauer and of others who denied the historicity of Jesus.

The agreement of Bultmann with Schweitzer is obviously of a more restricted kind. Nevertheless, it remains highly illuminating. The appraisal of the history of Jesus, and especially of his own conception of his person and mission, is quite divergent, though it may be remarked in passing that in a sense Schweitzer's final estimate of Jesus' conception of his mission was that it was also mythological. The agreement here may therefore perhaps be more precisely defined as an agreement with Johannes Weiss who enunciated a "consistent eschatological" view of the message of Jesus without applying this concept to the person of Jesus as Schweitzer came to do. In any case Bultmann agrees with both Weiss and Schweitzer that, for Jesus, the kingdom was thought of as supernatural and miraculous, wholly other and wholly future. Moreover, Bultmann admits that Jesus himself must have expected a violent eschatological drama, including the coming of the Son of Man, the resurrection of the dead, the judgment and the end of the world.[42]

In spite of this important difference, however, there emerges here an enlightening point of contact with Liberalism. Bultmann after all finds the eschatological no more congenial than do Harnack and Schweitzer and modern criticism as a whole. Harnack also recognized the historicity of the teaching of Jesus concerning the eschatological denouement. But by way of arbitrarily drawing a line between the eschatological and non-eschatological views of the kingdom he apparently supposed that he could jettison the former by the mere statement that it represented "an idea which Jesus simply shared with his contemporaries" while the other was his own original contribution.[43] Bultmann may be more consistent than Harnack in that he does not distinguish two strands in Jesus' teaching. But is he not as arbitrary when he dogmatically affirms that

42. The reference to the coming of the Son of Man is consistent with his denial of the historicity of the messianic consciousness, it may be recalled, because Bultmann maintains the thesis that Jesus distinguished between himself and the Son of Man.

43. Adolf Harnack, *Das Wesen des Christentums*, p. 35; *cf.* pp. 27f. (Eng. trans., p. 54; *cf.* p. 42).

the distinctively eschatological evaluation of Jesus' message concerning the kingdom likewise consisted of notions which Jesus shared with his contemporaries but do not constitute his real meaning or interest?

But what, according to Bultmann, is for Jesus the real meaning of his eschatological message?

> The real significance of the "Kingdom of God" for the message of Jesus lies in any case not in the dramatic events associated with its coming . . . . It does not interest Jesus at all as a condition, but rather as the transcendent event, which signifies for man the great either-or, which compels man to decision.[44]

In spite of the clear implication of Jesus' teaching to the contrary Bultmann says that the future kingdom of God is not something which shall come in the course of time. It is not a condition or possession or state which is realized in history or as the goal of history. It is not a future something which can ever become a present something; the future deliverance by God never arrives as a state of rest and salvation. Its significance is that it remains future and confronts man as the last hour, compelling him to face the great either-or of life.[45] At this point it is easy to detect the impact of the dialectical theology upon Bultmann. And one observes the devastating effect which its characteristic disjunction between history and faith has for exegesis.

What Bultmann has to say regarding the real meaning which Jesus found in eschatology is, moreover, of more than ordinary interest because it provides a substantial transition to his approach to the subject of the apostolic *kerygma* which was set forth in his famous essay on "The Problem of the Demythologizing of the New Testament Proclamation" which was first published in 1941. It can hardly be gainsaid that this essay, especially since its republication in 1948, has been in the very center of theological discussion round the world and is without serious doubt one of the most controversial, influential and provocative essays of all time. The opinion seems to be rather widely held that this essay represents a distinctly new phase in the development of Bultmann's thought, an opinion that might appear to find support in the violent eruption of protest against his views in the years that followed. To some extent indeed one can appreciate this evaluation. For now Bultmann centers

---

44. Bultmann, *Jesus*, p. 40 (Eng. trans., pp. 40f.). Quoted by permission.
45. *Cf. ibid.*, pp. 49ff. (Eng. trans., pp. 51ff.) .

attention upon the Christian proclamation as set forth in the
New Testament as a whole rather than narrowly upon the message of Jesus. He rejects this *kerygma* as mythological in a more
rounded and emphatic way. He centers attention upon the
necessity, from his own point of view — if there is to be no
personal *sacrificium intellectus* and the *kerygma* is to be preserved — of engaging in a demythologizing of the proclamation.
And associating his thought intimately with that of Heidegger,
he believes that it is possible to recover a genuine understanding
of human existence which was enshrined in myth. There may
therefore very well have been some development in Bultmann's
thought but the strong element of continuity should not be
overlooked. The later Bultmann is not really a new Bultmann
but one who merely works out with greater fullness, clarity and
force a basic feature of his earlier thinking.[46]

Bultmann's understanding of the Christian proclamation,
after the action of demythologizing, cannot be set forth here
in any truly adequate way. But it surely centers in what he
has to say concerning the preaching of the cross and the resurrection of Christ. For him the cross understood as concerned
with one who was the pre-existent, incarnate Son of God and
as such without sin, and who vicariously endured the punishment for sin on our behalf, is "a hotch-potch of sacrificial and
juridical analogies, which have ceased to be tenable for us
today."[47] Its real meaning, however, is to be discovered in the
following:

> To believe in the cross of Christ does not mean to concern
> ourselves with a mythical process wrought outside of us and
> our world, or with an objective event turned by God to our
> advantage, but rather to make the cross of Christ our own,

46. *Cf.* "Rudolf Bultmann's Jesus" in *PBA*, p. 148, n. 65. It is noteworthy
also that the influence of Heidegger on Bultmann's thought has been
traced back as far as 1927. *Cf.* L. Malvelez, *The Christian Message and
Myth* (London: SCM, 1958), p. 212.

47. Rudolf Bultmann, "New Testament and Mythology: The Mythological Element in the Message of the New Testament and the Problem of its
Re-interpretation" in *Kerygma and Myth*, edited by H. W. Bartsch and
translated by R. H. Fuller (London: S.P.C.K., 1957), I, 35. The essay,
"Neues Testament und Mythologie," in the original German was published
first in *Beiträge z. Ev. Theologie*, 7 (1941). Somewhat later, when it became the center of a burning theological and ecclesiastical controversy, it
was assigned the first place in Bartsch's work, *Kerygma und Mythos* (Ham-
burg: Reich, 1948), Volume I.

to undergo crucifixion with him . . . . In other words, the cross
is not just an event of the past which can be contemplated in
detachment, but the eschatological event in and beyond time,
for as far as its meaning — that is, its meaning for faith —
is concerned, it is an ever-present reality.[48]

In its redemptive aspect the cross of Christ is no mere mythical
event, but a permanent historical fact originating in the past
historical event which is the crucifixion of Jesus. The abiding
significance of the cross is that it is the judgement of the world,
the judgement and the deliverance of man. In this sense Christ
is crucified "for us", a phrase which does not necessarily imply
any theory of sacrifice or satisfaction. This interpretation of
the cross as a permanent fact rather than a mythological event
does far more justice to the redemptive significance of the
event of the past than any of the traditional interpretations.
In the last resort mythological language is only a medium for
conveying the meaning of the past event. The real meaning of
the cross is that it has created a new and permanent situation in
history. The preaching of the cross as the event of redemption
challenges all who hear it to appropriate the significance for
themselves, to be willing to be crucified with Christ.[49]

While the crucifixion of Jesus is an historical fact the resurrection, understood as the resuscitation of a corpse, is not. The
latter is simply incredible. It appears as a fact within the New
Testament, Bultmann acknowledges. But just as he was prepared to distinguish between Jesus' real interest in eschatology
and the eschatological message itself, so he is ready to say that
"the New Testament is interested in the resurrection of Christ
simply and solely because it is the eschatological event *par excellence.*"[50] The resurrection accordingly is an article of faith,
and "faith in the resurrection is really the same thing as faith
in the saving efficacy of the cross, faith in the cross as the cross
of Christ."[51]

The real Easter faith is faith in the word of preaching
which brings illumination. If the event of Easter Day is in
any sense an historical event additional to the event of the
cross, it is nothing else than the rise of faith in the risen Lord,
since it was this faith which led to the apostolic preaching. The
resurrection itself is not an event of past history.[52]

48. *Ibid.,* p. 36.
49. *Ibid.,* p. 37.
50. *Ibid.,* p. 40.
51. *Ibid.,* p. 41.
52. *Ibid.,* p. 42.

It thus appears that for Bultmann the real meaning of the proclamation of the death and resurrection of Christ, like Jesus' preaching concerning the coming of the kingdom of God, is to be found in the present encounter mediated by the present action of preaching. Both, as we have seen, are subsumed under the phrase "the eschatological event." As such, in spite of his reduction of the Jesus of history to a mere prophet and rabbi and his explicit denial of the historicity of the resurrection, this "eschatological event" is characterized by Bultmann as being "once for all."

> For this "once for all" is not the uniqueness of an historical event but means that a particular historical event, that is, Jesus Christ, is to be understood as the eschatological "once for all". As an eschatological event this "once for all" is always present in the proclaimed word, not as a timeless truth, but as happening here and now . . . . It is the eschatological once-for-all because the word becomes event here and now in the living voice of the preaching.[53]

It would take us beyond the scope of our present study to engage in a substantial critique of Bultmann's demythologizing of the New Testament proclamation. This would necessarily involve one in an examination of his philosophical and theological presuppositions, in an analysis of the basic features of his theological outlook, the validity of his historical criticism, the justification if any for his view, or views, of myth as applied to the New Testament, and the soundness of his exegetical evaluations. Most central of all, I am inclined to say, is the defectiveness of his doctrine of God. In spite of certain accents upon transcendence when he speaks of God as the Remote and Near, the biblical view of the transcendence of God as the sovereign Creator, Lord and Saviour is either forthrightly rejected or fails lamentably to come to its own rights. This is a point which appears in sharp focus, for example, when he speaks sympathetically of the modern conception of human nature "as a self-subsistent unity immune from the interference of supernatural powers."[54] The pervasively radical consequences of this approach for his understanding of nature and history, of religion and morality in general, of the person and work of Jesus Christ, and of the nature of the human response, need not be spelled out here in detail.

53. Bultmann, *Jesus Christ and Mythology*, p. 82.
54. Bultmann, "New Testament and Mythology," p. 7.

On the subject of Jesus Christ and the gospel, however, one final observation must still be made. It is that in spite of his valiant efforts to recover the supposedly real meaning of Jesus and of the Christian proclamation, his interpretation of the historical foundation of the Christian message does violent injustice to the plain import of the New Testament itself. Paul, for example, does not indicate any disparagement of the historical foundations when he speaks of not knowing Christ according to the flesh. For in keeping with the context as a whole, and II Corinthians 5:16a in particular, Paul makes clear that the phrase "after the flesh" is to be understood as qualifying the action of knowing. As a new creature in Christ Jesus he henceforth knows no man in a fleshly manner; it is obviously quite impossible to allow that Paul might be saying that after he became a Christian he had no knowledge of, or interest in, the history of any man. There was a time before his conversion when he evaluated every man from a sinful point of view, and this applied specifically and pre-eminently to Christ himself. But now he is concerned to live unto Christ who "died and rose again" (v. 15), "who knew no sin" but was "made to be sin on our behalf" and in whom God was reconciling the world unto himself (vv. 18-21). The wonderful riches of the present meaning of Christ's redemption on our behalf accordingly received powerful explication here. But this is not done in such a way as to suggest for a moment that the present benefits of redemption were conceivable and realizable apart from the truth of the message which confronts us first of all with the uniqueness and particularity of the history of Jesus Christ and of his death and resurrection.

In Bultmann's thought as a whole the element of continuity between Jesus and the Christian proclamation is therefore made to hang upon what, even from his own point of view, would have to be regarded as a very fragile and precarious basis. On his own fundamental analysis of the figure of Jesus as merely a prophet and rabbi, and of the Christian proclamation as set forth in terms of the redemption effected by a supernatural being, the pre-existent Son of God, it would be difficult to avoid the conclusion that Jesus was not really the founder of Christianity. And this situation is not genuinely relieved unless one is persuaded that Bultmann's hermeneutics provides a responsible way of interpreting Jesus and the gospel.

CHAPTER NINE

THE SELF - REVELATION OF
JESUS CHRIST

THE unquestionable verdict which a study of the main trends of modern criticism forces upon us is that the so-called historical Jesus cannot possibly be regarded as responsible for the gospel tradition as a whole and thus ultimately for the Gospels themselves. There may not be complete unanimity in detail with regard to this historical Jesus for there are various differences in the ways in which contents of the Gospels may be positively utilized or rejected as unauthentic. But in every case the "historical" Jesus differs radically from his portrayal in the Gospels. We must pursue the question therefore as to the true nature of the self-witness of Jesus as attested by the Gospels and whether it is not this Jesus who alone can account for the origin of the gospel tradition and its final inscripturation in the Gospels.

One may well begin with the simple though profound affirmation that Jesus claimed to be the Christ, the Messiah. What the evangelist John says with regard to the purpose of his own Gospel, namely, that "these are written that ye may believe that Jesus is the Christ, the Son of God" (20:31) might well have been said also by the other evangelists. And it is recognized universally, I believe, that the authors of the Gospels assume throughout that Jesus was indeed the Messiah and disclosed himself to be such in word and deed.

The number of recorded instances where Jesus himself uses the title Christ is very small. There are a few isolated instances such as that of Mark 9:41 where there is an assurance of reward "for whosoever shall give you a cup of water to drink, because ye are Christ's" and Matthew 23:10 with its warning: "Neither be ye called masters; for one is your Master, the Christ." In Matthew 22:42 Jesus introduces instruction concerning the messiahship by appeal to Psalm 110 with the question, "What

think ye concerning the Christ?", but without making a direct
claim at this point to be the Christ. For the rest, apart from
the birth narratives (Mt. 2:2, 4; Lk. 1:32f., 2:11, 26) and the
resurrection narrative of Luke (cf. 24:26, 42), the affirmations
of Jesus principally take the form of responding to the declarations or questions of Peter, the chief priests and Pilate (Mt.
16:16f., 20; 26:63, 64; 27:11, 17, 22 and parallels). Such reac-
tions on the part of others, however, as well as the mocking of
the soldiers and of the chief priests and the superscription upon
the cross (Mt. 27:29, 42; 27:37 and parallels) are not intelligible
apart from the supposition that Jesus had identified himself
as the Messiah.

In view of the relative paucity of such claims to be the Christ
it would appear that Jesus was somewhat restrained in the use
of this specific terminology, perhaps because of current misin-
terpretations and misunderstandings of the nature of the coming
of the messianic king. But in any case it is evident from the
total witness of the Gospels that Jesus determined to present his
messianic claims for the most part by the use of other titles
such as the Son of Man and the Son of God as well as by the
predications that he made concerning himself.[1]

Although the designation Christ or Messiah may not have
served most happily, in the given historical situation, to sum
up what Jesus thought concerning himself and his mission, its
place within the formulation of messianic hopes was so basic
that it could hardly be expendable. The fact, moreover, that

1. Cullmann does not make a convincing case for his view which tends
to reduce the positive significance even of the passages bearing upon Jesus'
claim of Christhood, and he is particularly far-fetched in his development
of the thesis that Jesus was confronted by the temptation in the wilderness,
by Peter's confession and at other points, to adopt a political conception of
messiahship. Cf. Oscar Cullmann, Die Christologie des Neuen Testaments,
2te Aufl. (Tübingen: Mohr, 1958), pp. 117ff., pp. 122ff., pp. 286ff.; Eng.
trans., The Christology of the N.T. (London: SCM, 1959), pp. 117ff., 122ff.
280ff.; Peter Disciple-Apostle-Martyr (Philadelphia: Westminster, 1953),
pp. 170ff.; The State in the New Testament (New York: Scribner's, 1956),
pp. 17f.; cf. pp. 9, 16, 24, 27, 30, 40. The response of Jesus to Peter's
confession in Mt. 16, e.g., teaches indeed that Peter had an inadequate
conception of messiahship, and in particular that he did not reckon with
the program of suffering which was to precede the messianic glory. But
nothing suggests that Peter conceived of messiahship at this time in
political terms, and that Jesus in correcting Peter's, "Far be it from thee,
Lord," intended to reject a temptation to assume political leadership. See
my comments in WTJ, XVI (May, 1954), p. 188; XIX (Nov., 1956),
pp. 77f.

in the writings of the New Testament outside of the Gospels the name Christ was so constantly associated with that of Jesus gives eloquent testimony to the conclusion that the Christian church did not contemplate her Lord apart from the place which he was recognized as occupying as the Messiah who fulfilled the hope of Israel.[2]

Analysis of Messiahship

In seeking now to pursue further the question of the meaning of the messiahship within the New Testament we are clearly brought under obligation to turn back first of all to the Old Testament. This is a necessity which the New Testament itself places upon us because it so constantly confronts us with the thought that Jesus made his messianic claims and acted as Messiah because of his understanding of the Old Testament and its application to himself. There is surely no need to review here all the evidence for this conclusion. But the point is made perfectly clear when one contemplates the feature of the Christian message which traces *the necessity of the passion* of the Messiah to the fulfillment of the divine Scriptures. Thus Peter in his discourse in the temple, as reported in Acts 3, having declared that the men of Israel were guilty because of the death of Jesus, the Holy and Righteous One and the Prince of Life (vv. 14f.), announces:

> But the things which God foreshowed by the mouth of all the prophets, that his Christ should suffer, he thus fulfilled (v. 18).

And Paul in the synagogue of the Jews at Thessalonica

> For three sabbath days reasoned with them from the Scriptures, opening and alleging that it behooved the Christ to suffer, and

---

2. The very frequency of the use of the name "Christ", including over 400 instances in Paul, is hardly explicable apart from a recognition of this fact. In many cases, to be sure, there is much to be said for the view that, especially in the combination "Jesus Christ" and at times in the simple designation "Christ", it has become a proper name, and does not necessarily involve reflection on its etymological force or historical background. Nevertheless, even the use as a proper name points to the conclusion that it owes its origin to a situation in the Church where its meaning was reflected upon in relation to messianic expectations. Moreover, the fact that Paul repeatedly uses the order "Christ Jesus" tells against any view that the name was largely formal; this is likewise at least possible of many cases where "Christ" is used alone. *Cf.* especially Acts 4:26f. and II Cor. 1:21 where the name Christ is mentioned in connection with anointing.

to rise again from the dead; and that this Jesus, whom I proclaim unto you, is the Christ (17:1-3).

And this pattern of apostolic proclamation simply follows that of our Lord's own teaching as reported in the Gospels. Luke is perhaps most explicit in this regard when he quotes the risen Lord as saying to his disciples:

> These are my words which I spake unto you, while I was yet with you, that all things must needs be fulfilled, which are written in the law of Moses, and the prophets, and the psalms, concerning me. Then opened he their mind, that they might understand the scriptures; and he said unto them, Thus it is written, that the Christ should suffer, and rise again from the dead the third day; and that repentance and remission of sins should be preached in his name unto all the nations, beginning from Jerusalem. Ye are witnesses of these things (24:44-48; cf. 24:25-27).

Though spoken following the resurrection this discourse does not introduce a new theme but, as the quotation explicitly indicates, it is offered as a summary of the proclamation of Jesus in his public ministry.

Although utterances concerning the passion or reflections upon it are not completely absent from the earlier chapters we all know that they are specially conspicuous in the latter half of the Gospels following the confession of Peter. And in fact they are so frequent and so largely explain the actual course of events that all these latter chapters, as has been observed above, may, with very little exaggeration, be characterized as passion narratives. One may not overlook the fact that Jesus' pronouncements concerning his passion characteristically speak of "the Son of Man" rather than "the Messiah." But there is genuine continuity between the confession of Jesus as the Christ, elicited from the disciples by Jesus himself as the appraisal that stood over against ordinary opinion, and the instruction which Jesus immediately undertook to bring forcefully home to them, the messianic program of passion, of crucifixion and of resurrection which awaited him. This connection is indeed especially clear in Matthew (cf. 16:17ff., 20, 21), but it is surely implicit also in Mark (8:27-33) and Luke (9:18-22). The passion and resurrection pronouncement of this occasion is substantially repeated on two other occasions.[3] In these passages there is a

---

3. Mk. 9:30-32 and 10:32-34 and parallels; cf. Mk. 9:12; Mt. 17:12; Lk. 17:25; Mk. 10:45. The survey of the contents of Mark, pp. 71ff. above, bears on this point as well as more broadly on the theme of this chapter.

solemn emphasis upon the necessity of the messianic passion, and this necessity must evidently be thought of as that which was involved in the requirement that God's plan of redemption should be fulfilled. The declaration of the divine plan is not traced at every point to the teaching of the Scriptures of the Old Testament. But it does come to explicit expression not only in the passages from Luke 24 which have been quoted above but also in Mark 14:21 where Jesus says: "The Son of man goeth as it is written of him" (cf. Mt. 26:24; Lk. 22:22. See also Mk. 9:12; 12:10; Lk. 22:37).

As one turns to the Old Testament one is impressed with the observation that nowhere does the title "the Messiah" appear nor is messiahship considered in the abstract. Rather the evidence which is pertinent to our study is that in which various persons are described as God's anointed or, to follow the common LXX rendering which also finds expression in the formulation of Simeon's expectation in Luke 2:26, the anointed of the Lord. Thus Saul, who was chosen and appointed by God to exercise rule over his people Israel, was at God's command anointed by Samuel to the royal office (I Sam. 9:16f.; 10:1) and in view of the relationship which he thereby sustained to God he was called the Lord's anointed (I Sam. 24:6). It was pre-eminently David, however, who as king and as the one to whom the promise came that the throne of his kingdom would be established forever, who is described in these terms (Ps. 2:2; 18:50; 89:20-37; 132:10ff., 17; cf. II Sam. 7:12ff.). And our understanding of the meaning of the relationship with God sustained by one who was anointed is enlarged when one recalls that at David's anointing by Samuel "the Spirit of God came mightily upon David from that day forward" (I Sam. 16:3, 13; cf. I Sam. 10:1ff., 9ff.; Isa. 61:1). There is no record of the anointing of Cyrus, but even this heathen ruler could be designated by God as "his anointed" in virtue of the fact that he was commissioned and qualified by him to perform a special task in the fulfillment of God's purpose.[4]

Those who were anointed of God were not restricted to kings. Prophets were not ordinarily anointed; Elisha appears as an exception (I Kgs. 19:16). But priests were regularly anointed as they were consecrated to minister in the priest's

4. Cullmann, *Die Christologie des Neuen Testaments*, p. 144 (Eng trans., p. 114).

office (cf. Ex. 28:41; Num. 3:3). And the high priest of Israel was designated, with the employment of the same verbal noun used to speak of the anointed king, as "the anointed priest" (Lev. 4:3, 5, 16).

If now one asks what these various references to divine anointing have in common or, to put it more precisely, what divine action or actions are essential for the understanding of the relationships which the anointed ones sustained to him, I believe that they may be subsumed under two main heads. The first concerns the fact of *divine commission,* the second that of *divine endowment.*

(1) One who is anointed of the Lord is viewed as having received his office by divine appointment through his being anointed as an individual. And thus even in such a case as the Davidic dynastic succession, the authority of the kings does not stem simply from filial succession but from the divine initiative and action. The anointed ones therefore are Representatives of God and are clothed with his authority in carrying out the functions of their office. One should add at once, however, that there is another side to this coin. Those who are appointed to exercise authority are under appointment to perform the will of God; theirs is a divine commission but they are in duty bound to fulfill the terms of their commission; they are *the Representatives of God* but they are also *the Servants of the Lord.*

(2) Those who are appointed to office by God through his action of anointing are therewith also qualified to carry out the obligations of their office. And as we have seen from this point of view the enduement is on various occasions described as the coming of the Holy Spirit upon a person.[5] In a recent article W. C. van Unnik, writing on the theme, "Jesus the Christ," singles out the feature of bestowal of the Spirit as virtually

5. This analysis of messiahship follows rather closely that of Geerhardus Vos in *The Self-Disclosure of Jesus* (New York: Doran, 1926; rev. ed. Grand Rapids: Eerdmans, 1954), pp. 107ff. Vos adds a third feature which he describes as "the close association with God and the consequent sacrosanctness of the one on whom the anointing has been bestowed" (p. 109), an element which is no doubt present in certain Old Testament contexts. Nevertheless, at best this feature seems to be a consequence of the other ingredients rather than of the very essence of the meaning of anointing. Moreover, Vos does not seem to me to be thoroughly convincing when he seeks to find evidence of the reflection of this third feature in the history of Jesus (cf. p. 110).

synonymous with anointing.[6]   And applying this analysis to
the New Testament he declares that the essential element in
the messiahship for Jesus and the early Christian church was
"not the outward activity of the king, but *the person possessed
by the Spirit."*[7]   Although van Unnik's thesis may seem to be
somewhat too simple in view of the omission of the first factor
outlined above, it may be acknowledged as being, so far as its
main thrust is concerned, largely in agreement with the approach taken here.   The element of divine commission is basic,
but I would hasten to add that in my opinion it does not necessarily enjoy temporal, but at most logical, priority.   Appointment and endowment coincide in the one action of anointing.

On the background of the insights gained by means of linguistic analysis concerning the meaning of anointing, one may
fruitfully turn to a study of messianic prophecy in the Old
Testament.   Obviously, however, this is a subject which is far
beyond the scope of the present work.   A few general remarks
must suffice.   In the first place, the New Testament itself is
constantly affirming or presupposing the presence of such
prophecy in the law, the prophets and the psalms (*cf.* Lk.
24:44).   Moreover, the expectation of the coming of the Messiah as disclosed in the Old Testament is clearly not an isolated one; where it appears it is rather a feature of the broader
expectation of the eschatological salvation of the people of God.
Nor do we encounter a systematic delineation of the figure of
the future Messiah.   There is no messianic stereotype.   There
is no prophecy in which in clear-cut fashion we are confronted
with one who is supremely the Anointed of the Lord and in
whose office there is a converging of the lines of kingly, priestly
and prophetic activity.   Rather there are many strands of messianic prophecy with a variety of designations and with now
one function and again another coming to expression.   The
Isaianic Servant of the Lord, although not specifically designated
as the Messiah, comes closest to providing such a comprehensive delineation.   For he is the chosen servant of God upon
whom the Spirit of God has been placed (Isa. 42:1), who is
the kingly judge and leader and commander to the peoples, a
witness to the peoples and a light to the Gentiles and one who
freely, that the divine plan of redemption might be accom-

6. *NTS,* 8 (January, 1962), pp. 101ff.
7. *Ibid.,* p. 115; *cf.* p. 113.

plished, gave up his life as a trespass-offering for many (*cf.* Isa. 42:2-4; 55:4; 49:5f.; 52:13-53:12.   See also 61:1-4).

But all of the messianic prophecies together and those concerned with the Servant of the Lord in particular, however indispensable and pertinent they are for our understanding of their fulfillment in Christ, must be thought of as *partial and preliminary* to the fullness of revelation which came to manifestation in Christ himself. The concept of the fulfillment of the Old Testament revelation appears within the New as marking not merely the realization in history of what had been disclosed beforehand through the prophets, but as itself constituting a new age of revelation continuous with the Old and yet transcending it because of the absoluteness and finality of Christ himself. This is a perspective which is delineated with special clarity and emphasis in the Epistle to the Hebrews, as even its opening words reflect: "God, having of old times spoken unto the fathers in the prophets by diverse portions and diverse manners, hath at the end of these days spoken unto us in a Son, whom he appointed heir of all things, through whom also he made the worlds. . . ." But what Hebrews says so unambiguously appears, when the New Testament evidence is examined in detail, to be the point of view which underlies the whole of it.

The question whether Jesus himself transformed the concept of messiahship has often been raised in connection with evaluations of the data of the Gospels and particularly as the historicity of the messianic consciousness of Jesus has been debated. Certainly the term "transformation" is none too strong when one thinks of Jesus' evident reaction to various contemporaneous messianic expectations and especially those of a nationalistic character which in effect made the Messiah subservient to the supposedly best interests of the nation and people rather than to God. As Geerhardus Vos has said,

> The dominating characteristic of Jesus' Messiahship in the Gospels consists in its being absolutely God-centered. The office exists primarily for the sake of God. It is commonly admitted by those who believe in the Messianic consciousness as the center of His religion that He made the idea far more profoundly spiritual and ethical than it had ever been before. But this is only a smaller and more obvious half of the truth. The other half, possessing a far deeper source and a far wider reach, consists in its God-centered character. He felt that as the Messiah He had come to give God what was God's, and that in the discharge of all the functions pertaining to the Messianic pro-

gram this was so much the chief interest at stake as to render compliance with any peripheral feature, or even the apparent frustration of any secondary end, relatively unimportant, provided only the one great purpose of glorifying God might find fulfillment . . . . As a matter of fact Jesus found Himself at this point in sharp antithesis to the Judaistic Messianic concept, which had increasingly been tending toward a man-centered form of hedonism. Not God but Israel was in it the chief figure of the world to come, and the Messiah appeared as the agent who would raise Israel to this greatness. Jesus resolutely turned His back upon this irreligious perversion of the idea, and set His face toward the fulfillment of that God-centered form of it, which He recognized as already outlined in the Isaianic Servant of Jehovah.[8]

Since as we have seen the very term "God's anointed" emphatically confronts us with the God-centered character of messiahship, and the study of the messianic prophecies of the Old Testament powerfully confirms this estimate, the use of the term "transformation" with reference to Jesus' response to the Old Testament prophecies would be misleading and erroneous. For then the basic factor of continuity would be obscured or set aside. Nevertheless, it should not be overlooked that *Jesus himself in the fullness of his self-disclosure, in the precise way in which he employs various titles as self-designations and describes the various activities of his ministry, provides the final and complete portrayal of what it meant to be the Messiah.* He it was who by his names and claims and the active exercise of divine authority in word and deed brought to light and life the full meaning of what was entailed in being God's anointed Representative, while at the same time, as the Servant of God who was under divine orders, he constantly displayed the marks of restraint and reserve, of humility and even of passivity, in the disclosure and exercise of his messiahship. And he it is who acts and speaks out of the consciousness that in a preeminent way the Spirit of God has come upon him to qualify him for the performance of his task (*cf.* Lk. 4:18; Mt. 12:28).

For such a one surely the messiahship could never have been a merely formal concept or one of peripheral concern. *Unless his sense of messiahship held absolute sway over him,* no one could have claimed such relationships with God for himself, such dignity and authority and favor, or have brought to expression such unqualified obedience to the will of God as finds its

8. Vos, *op. cit.,* p. 59.

unique expression in that story — more sorrowful and poignant than any other and yet likewise more charged with blessing — that story of the obedience of the Messiah even unto the death of the cross.

The Deity of the Messiah

So far our thoughts have been largely occupied with messiahship as an office involving the performance of various functions. And thus the Messiah has been seen to be a figure in history in the midst of the life of men, and accordingly in the discharge of his commission the element of submission and subordination to God has been conspicuously present. Nevertheless, in thus reflecting upon the mission of Jesus Christ one has not done full justice to Jesus' own self-disclosure. For beyond the idea of messiahship in the strictest sense of the term, there emerges the issue of ontology. The tendency in the modern discussion concerning Jesus Christ is to suppress or deny this issue because it is taken for granted that ultimately Jesus was a mere man, and anything said about his messianic consciousness must be envisioned within the framework of his essential humanity.[9] In my judgment, however, the Gospel data do not permit us so lightly to turn aside from the question of the nature of Jesus. Theologically one is involved here in the total question of the reality of the incarnation and of the deity of Christ. And in terms of our previous reflections we must inquire concerning the identity of the person appointed to be the Messiah. It must of course be freely admitted that the doctrine of the two natures of Christ as formulated at Chalcedon is not simply a precise summary of the teaching of Jesus or of the New Testament as a whole but presupposes a process of theological reflection. Moreover, we have as much antipathy to a docetic view of Christ's person as any Liberal. But the full acceptance of the humanity of Jesus Christ does not require the acceptance of an adoptionist christology or any comparable view which denies the deity of Christ.

Since within the Synoptic Gospels, in contrast with John and other parts of the New Testament, the teaching concerning the coming of the kingdom of God is rather pervasively in the fore-

9. It is a grievous defect even of Cullmann's *Christology of the New Testament* that it does not seriously allow for this element. (*Cf.* pp. 3ff. and *passim.*) This tendency may be recognized as another factor connected with the persistence of Liberalism.

ground of attention and that of the person of Christ somewhat subordinate, it is not surprising that reflection upon the deity of Christ is not especially prominent in the Synoptic tradition. Nevertheless, it is unmistakably present.

The evidence which perhaps most pointedly involves the claim of deity relates to the pre-existence of the Messiah. In Matthew 22:41-45 and parallels Jesus undertakes a correction of certain inadequate or erroneous conceptions of the nature of messiahship by appealing to Psalm 110. There was a widely held, if not dominant, view that the Messiah could be thought of simply as the son of David, a title which could be used to advantage by those whose messianic hopes were basically nationalistic in character. In view of the fixed place which the messianic descent from David occupies within the christology of the New Testament, including, for example, Romans 1:3f., Jesus may not fairly be understood as repudiating outrightly the propriety of using this title. Nevertheless, his aim in the present context is to show that the title, to say the least, is inadequate inasmuch as David himself spoke of the Messiah as his Lord:

> How then doth David in the Spirit call him
> Lord, saying,
> The Lord said unto my Lord,
> Sit thou on my right hand,
> Till I put thine enemies underneath thy feet?
> If David then calleth him Lord, how is he his son?

Jesus is teaching therefore that in this Davidic Psalm, which was given by inspiration of the Spirit, David was already reverently acknowledging the Messiah as his Lord. This amounts, according to Johannes Weiss, to saying that the Messiah was "a heavenly being who would appear from above in divine glory,"[10] and this figure he identifies further as the Son of Man. On his approach, however, this transcendent conception of messiahship must be thought, it is felt, to reflect the theology of the early church rather than Jesus' own estimate of himself.[11]

---

10. *SNT*, I, 189.

11. See also Bousset, *Kyrios Christos* (Göttingen: Vandenhoeck & Ruprecht, 1913), pp. 5, 51, and 83, n. 1; Bultmann, *Die Geschichte der synoptischen Tradition* (Göttingen: Vandenhoeck & Ruprecht, 1931², 1958⁴), pp. 145ff. The latter is not quite so specific and definite in his exegesis and interpretation of the passage but does say that on the view that the figure might be understood as having reference to the Son of Man there would be the "fantastic" implication of pre-existence.

This leads us naturally to a brief consideration of the significance of the title "the Son of Man" as that appears again and again on the lips of Jesus. Since I have expressed myself rather fully on this subject in another place,[12] I may perhaps be content with a few summary statements. In the first place the connection between the sayings of Jesus and the vision of Daniel in 7:13, 14 seems unmistakable. In Daniel, to be sure, the specific title is not found but rather the description of a figure represented symbolically, in contrast with the beasts, as "like unto a son of man." But the description of this figure as sharing in the glory and sovereignty of the Ancient of Days, and especially his theophanic manifestation with the clouds of heaven as he comes to the Ancient of Days, provides us with a representation of a pre-existent celestial being. And it is this figure, understood as being reflected upon in the title, that provides the indispensable background for the understanding of the various predications of Jesus. This is widely admitted so far as the so-called apocalyptic or eschatological group of Son of Man sayings is concerned. But it is no less essential for the explication of the so-called passion utterances. At first blush such sayings might seem to point in quite an opposite direction. But these are not ordinary sayings about the human experience of suffering; they tell rather of the unique ministry of Jesus Christ in which, in a way that was beyond human understanding and was incongruous from a purely human point of view, he humbled himself to this program of suffering and death in order that the divine plan of redemption might be accomplished. Although it would have been appropriate for the Son of Man to have been ministered unto, he came rather to minister and to give his life a ransom for many (Mk. 10:45). "The Son of man goeth as it is written concerning him, but woe to that man through whom the son of man is betrayed" (Mt. 26:24). And most of the other Son of Man sayings, which are not readily or immediately subsumed under the two classes which have been mentioned, including in particular Mark 2:10, 28; Matthew 8:20, and Luke 19:10 are, to say the least, highly consonant with the thought that the Son of Man because of his heavenly provenience possessed divine authority and dignity.[13]

12. Cf. *WMMC*, pp. 251ff.
13. For the very reason that the Son of Man title, if taken in full earnest, would be expressive of the heavenly and pre-existent character

One of the clearest evidences of what is tantamount to a claim of deity on the part of Jesus is to be found in Matthew 11:27 (Luke 10:22) where the full correlativity of the Son's knowledge with that of the Father is enunciated. That Jesus is speaking about unique divine knowledge when he reflects upon the knowledge which the Father possesses is surely beyond dispute. It is this simply by virtue of the fact that it is the knowledge of the Father whom Jesus addresses as Lord of heaven and earth. It is moreover indicated to be divine because of its exclusive character: "No one knoweth the Son save the Father." The Father's knowledge is obviously not acquired in history but is present and continuous, as the present tense of the verb "knoweth" indicates. And the divine character of this knowledge is further emphasized by the observation that it is known to men only through revelation, and this revelation itself is described as a sovereign divine action:

> I thank thee, O Father, Lord of heaven and earth, that thou didst hide these things from the wise and understanding, and didst reveal them unto babes; yea, Father, for so it was well-pleasing in thy sight (11:25, 26).

But Jesus reflects upon the Son's relation to the Father as well as the Father's to the Son, and does so in terms of the mutuality of knowledge in such a way as to leave no room for subordination. The Son's knowledge of the Father is likewise exclusive, present and continuous: "Neither doth any know the Father save the Son." The Son's knowledge of the Father likewise may be known to men only by way of sovereign revelatory activity on the part of Jesus: "Neither doth any know the Father save the Son and he to whomsoever the Son willeth to reveal him." The import of the passage is therefore not to the effect that God may not be known; it quite emphatically states the contrary both with respect to the Father and the Son. But the knowledge possible to men, which is to be received by way of revelation and by divine sovereign determination, is the knowledge which man as a creature may acquire of God as Creator, Lord and Saviour. But the knowledge which the Son as Son possesses of the Father like the knowledge which the

---

of Jesus' person, it is widely rejected as utterly inconceivable and fantastic on the lips of Jesus, and so as unauthentic. *Cf. e.g.*, Bultmann, *Theology of the N.T.* I, pp. 29ff.; J. Knox, *The Death of Christ* (New York: Abingdon, 1958), pp. 56ff.

Father as Father possesses of the Son, is not subject to such human limitations.[14] The transcendent claims which Jesus makes regarding his person are by no means confined to his use of various titles such as Son of God, Son of Man and Lord. For often in speaking about the commitment which men ought to sustain to him he assumes a level of dignity and self-importance which surpasses that of human relationships and cannot even be explained by the extraordinary character of his messianic claims. Consider, for example, that paradoxical saying found in Luke 14:26:

If any man cometh unto me, and hateth not his own father and mother, and wife and children, and brethren and sisters, yea, and his own life also he cannot be my disciple.

In view of the plainness with which Jesus teaches the requirement of love in all human relationships one must recognize in this statement the element of rhetorical hyperbole. Nevertheless, that which Jesus sets forth as a requirement of hate only serves to place his meaning in the sharpest possible focus. His teaching is to the effect that there is nothing in life as important as being a disciple of his, and that in order to be his disciple one must be involved in a love to him that is absolutely unique and which will mean the subordination of all other

---

14. The authenticity of Mt. 11:27 as a saying of Jesus is commonly rejected. *Cf.*, *e.g.*, E. Norden, *Agnostos Theos* (Berlin: Teubner, 1913), pp. 277ff.; Bultmann, *Geschichte d. syn. Tradition*, pp. 171ff.; M. Dibelius, *Die Formgeschichte des Evangeliums*, 2te Aufl. (Tübingen, Mohr, 1933), pp. 279ff.; Eng. trans., *From Tradition to Gospel* (New York: Scribner's 1935), pp. 279ff. O. Cullmann, *Die Christologie des Neuen Testaments*, pp. 292ff. (Eng. trans., pp. 286ff.), defends its genuineness and with some hesitation allows for the possibility of a consciousness of pre-existence, but holds that the saying in any case has to do primarily with "revelatory *action*" in which Jesus continuously experiences his oneness with the Father" (p. 288). Prior and basic to the revelatory action, however, is the central teaching concerning the full correlativity of the mutual knowledge of the Father and the Son, which is not viewed as acquired, or otherwise conditioned by, history. Harnack's bold reconstruction of the text, whereby its significance is reduced to the point where, in accordance with the Liberal estimate of Jesus, it expresses merely the thought that Jesus in history acquired a peculiarly intimate knowledge of the Father, may also be recalled. *Cf.* Adolf Harnack, *Sprüche und Reden Jesu* (Leipzig: Hinrichs, 1907), pp. 196ff.; Eng. trans., *The Sayings of Jesus* (New York: Putnam, 1908), pp. 272ff.; *Das Wesen des Christentums*, pp. 80ff. (Eng. trans., pp. 127ff.). See *WMMC*, pp. 212ff. For a recent review of the issues, cf. A. M. Hunter, "Crux Criticorum — Matt. xi. 25-30 — A Re-appraisal," *NTS*, 8 (April, 1962), pp. 241.

affections to the supreme love of which he alone is worthy. This teaching, it may not be forgotten, is by one who said, "Thou shalt love the Lord thy God with all thy heart, and with all thy soul, and with all thy mind" (Mt. 22:37).

Hardly less illuminating for the understanding of Jesus' ultimate self-appraisal are his words which speak of the consequences of confession or denial of himself:

> Everyone therefore who shall confess me before men, him will I also confess before my Father who is in heaven. But whosoever shall deny me before men, him will I also deny before my Father who is in heaven (Mt. 10:32f.; Lk. 12:8f.; cf. Mk. 8:38; Lk. 9:26).

Jesus makes the entire position of men in the world to come, whether for weal or woe, to depend upon their relationship to and attitude toward him in this present world. Is this a claim which any mere man might have made? Do we not encounter here essentially the exclusiveness of Acts 4:12, "And in none other is there salvation; for neither is there any other name under heaven, that is given among men, wherein we must be saved"? And thus we also hear Jesus speaking with unqualified sovereign authority and self-assurance:

> Come unto me, all ye that labor and are heavy laden, and I will give you rest. Take my yoke upon you, and learn of me; for I am meek and lowly in heart; and ye shall find rest unto your souls. For my yoke is easy, and my burden is light (Mt. 11:28-30).

Conclusion

As we reflect upon the disclosure of Jesus concerning his person and messiahship we observe that a distinctive view of history — and especially of the gospel history — confronts us. And this view of history is in irreconcilable conflict with others which have dominated the thinking of many modern students of the Gospels. Historicism is clearly found wanting. For it lays violent hands upon the witness of the Gospels. In the name of criticism and exegesis, it modernizes that witness, first, as it relativizes the absolute and unique in the person of Jesus Christ and, subsequently, in the interest of abiding religious value, seeks, after a fashion, to absolutize the so-called historical Jesus. And the virtual repudiation of the significance of history for Christian faith, whether inspired by Hegel or Heidegger, as it has come to expression in Strauss, Schweitzer and Bultmann, is thoroughly at variance with the once-for-all place assigned to the history of Jesus in the gospel as both Jesus and the apostles proclaimed it.

Nor is the modern approach which distinguishes between two kinds of history, *Historie* and *Geschichte,* one that offers any genuine clarification. Quite the contrary. To be sure, there is some ambiguity in the use of these terms. But they commonly assume two worlds or planes of reality, one of nature and the other of freedom, which is not genuinely biblical. On this approach, on the one hand, there is one kind of history (*Historie*) which deals with nature or history so far as it is thought of in terms of natural cause and effect. Then, by allegedly impartial and scientific methods, the merely human Jesus, the supposedly historical Jesus, might be understood "as part of the nexus of history." But there is a quite different history (*Geschichte*) concerned with aspects of human experience which transcend the realm of the determined and allow for a free decision. And it is in the latter that Bultmann, for example, finds a place for Christian faith and what he speaks of as that which "God has wrought in Christ, that is . . . the eschatological event."[15] The Gospel witness concerning the divine Messiah who came to effect the redemption of his people by his life and death on their behalf can never be brought into focus with this distinction between two kinds of history because its view of God and man and of history itself is so sharply divergent from this modern philosophical point of view.

In the gospel there is no antithesis or disjunction between history and revelation. For the history of the divine Messiah in its entirety, including the resurrection as well as his life and death, because of its intrinsic character partakes of the nature of revelation. It is a revelation in history and a history that is truly revelatory. These observations apply not only to the biblical conception of revelation in history as a whole but also particularly to Jesus' own teaching. To borrow Harnack's terminology, supreme reverence for his own history came to manifestation in Jesus' own teaching and work as the divine Messiah;[16] it did not, as Harnack supposed, represent some later stage of christological reflection. Jesus came bringing the gospel with him and from the first, expressly or by implication,

15. Bultmann, *Jesus Christ and Mythology,* p. 80; *cf.* Malvelez, *op. cit.,* p. 188.
16. See pp. 176ff. above.

Jesus himself was assigned an indispensable place within it. He was both the revealer and the revealed.[17]

Only if the witness of the Gospels to Jesus and that of Jesus' self-revelation are taken at face value, therefore, will one be able to establish genuine continuity between Jesus and the Gospel tradition. And once it is acknowledged that the divine Messiah alone can explain the origin of that tradition will one be in a position to discern how, as a part of a single historical movement, the Gospels not only as matchless historical documents but as integral parts of Holy Scripture came into being. Only if he was the divine Messiah, can we understand the history in which those who from the beginning were eyewitnesses and ministers of the Word, acting with his authority, delivered over to the Church a knowledge of the Gospel tradition. And this history is intelligible also only as we grasp the fact that the divine Messiah, who was endowed with the Spirit of God in a unique fashion, himself qualified his spokesmen and representatives with an enduement of the Spirit from on high that they might bear faithful witness to him.

17. This subject of the philosophy of history, including particularly that of the biblical view of history, is one of profound proportions and admittedly of exceptional difficulty. No issue in the present debate is more fundamental; and the literature is voluminous. Regrettably I have felt it necessary to limit myself here to a few general observations.

INDEX OF SUBJECTS

Allegory, 39, 40, 42

Apostolic, men, 7-9; proclamation: Catechism 139, 140; didache, 135-137, kerugma, 4, 8, 117, 128, 130, 135-137, 139-141, 152, 172-174, message, 129, 132ff., tradition, 116, 127, 128, 142-147; transmission, 38, 113ff., 141

Atonement, 151, 172

Early Church, The ("Community"), 27, 34, 39, 115, 118, 123, 138-141, 148, 154, 158, 159, 168, 182, 186

Eschatology, 104, 137, 151, 161-165, 167, 170-174, 182, 191

Form Criticism, 37, 114, 138-140

"Four Document" Theory, 51

Gospel origins, 111, 146ff. 155

Harmony, of the Gospels, 93ff., 107-109

Heresies, 4-7

Historicism, 155, 165, 190

History, 133, 144, 160ff., 183, 190-192

Interdependence, 57, 76, 79, 80, 111, 113, 140, 146; direct dependence, 64; indirect dependence, 59

Kingdom of God, The, 134, 135, 151, 157, 161, 164, 170ff.

Law, 99ff.

Lexical knowledge, 120-122

Liberalism, 53, 149ff., 161, 165-170, 185

Literary sources, 64, 84, 114, 128, 138, 146

Luke, Gospel of, Prologue, 116, 118ff., 132; relation to Mark, 49, 96f.

Matthew, Gospel of, authorship, 2ff., 19ff., 45; date of composition, 26; literary character, 103, 108; original language, 83-90

Mark, Gospel of, abridgement of Matthew, 73; authorship, 2; language, 61, 78ff.; priority, 22, 49ff., 110-112, 158; raison d' être, 71, 72

Messiah, the, 176ff., 185-190

Messianic consciousness, 156, 158, 160, 163, 166, 191, 192

Messianic secret, theory of the, 112, 158, 161, 168

Myth, 155, 156, 159, 170-174

Neo-orthodoxy, 168

Oral tradition, 13, 114, 115, 128, 138, 139, 146

Order of the Gospels, 55, 91; of events in the Gospels, 66-69

Parables, 34ff.

Presuppositions, 24ff., 37, 38, 139, 150, 153-155, 163, 174

Prophecy, 42, 182-184

"Q," 13, 15, 52, 62, 79, 80, 84, 145, 153

Qumran, 86, 87

Resurrection, the, 117, 129, 144, 151, 153, 173ff., 179

Scripture, the doctrine of, 1, 5, 11, 47, 54, 109, 110, 134, 148, 152

Self-witness (internal evidence), 1, 19ff., 46

Septuagint citations, 84ff.
Sermon on the Mount, the, 156, 157, 166, 167
Servant of the Lord, 183, 184
Single-source theory, 64
Sitz im Leben, 34, 37, 56, 87, 139, 142
Son of Man, 186, 187
Superscriptions, 15-18

Synoptic problem, the, 48ff., 76, 77, 92

Tendency criticism, 31ff., 156
Tradition (external evidence), 1, 4ff., 22, 54-56, 75-77, 89ff.
Two-document theory, 51, 52, 145

"We Sections" in Acts, 124ff.

INDEX OF NAMES

Abbot, E. A., 58
Allen, W. C., 27
Augustine, 50, 57

Bacon, B. W., 14, 30, 45, 91
Baird, W., 135
Bartsch, H. W., 172
Bauer, Bruno, 170
Baur, Ferdinand Christian, 21, 154, 156-158
Bavinck, H., 118
Berkhof, L., 110
Black, Matthew, 39, 83, 84
Bornkamm, G., 26, 35-37, 39, 40, 42, 99, 100, 102
Bousett, 186
Brouwer, A. M., 39
Brown, J. P., 62
Bruce, F. F., 86
Bultmann, Rudolph, 25, 159, 168-175, 186, 188-191
Burkitt, F. C., 14, 27, 28
Bussmann, W., 58
Butler, B. C., 59, 60, 63, 65, 75, 79-83, 145

Cadbury, Henry J., 49, 118-127, 130, 134
Calvin, John, 38, 73
Chapman, John, 50, 51, 59, 73-76, 78, 83, 85, 89
Clement of Alexandria, 10, 46, 55
Coates, J. R., 147
Conzelman, 104
Creed, J. M., 41
Cross, F. L., 7
Cullmann, Oscar, 147, 148, 168, 177, 180, 185, 189

Daube, D., 26, 28
Davies, W. D., 26
DeBruyne, 10
De Solages, Bruno, 52, 53

Dibelius, M., 189
Dodd, C. H., 37, 39, 135-138, 168
Doeve, D., 30

Easton, B. S., 41
Ellis, E. E., 87
Enslin, Morton S., 51
Eusebius, 4, 11, 13, 14, 55

Farmer, W. R., 59, 60, 63
Farrer, Austin M., 51, 80
Feine, P., 58
Filson, F. V., 15, 23
Fitzmyer, Joseph A., 53
Fuller, R. H., 172

Gerhardsson, B., 138
Geldenhuys, Norval, 41, 147
Gieseler, J. C. L., 58, 140
Gilmour, S. M., 41
Goodspeed, Edgar, J., 20, 21
Gould, 27
Grant, F. C., 2, 27, 54, 55, 168
Grant, Robert M., 54
Grayston, K., 52
Greijdanus, S., 41
Grobel, Kendrick, 7
Gutwenger, Engelbert, 10

Harnack, Adolf, 10, 149-154, 158, 170, 189, 191
Hawkins, Sir John C., 61, 62, 81, 82, 85, 94, 110
Hegel, G. W. F., 190
Heidegger, Martin, 172, 190
Herdan, G., 52
Hilgenfeld, 60
Hodge, A. A., 110
Howard, W. F., 10
Huck, 10
Hunter, A. M., 189

Ignatius, 46
Irenaeus, 4-7, 9-12, 17, 53, 55

Jeremias, J., 34, 38, 39, 41, 168
Jerome, 91
Johnson, 27
Jülicher, A., 14, 23, 39

Kant, Immanuel, 153, 154, 156
Kähler, M., 72
Kilpatrick, G. D., 14, 15, 17, 24-26,
    29-35, 37, 42, 44-46, 83
Kittel, G., 13, 14
Kleinhans, K., 53
Knox, J., 188
Know, W. L., 144, 145
Kuyper, A., 110

Lachman, 63
Lantero, Erminie H., 169
LaGrange, M. J., 85, 88-90
Lessing, G. E., 58
Lightfoot, J. B., 11, 14, 15
Lotze, 154
Ludlum, John H., Jr., 59

Machen, J. Gresham, 160
Mackintosh, H. R., 95
Malvelez, L., 172
Marcion, 6-9
McNeile, A. H., 10, 23, 39, 103
Menzies, 27
Meyer, 27
Miller, A., 53
Moffat, James, 23
Moore, G. F., 29, 30
Murray, John 27, 28, 109, 110

Nineham, D. E., 51
Norden, E., 189

Papias, 10-15, 18, 43, 44, 90-92
Piper, O. A., 135
Plummer, Alfred, 16, 41
Polycarp, 11

Rawlinson, A. E. J., 88
Rengstorf, K. H., 41, 147
Ridderbos, Herman, 147
Riesenfeld, Harald, 138-144, 148
Ritschl, Albrecht, 156

Robinson, James M., 160, 161
Ropes, James Hardy, 14-16, 22, 51,
    127

Schmiedel, Paul, 53
Schniewind, Julius, 108
Schürer, E., 20
Schwartz, 12-14
Schwitzer, Albert, 160-168, 170, 190
Siegman, E. F., 53, 54
Smith, Louise P., 169
Stendahl, Krister, 85-89
Stonehouse, Ned, 2, 3, 7, 19, 26, 27,
    64, 66, 71, 87, 102, 104, 119, 124-
    126, 147, 148, 158, 172, 177, 187,
    189
Strack-Billerbeck, 27
Strauss, David Fredrich, 154-156, 160,
    190
Streeter, B. H., 14, 43, 44, 56, 58-64
    78, 79, 81, 94, 110, 145

Tasker, R. V. G., 39
Taylor, V., 27, 28, 83, 88, 94, 95, 110
Tertullian, 7-9, 17, 55
Tisserant, Cardinal, 52
Trench, R. C., 41
Turner, C. H., 145

Valentinus, 6
van Unnik, W. C., 7, 181, 182
Vincent, J. J., 39
von Dobschütz, E., 30
Vos, Geerhardus, 133, 134, 181, 183,
    184
Vosté, Jacques M., 51, 52; 89

Warfield, B. B., 13, 95, 98, 102, 110
Weiss, Johannes, 170, 186
Westcott, B. F., 58, 141
Wikenhauser, A., 39, 43, 49, 52, 53,
    89
Wood, H. G., 65, 69
Wrede, Wilhelm, 112, 158-161, 165,
    168-170

Zahn, T., 14, 15, 20, 41, 49, 52, 60,
    83-85, 91

INDEX OF SCRIPTURE

EXODUS
28:41   181

LEVITICUS
4:3   181
4:5   181
4:16   181

NUMBERS
3:3   181

I SAMUEL
9:16f   180
10:1   180
10:1ff   180
10:9ff   181
13   180
16:3   180
24:6   180

II SAMUEL
7:12ff   180

I KINGS
19:16   180

PSALMS
2:2   180
18:50   180
80:1   6
89:20-37   180
110   176, 186
132:10ff   180

ISAIAH
29:13   88
42:1   182
42:2-4   183
49:5f   183
52:13-53:12   183
55:4   183
61   133
61:1   180
61:1-4   183

DANIEL
7:13, 14   187

AMOS
5:14f   101

MATTHEW
1   70
2   70
2:15   87
2:23   87
3:7   32
3:7f   32
3:9   32
3:18   20
4:17   134
4:18-22   66
4:18-9:34   66
4:23   134
5-7   68
5:3-7:27   67, 70
5:11   33
5:20, 21ff   32
5:32   27, 28
5:48   101
8   67, 68
8:1-4   67
8:1-9:34   67
8:5-13   67
8:11ff   41
8:14, 15   67
8:16   69
8:18-22   67
8:20   187
8:23-27   67
8:28-34   67
9   67, 68
9:1-8   67
9:9   44, 45
9:9-13   20, 67
9:11   32
9:14-17   67
9:16, 17   67
9:18-26   67

197

9:27-31	67	19:17a	97
9:32-34	67	19:17b	97, 101
9:34	32	19:18a	101
9:35	134	19:19b	97
10:3	20	19:21a	97, 101
10:5-43	70	19:27	103
10:7	134	19:28	96, 97, 100, 104, 106, 111
10:17	33, 34	19:29	96, 104
10:23	33, 34	21	41
10:32f	190	21:33-44	40
10:40	147	21:35	33, 34
11:1	137	21:39	62
11:2-30	70	21:46	41
11:25, 26	188	22	41
11:25-30	189	22:1-10	35
11:27	148, 188, 189	22:1ff	36
11:28-30	190	22:2	177
12	29	22:4	177
12:2	32	22:5, 6	39
12:24	32	22:6	33, 34, 35
12:21ff	32	22:6, 7	40
12:25ff	32	22:7	35
12:28	184	22:8-14	40
12:31f	32	22:9	40, 41
12:34	32	22:23	31
12:35	101	22:37	190
13:3-52	70	22:41-45	186
13:19	134	22:42	176
13:58	94	23:2f	32
15:2	32	23:10	176
15:3	32	23:34	33, 34
15:6	32, 88	24	80
15:8f	87, 88	24:4-25:46	70
15:12-14	32	24:10	33
15:14	32	24:37-25:46	80
15:19	33	25	80
16	177	26:24	180, 187
16:12	32	26:63, 64	177
16:16f	177	27:9, 10	87
16:17-19	70	27:11	177
16:17ff	179	27:17	177
16:20	177	27:22	177
17:12	179	27:29	177
18:3-35	70	27:37	177
19:3	29, 32	27:42	177
19:9	27, 28, 30	28:9-20	70
19:16	97, 107		
19:16, 17	101, 108	MARK	
19:16-30	95	1:1	70
19:17	93	1:14	137
		1:15	134

1:16-20	66	10:17	96, 97, 107
1:16-2:22	66	10:17-19	97
1:21f	137	10:17-22	97, 99
1:21-28	66	10:17-31	95
1:21-35	66, 68, 69	10:18	93, 96, 106
1:23-28	70	10:19	101
1:29-31	66, 67	10:21	96, 97, 98, 108
1:32	69	10:22	96, 97
1:32-34	66, 67	10:23	96, 97
1:35	66	10:23-31	97
1:35-38	70	10:24	96, 97
1:36-38	66	10:26	96
1:38f	137	10:26, 27	102
1:39	66	10:28, 29	106
1:40-45	66	10:28ff	103
2:1-12	66, 67	10:29	96, 108
2:10	187	10:29, 30	103
2:13-17	66, 67	10:30	96, 97
2:14ff	20	10:32-34	179
2:18-22	66, 67	10:45	179, 187
2:27	70	12:8	62
2:28	187	12:10	180
3:4	101	12:18	31
3:17	82	12:40-44	70
3:20, 21	70	13:9	33
3:31-35	63	13:33-37	70, 80
4:21-24	70	14:21	180
4:23-35	66	14:36	82
4:26-29	69	14:51-52	70
4:35-41	67	15:22	82
5:1-20	67	15:34	82
5:21-43	67		
5:41	82	LUKE	
6:5	94	1:1	122, 132
6:30	70	1:1, 2	118
7:3-4	70	1:2	116, 119, 122, 124 127
7:8	88	1:3	118, 119, 124, 126
7:11	82	1:4	118, 126
7:32-37	69	1:32f	177
7:34	82	2:11	177
8:22-26	70	2:26	177, 180
8:27-33	179	4:18	184
8:38	190	4:18, 19, 21	133
9:12	179, 180	4:43	134
9:29	70	5:27ff	20
9:30-32	179	6:13	117
9:38-41	70	6:15	20
9:41	176	6:22	33
9:48, 49	70	6:45	101
10:12	27, 28, 30	7:22	133

9:1 — 117
9:2 — 117, 134
9:10 — 117
9:11 — 134
9:18-22 — 179
9:26 — 190
9:60 — 134
10:22 — 188
10:25-28 — 98
10:25-37 — 100
10:29-37 — 98
12:8f — 190
14 — 35
14:12-14 — 42
14:15 — 42
14:16-24 — 35
14:16ff — 36
14:21 — 41
14:23 — 38, 41
14:26 — 189
16:16 — 133, 134
16:29 — 98
16:31 — 98
17:5 — 117
17:25 — 179
18:18 — 96, 107
18:18-30 — 95
18:22 — 108
18:25 — 96
18:29 — 96
19:10 — 187
20:15 — 62
22:14 — 117
22:22 — 180
22:28-30 — 104
22:37 — 180
24 — 180
24:10 — 117
24:25-27 — 179
24:26 — 177
24:27 — 87
24:42 — 177
24:44 — 182
24:44-48 — 179

JOHN
5:29 — 101
5:39 — 87
13:16 — 147
13:20 — 147

13:23ff — 19
19:26f — 19
19:35 — 19
20:2ff — 19
20:31 — 176
21:24f — 19

ACTS
1:1 — 132
1:2 — 111
1:3 — 117
1:8 — 117, 130
1:13 — 20
1:21, 22 — 130
1:21f — 117
2:32 — 131
3 — 178
3:14f — 178
3:15 — 131
3:18 — 178
4:4 — 134
4:12 — 190
4:26f — 178
4:29 — 134
4:31 — 134
5:32 — 131
6:2 — 132
6:4 — 134
8:4 — 134
8:14 — 134
8:25 — 134
10 — 130
10:36 — 134
10:36-39 — 143
10:44 — 134
11:1 — 134
11:19 — 134
13:5 — 134
13:7 — 134
13:26 — 134
13:44 — 134
13:46 — 134
13:49 — 134
17:1-3 — 179
19:8 — 134
20:24f — 134
22:15 — 131
26:16 — 131, 134
28:23 — 134
28:31 — 134

ROMANS
1:3f   186
2:10   101
4:25   152
6:17   129
7:12   101
12:2   101
13:3   101

I CORINTHIANS
11:2   129
11:23   129, 147
15   128
15:8-10   129
15:11   129
15:15   129

II CORINTHIANS
1:21   178
5:15   175
5:16   166
5:16a   175
5:18-20   175

GALATIANS
1:9   129
6:10   101

EPHESIANS
4:28   101

PHILIPPIANS
4:9   129

I THESSALONIANS
4:1   129

II THESSALONIANS
2:15   129

HEBREWS
4:15   95
5:8   95

REVELATION
4:7   54, 55

twin brooks series BOOKS IN THE SERIES

THE ACTS OF THE APOSTLES ....Richard B. Rackham
APOSTOLIC AND POST-APOSTOLIC TIMES (Goppelt) ....Robert A. Guelich, tr.
THE APOSTOLIC FATHERS ....J. B. Lightfoot
THE ATONEMENT OF CHRIST ....Francis Turrettin
THE AUTHORITY OF THE OLD TESTAMENT ....John Bright
BACKGROUNDS TO DISPENSATIONALISM ....Clarence B. Bass
BASIC CHRISTIAN DOCTRINES ....Carl F. H. Henry
THE BASIC IDEAS OF CALVINISM ....H. Henry Meeter
THE CALVINISTIC CONCEPT OF CULTURE ....H. Van Til
CHRISTIAN APPROACH TO PHILOSOPHY ....W. C. Young
CHRISTIAN PERSONAL ETHICS ....Carl F. H. Henry
COMMENTARY ON DANIEL (Jerome) ....Gleason L. Archer, Jr., tr.
THE DAYS OF HIS FLESH ....David Smith
DISCIPLING THE NATIONS ....Richard DeRidder
THE DOCTRINE OF GOD ....Herman Bavinck
EDUCATIONAL IDEALS IN THE ANCIENT WORLD ....Wm. Barclay
THE EPISTLE OF JAMES ....Joseph B. Mayor
EUSEBIUS' ECCLESIASTICAL HISTORY
FUNDAMENTALS OF THE FAITH ....Carl F. H. Henry, ed.
GOD-CENTERED EVANGELISM ....R. B. Kuiper
GENERAL PHILOSOPHY ....D. Elton Trueblood
THE GRACE OF LAW ....Ernest F. Kevan
THE HIGHER CRITICISM OF THE PENTATEUCH ....William Henry Green
THE HISTORY OF CHRISTIAN DOCTRINES ....Louis Berkhof
THE HISTORY OF DOCTRINES ....Reinhold Seeberg
THE HISTORY OF THE JEWISH NATION ....Alfred Edersheim
HISTORY OF PREACHING ....E. C. Dargan
LIGHT FROM THE ANCIENT EAST ....Adolf Deissmann
NOTES ON THE MIRACLES OF OUR LORD ....R. C. Trench
NOTES ON THE PARABLES OF OUR LORD ....R. C. Trench
OUR REASONABLE FAITH (Bavinck) ....Henry Zylstra, tr.
PAUL, APOSTLE OF LIBERTY ....R. N. Longnecker
PHILOSOPHY OF RELIGION ....D. Elton Trueblood
PROPHETS AND THE PROMISE ....W. J. Beecher
REASONS FOR FAITH ....John H. Gerstner
THE REFORMATION ....Hans J. Hillebrand, ed.
REFORMED DOGMATICS (Wollebius, Voetius, Turretin) ....J. Beardslee, ed., tr.
REFORMED DOGMATICS ....Heinrich Heppe
REVELATION AND INSPIRATION ....James Orr
REVELATION AND THE BIBLE ....Carl F. H. Henry
ROMAN SOCIETY AND ROMAN LAW IN THE NEW TESTAMENT ....A. N. Sherwin-White
THE ROOT OF FUNDAMENTALISM ....Ernest R. Sandeen
THE SERVANT-MESSIAH ....T. W. Manson
STORY OF RELIGION IN AMERICA...................................Wm. W. Sweet
THE TESTS OF LIFE (third edition) ....Robert Law
THEOLOGY OF THE MAJOR SECTS ....John H. Gerstner
VARIETIES OF CHRISTIAN APOLOGETICS ....B. Ramm
THE VOYAGE AND SHIPWRECK OF ST. PAUL (fourth edition) ....James Smith
THE VIRGIN BIRTH ....J. G. Machen
A COMPANION TO THE STUDY OF ST. AUGUSTINE ....Roy W. Battenhouse, ed.
STUDIES IN THE GOSPELS ....R. C. Trench
THE HISTORY OF THE RELIGION OF ISRAEL ....John Howard Raven
THE HISTORY OF CHRISTIAN DOCTRINE (revised edition) ....E. H. Klotsche
THE EPISTLES OF JUDE AND II PETER ....Joseph B. Mayor
THEORIES OF REVELATION ....H. D. McDonald
STUDIES IN THE BOOK OF DANIEL ....Robert Dick Wilson
THE UNITY OF THE BOOK OF GENESIS ....William Henry Green
THE APOCALYPSE OF JOHN ....Isbon T. Beckwith
CHRIST THE MEANING OF HISTORY ....Hendrikus Berkhof